6/17/98

Mastering
the Art of
Creative
Collaboration

Robert Hargrove

Other BusinessWeek Books

TransCompetition
Harvey Robbins and Michael Finley

Conquering Uncertainty
Theodore Modis

Mastering

the Art of

Creative

Collaboration

Robert Hargrove

 **BusinessWeek Books**

McGraw-Hill

New York   San Francisco   Washington, D.C.   Auckland   Bogotá
Caracas   Lisbon   London   Madrid   Mexico City   Milan
Montreal   New Delhi   San Juan   Singapore
Sydney   Tokyo   Toronto

McGraw-Hill

A Division of The **McGraw·Hill** *Companies*

1 2 3 4 5 6 7 8 9 0 DOC/DOC 9 0 2 1 0 9 8 7

ISBN 0-07-026409-0

The sponsoring editor for this book was Susan Barry, the editing supervisor
was Bernard Onken, and the production supervisor was Tina Cameron.
Packaged for McGraw-Hill by backbone books and Future Studio,
Los Angeles.

I would like to dedicate this book
to all individuals in this world
who have a passion to make a difference.
My contribution is to offer you assistance
in fulfilling your passion through
these stories of enterprising, creative,
far-flung collaborations, and
deep human understanding and compassion.

Contents

In 1776, the Human Agenda Reflected Deep Human Values

If you and I had lived 200 years ago—around the time of Thomas Jefferson—people might have said that we were moving from a period of monarchy and despotism, where the king could cut out your tongue for expressing your views, tax you without representation, or quarter his horses in your church, to an era of democracy and equal rights. The new human agenda at that time, not only in America but in other parts of the world, was based on deeply spirited, generative conversation about human rights.

Even today, when we hear the words "We hold these truths to be self-evident: that all men are created equal; that they are endowed by their creator with certain inalienable rights . . ." our spirits are generally stirred much more so than when we hear about the latest economic growth indicators or the Clinton administration saying we are living in an era of peace and prosperity, or even when we dial directory assistance only to hear James Earl Jones in his best Darth Vader, cyber-speak accent, Wel Kolm to Bel Atlantikk."

The way the human agenda of the Founding Fathers was achieved had to do with fighting a revolution, framing a constitution—which historian Pauline Maier refers to as the "American scriptures," something sacred—and laying down the tracks of westward expansion through the building of the railroads. This remained pretty much the track of the human agenda, and the human agenda began to shift.

By the time I was born as a "baby boomer" in Boston, Massachusetts, went to school and read about Thomas Jefferson and John Quincy Adams, the human agenda had shifted dramatically. It seems that the three biggest issues, the ones that made it to the top of the human (or national agenda) were: (1) winning the superpower battle between the United States and the Soviet Union in the Cold War; (2) achieving science and technological breakthroughs; and (3) spurring economic growth, which some consider as the period when there was the most profligate consumption of economic goods the world has ever known.

I can remember exactly where I was standing as a young boy when I heard that the Russians had put Sputnik, the first satellite, into space. It was very depressing for my whole neighborhood, as was the day in the Kennedy-era of the 1960s when my father came home and pointed to the newspaper heading that read, "Khrushchev Walks Out of Summit Conference," and said, "There's going to be a war"—which, to us, meant nuclear. I remember that when I grew up in the suburbs, to be a respected family in the neighborhood, you had to have a new car every two years—hopefully one model up from a Chevy BelAir to at least an Impala. That bit of conspicuous consumption went with the house with a white picket fence and our images of personhood. "You are what you own. The more you own, the more you are," was the mantra of the day.

Later, I went to college and graduated to more sophisticated strivings. I spent my academic years as a cultural historian. I found memorizing facts and dates boring but cultural history extremely interesting. It allowed me to see what had happened over a certain period of time by examining the underlying trends and patterns that are invisible to most people. I studied the writings of many cultural historians, from Alexis DeTocqueville's *Democracy in America* and Oswald Spengler's *Decline of the West* to more contemporary ones like Lewis Mumford's *The Human Prospect*. Working as an editor and journalist after I finished school, I started hearing about Marshall McLuhan's "global village," Daniel Bell's "post-industrial society," Alvin Toffler's "third wave," and then later, a book by a friend, Paul Hawken, entitled *The Next Economy*.

These books would always begin by examining a profound shift in human cultural evolution. But it was a different shift in nature than the shift from the divine right of kings to democracy, and it reflected how much the human agenda had changed. The opening sentence would always be something like: "We are going through a period of global transition just as profound as the shift from the hunting-and-gathering stage to the Industrial Revolution. We are moving into a new Information Age that is destined to transform every aspect of our lives."

One problem I had with this interpretation of human cultural evolution is that it views what it means to be a human being as a matter of technology and economic wherewithal, not the other way around. Instead of our deeper human qualities surrounding and shaping our economic desires and technologies, as William Irwin Thompson points out in his 1997 book, *Passages About Earth,* in this interpretation our economic desires and technologies are seen as surrounding and shaping us. Although there is certainly abundant evidence to support such an interpretation, it has perhaps led people toward pursuing goals of economics without pursuing corresponding goals of humanity. This has not only resulted in the unrestrained production and consumption of goods but also in wars, pollution, and a way of living that will not give humanity a sustainable future on the planet.

It would be foolish to say that the technological and economic growth track we have been on for the last fifty years or so is a bad thing for the world—as many people did in the 1970s when they espoused a new gospel of planetary mysticism and went back to the woods to read *The Whole Earth Catalog* in reaction to Marshall McLuhan's notion of a global electronic village.

As it says in the Book of Ecclesiastics, "To everything there is a season and a time for every purpose under heaven." There was a time for the new human agenda of superpower over the "Evil Empire," a time for unrestrained economic growth and technological push, a time for the intensification of the factory system after World War II (which brought about the beginning of the end of the factory system), a time for the shift from hardware to information, from coal and iron to oil and plastics, from bookkeeping to electronics. And now there has come a time for a new human agenda and a new means to reach it.

I am talking about a powerful new interpretation of human prospect as we stand at the edge of history only a few years from the millennium, which is more grounded in human values. It is time to lay down a new track. I am talking about a new era in which these human values surround and shape economic means and technology rather than the other way around. Not only to bring about a more civil, decent, and just society but because all of the technological and economic growth that we have experienced has little or no impact on complex human problems—such as suicide bombings in Jerusalem, shoot-em-ups by U.S. Postal Service employees, the divorce rate and distortion of family values, the lack of adequate education to ensure that our young people possess the necessary skills for the year 2020, the slashing and burning of the rain forests, or business enterprises that are climates of profound resignation rather than possibility.

Perhaps now that the Berlin Wall has come down, the Cold War is over, and we are living in a period of prosperity, we are strong enough, secure enough, and prosperous enough to honestly acknowledge these breakdowns and the need to address them through a different means. Perhaps now we are willing to say that it is time to declare a new era—a new human agenda—that is creative and bold, and to call that forth from ourselves with the courage and commitment our founding fathers used 250 years ago. Perhaps by the year 2020, cultural historians can rightly proclaim, "We are in the middle of a shift today, as profound as the shift from the birth of democracy to the Industrial and Information Ages, a shift to an era of creativity and collaboration, a shift to an era of reconciliation, an era of compassion that will help to solve some of the world's worst problems."

Of one thing we can be certain: Whatever it is called, the breakthroughs of the twenty-first century will come from an expanding concept of what it is to be a human—something we call being a collaborative person, not just the desire for economic and technical growth. As John Seely Brown, chief scientist at Xerox's Palo Alto Research Center (a man well familiar with business and technology) says, "Knowledge is a social activity." Complex problems cannot be solved by specialists thinking and working in isolation, but in coming together through a process of dialogue, deeply informed by human values that are grounded in practical problems. "This not only applies to social and environmental issues," Brown emphasizes, "but to every corporation that desires to compete in the world today."

I believe that, if we continue down the same track we have been on, we will never find a solution to the complex problems we face, no matter how hard or intelligently we try. I am reminded of a story: A student once asked Jay Forester of MIT—the founder of Systems Dynamics who also happened to invent the first IBM computer back in the 1960s—why he got out of the computer field so early, at a time when the industry was about to explode. Forester said, "Son, most technology, and particularly computers, will always be used to do the things people have always done, only faster, but not to create things that never existed before."

If this story doesn't make it clear, perhaps another example will. Today people from all over the world have the capacity to communicate by e-mail and to participate in electronically distributed meetings using something called "groupware," but Peter and Trudy Johnson-Lenz, who coined the term, nonetheless note that "The technology has, in most cases, increased the quantity of interactions people are having, not the quality of interactions." To do this will require a shift in thinking and attitudes toward being more creative and collaborative.

What will the new human agenda of the year 2020 be? I believe it will represent lateral thinking, not just thinking down the lines of the same track. Perhaps a few proposals might serve as a good starting point: (1) seeing each person as a creator and author, one with the educational opportunities to allow them to allow fulfillment of one's highest aspirations and provide for one's basic human needs; (2) fostering enterprising organizations in every sector that have the vision, collaborative attitudes, and knowledge-creating skills needed to meet both social and economic needs; (3) finding better ways to deal with difficult conversations, disputes, and regional conflicts than coercion, compliance, or war; (4) creating a more decent, civil, and just society and a sustainable environment for the future.

To realize this kind of new human agenda will require leaders who dare to take a stand for something difficult or who can assemble a creative, daring combination of people from different specialties to engage in truly collaborative conversations where they "marinate a problem" by thinking and working together on it and then by brainstorming to crack it wide open.

* * * * *

The new human agenda has been the background which, by and large, has defined who I am and the kind of work I have done since the 1970s. It was what was in the back of my mind and represented what was really important to me, even as I struggled to articulate it or live in a manner that was consistent with this new agenda. As I said earlier, I was inspired and interested by thinkers and writers that had a big panoramic view of the world and of human cultural evolution, but I wanted to do something more with my life than merely to describe or explain something.

I had a passion to make a difference, to have an impact, not just to tell people about ideas that would open up new possibilities, but to touch them. I spent a good part of the 1970s studying the ideas of personal transformation—Eastern and Western, ancient and modern, practical and esoteric. In 1976, I started an organization that provided personal transformation seminars—Relationships, an educational corporation. These seminars impacted the lives of thousands of people.

Yet, at some point I realized it was time to move from thinking in terms of transforming individuals to transforming people in groups or organizations. By the 1980s, I had romantic notions of taking what I had learned and going to do a project with NASA, or going to the Middle East and making a qualitative contribution to the Arab-Israeli crisis, or perhaps doing something about the environment. These ambitious dreams never materialized, as I had a family and organization to support and because, while I was somewhat masterful at transforming individuals, I didn't know enough about how to transform people in groups or complex human systems.

Therefore, with these purposes in mind, I spent almost 15 years as an executive coach and consultant in the area of enabling organizations to collaborate more effectively. Yet, for most of that time, I found that many of the qualities that transformed an individual did not necessarily impact a group, and vice versa. So I continued to pursue the inquiry in a broader and deeper way. In the process, I came up with ideas that I believed could offer any individual assistance in making a difference in their world.

I found some of the missing pieces in conversations with business leaders. Yet, the many of the conversations with people on the forefront of international affairs, science, government, enterprise, education, and law enforcement are what helped me to formulate and articulate the three or four central ideas put forward in this book—such as lateral leadership, creative collaboration, and deeply spirited, generative conversations.

This book, then, is for me a culmination of a long journey, written with the following purposes: First, to declare and clearly articulate for myself and for others this new human agenda so it can be heard and, if worthy, adopted. Second, to share what I have learned about lateral leadership, creativity, and collaboration as they apply to reaching shared understood goals and to solving complex problems in almost every domain of human concern. And, finally, to create a platform for an organization my colleagues and I have created called the Institute for Creative Collaboration.

I would like to close this preface with a quotation from Mikhail Gorbachev from his book, *The Search for a New Beginning—Developing a New Civilization:* "In order to solve pertinent problems, there is no other way but to seek and implement new forms of [relationship and inter-action]. Only the creative interaction of divergent groups which constitute our society, will allow for the answers we all seek to emerge" . . . and guide us as we shape the next phase of human development."

Acknowledgments

While I am the principal author of this book, I have had many collaborative co-authors, in a sense, as this book is the result of conversations or a network of conversations with many. Yet, whatever credit is due for the writing of this book, I must share fully and wholly with two people.

First is my partner in life, Susan Youngquist, who has been my inspiration in this project, especially in making it possible for me to talk to so many extraordinary people, while providing a practical anchor on every conceivable aspect of this book.

Next, enormous credit is owed to Leslie Whitaker for the powerful assistance she has provided through her listening to help elicit ideas, through her writing of first drafts, through her encouragement of my redrafts, and through her editing of finished pieces.

Both Leslie and Susan were excellent collaborators, simply the best I have ever been involved with. At all times they remained focused on the vision of the book, on what was next or what was missing, where value could be added, and never on what was wrong or the problem. Each was always available to do what was needed down to the last detail.

I would like to acknowledge my dear friend and colleague, Carl Kaestner, for his indefatigable support at all times, under all circumstances and conditions. Carl was a powerful factor in helping me to conceive the book, as well as setting up meetings with remarkable men and women—such as Michael Schrage and Maggie Herzig of the Public Conversations Project—who helped us to map the territory of creative collaboration and collaborative conversations.

A special acknowledgment goes to my stellar agent, Robin Davis. Robin had a vision of who I was and what could be accomplished through this book and who made it possible for me to move to a larger stage, in part by helping me create a relationship with my editor, Susan Barry of McGraw-Hill.

I very much appreciate the fact that Susan fully supported me in taking a global, multiple-perspective, cross-disciplinary approach that allowed me to cross-fertilize ideas on creative collaboration in government, business, law, education, and the arts. I believe this gave the book wings and has resulted in one that is much more dynamic and interesting to read than it otherwise might have been.

The people I have acknowledged here are the book's primary stakeholders. I would also like to acknowledge others who contributed through many conversations that not only led to a higher level of understanding but also to co-constructing new insights into the topic. These people are acknowledged in various ways in other parts of the book.

Finally, I would like to acknowledge my children for their enthusiasm, encouragement, and support during the time I wrote this book—Vanessa, Adam, Morgan, and Roc.

Introduction

What This Book Is Designed to Do

Creative collaboration is a big, new, exciting idea. Think of this book like a stick of dynamite. It is based on a big idea that has the power to unleash the human spirit into action and create new openings for possibility in every domain of human concern. It also has the power to explode some of the prevailing myths that have shaped institutions—government, the corporation, the university—as well as the way you and I tend to think and interact. These myths include the desire or need for power and control, the division of knowledge, and the division of labor.

As with any idea whose time has come, just mention the words "creative collaboration" and you will see people's eyes light up, signaling a moment of recognition. Suddenly, you will notice that they have given you the gift of their presence, listening with a high quality of attention that you may not be accustomed to. "Tell me a bit more about the idea," they will request. When you respond with, "It is not just about what extraordinary people can create on their own, but about what extraordinary, creative combinations of people can create together," you will almost hear the click as their minds switch on.

Immediately, from just a few things they say, you can see how they have already started to conjure up the possibility that, right in front of them, might be a way to deal with some of the really big challenges the world faces as we approach the millennium. You can also tell from the expression on their faces that they are thinking that it might be possible to find a new way to think and work together on the bothersome issues and problems they face in their lives, one that might result in surprising, thrilling, creative, entrepreneurial, breakthrough solutions.

You can tell from the curious questions people ask that they have a vague intuitive feeling that they are hardly able to articulate. Perhaps, they think, here might be a set of guiding ideas, methods, or tools that will have practical, down-to-earth application to help them reach goals, solve problems, and resolve conflicts.

The Purpose and Intent of This Book

John Mack, a friend, noted psychiatrist, and author of the Pulitzer Prize-winning biography of Lawrence of Arabia, once asked his son, "How do you make a difference in the world?" His son replied, "By taking action." Mack responded, "No, you make a difference with ideas . . . then you take action." The purpose of this book is to offer you ideas—like lateral leadership and creative collaboration—that will inspire you to make a difference in your world, as well as to offer you the guiding principles and methods that will assist you in demonstrating the power of collaborative action.

At a certain point early on in the process of writing this book, my colleagues and I reached a fork in the road. One road had a sign that said *Panoramic View.* This road would take us to a higher viewing place where we could have a broader and deeper view of how creative collaboration was being applied in many different fields, such as science, business, government, education, and the arts. The other road, in effect, said *Close Up.* This road would give us a more in-depth view of how creative collaboration was being applied in one field, such as government or business.

We chose the former road—the *Panoramic View*—to start out with. From the beginning, we had the idea that creative collaboration was a big idea whose time had come. Yet, when we started doing research, it was truly fascinating to see how creative collaboration kept showing up in every field and, furthermore, how excited people were to talk about it and how proud they were of the results that they had achieved with it.

I am speaking of heads of state like Shimon Peres, brilliant scientists and engineers like Rob Manning of the Mars Project, CEOs and executives like Roger Ackerman of the fast-growth Corning Incorporated, police officials such as staff sargeant Rick Murphy in Ottawa. Historian Pauline Maier, who wrote the book *American Scriptures* where she reinterpreted the writing of the Declaration of Independence as a collaborative effort, not an individual one, told us, "This is the only way to go." According to John Seely Brown at Xerox, "It is the way *everything* is going." All this was heady stuff.

At the same time, while we took the Panoramic View, we doubled back and went the Close-Up route to see how creative collaboration was being applied in specific fields, illustrating with profiles on the Mars Project, the Israeli-Palestinian conflict, Xerox and Corning corporations, the Hunger Project, and much more. We chose to do this for several reasons.

The first was to ground the idea of creative collaboration in some specific work settings that readers in the same or related fields could learn a lot from. The second was that, by doing more robust case studies of successful collaborations, we could draw out many lessons about what to do when faced with an impossible goal, a difficult problem, or a seemingly irresolvable conflict.

Third, we wanted to make it possible for any elected official or businessperson to see collaborative projects from a variety of perspectives that they could then "triangulate," juxtaposing the various approaches to come up with one that would apply to their own situation. We believe that this approach will make richer, more enjoyable reading.

There's a certain structure to the book that we feel is creative, effective, and definitely eclectic. The main chapters are largely intended to provide guiding ideas, tools, and methods. These are interspersed with interludes that are based on the conversations we had with collaborative people in different genres in which they told their stories. The intention of the interludes is to inspire the reader and to make sure you do not get a case of "information overload." Let's take a closer look at the various chapters and interludes.

Chapter One: *Creative Collaboration: An Idea Whose Time Has Come.* The book begins with a big, spiraling chapter that shows how an age of specialization is colliding with an age of complexity—making collaboration an idea whose time has come. The chapter shows how creative collaboration is impacting many different professions. A recipe at the end of the chapter can be practically and immediately applied.

Interlude: *The Mars Pathfinder Mission.* This powerful story drawn from conversations with people at NASA's Jet Propulsion Lab in La Cañada, California, shows how Phase One of the Mars Exploration Program—sending a lander and a remote control rover to Mars—is not only a pathfinder mission in terms of science and technology but also in terms of people thinking and working together.

Chapter Two: *How to Become a Collaborative Person.* The idea in this chapter is that collaboration isn't just something that is a matter of technique, but attitude. It requires learning to be a collaborative person who has the thinking and attitudes to make collaborations happen. Often, the people who could most benefit from collaboration —and think they are quite good at it—are often not very good at it at all. The chapter offers insights on how to learn to be a collaborative person, as well as unlearn old patterns of thinking and behavior that are counterproductive.

Interlude: *Passionate Diplomacy in the Middle East.* This is an inspiring story of how an ordinary person can make a difference by bringing together an extraordinary combination of people. The story shows how Terje Larsen, a Norwegian citizen, saw that the Washington talks between the Israelis and the Palestinians (the front channel) was designed for failure and created a secret backchannel in Oslo, Norway, that led to an historic breakthrough. The story provides a seldom seen, behind-the-scenes look at what happens on a human level in a high-tension, international negotiation.

Chapter Three: *The Building Blocks of Creative Collaboration.* As my friend Bob Fritz, author of *Creating,* says, "Structure influences behavior." This chapter delineates the building blocks—such as lateral leadership, shared goals, lots of time in dialogue—needed to ensure the success of collaborative projects.

Interlude: *The Future of the Firm.* This interlude reminds me of a quotation I read from Oliver Wendell Holmes: "A mind stretched by a new idea cannot find a way to get back into its previous container." This story provides insights on how to build a creative and collaborative corporation. It is based on conversations with Roger Ackerman, CEO of Corning Incorporated, a company that is exploding with growth, and with John Seely Brown, chief scientist at Xerox's Palo Alto Research Center, largely responsible for the PC revolution. While Ackerman has powerful and simple ideas that are very implementable, Brown dazzles with his innovative ideas that are grounded in practical results.

Chapter Four: *Close Encounters of the Creative Kind: Launching Your Collaboration.* While chapters two and three show the basics of collaboration—being a collaborative person and the building blocks—this chapter shows you how to launch your own creative collaboration. It will offer you a powerful assist in deciding what you want to collaborate on, help you design an extraordinary combination of people that will bring different perspectives and spark creativity, as well as prepare you for the first meeting of your collaborative project.

Interlude: *Joan Holmes and the Hunger Project.* In today's corporation (or other institutions), issues like eradicating world hunger and poverty or creating a sustainable environment usually don't show up on the radar screen as priorities. Yet those of us who work in these corporations are also human beings, who on some level care deeply about these issues—even while we may tend to bury the fact. This story about Joan Holmes, director of Hunger Project, will help you unearth the fact that you care, whether it is about issues like hunger, or your neighborhood, or your children's schools. It will also give you a great example of a unique approach to creative collaboration called "strategic planning in action" that can be applied to any social issue or complex management problem.

Chapter Five: *It Happens in Conversations: An Introduction.* Dr. Louis Koster, a prominent physician and a consultant to international organizations, estimates that 50 percent of the communication in most groups consists of arbitrary opinions, gossip, or complaining that does not contribute to creativity, team collaboration, or productive results. This chapter shows how a collaborative conversation is distinct from the conversations most people usually indulge in. It will also provide an introduction to the five phases of a collaborative conversation offered in the next chapter.

Chapter Six: *The Five Phases of a Collaborative Conversation.* This chapter shows you how to clarify or frame the purpose of a collaborative conversation so that it produces the desired results. It also shows how to gather different views and perspectives, build shared understanding, and deal with these seemingly incompatible views in a creative rather than destructive way. This and the first chapter are probably the two most instructive chapters in the book, which you can decide for yourself as you put this information into practical application.

Chapter Seven: *Coaching, Practical Applications, and Tools of Creative Collaboration.* This chapter will provide a number of strategies for the lateral leader as facilitator, as they apply to various issues. Specific conversation recipes (distinct from the five phases) will be provided that will assist you in facilitating groups to reach stretch goals, solve problems, or resolve conflicts. The chapter also creatively interweaves examples from people who have deep experience in negotiation, mediation, and facilitation—such as Roger Fisher and Bill Ury of *Getting to Yes,* and Robert Bush and Joe Folger, of *The Promise of Mediation.*

Note: *Why the book is voiced in both "I" and "we":* It's important to clarify that, while I am the creator and author of the book and that it distinctly reflects my writing and thought process, the book was, in another sense, created and authored by a very creative and collaboration relationship, including Susan Youngquist, my partner in life, and Leslie Whitaker, an editorial consultant and writer. I use the word "we" in the main chapters to express the spirit of our collaboration, and the word "I" in the interludes to express the personal relationship and insights that were developed one-on-one with the people I spoke to.

Chapter One

Creative Collaboration:

An Idea Whose Time Has Come

Imagine the possibility of achieving dreams and aspirations that were never attainable to you on an individual basis.

Imagine thinking and working together with others who see and respond differently to the world than you do but whom you find endlessly curious, intriguing, and compelling.

Imagine participating in deeply spirited, generative conversations that result in new shared understandings, as well as in creating something that never existed before.

Imagine what it would be like to be part of a community of commitment, where learning and questions were more important than knowing and certainty.

To Step into the Future, We Must Shift Our Weight to the Opposite Foot

Extraordinary individuals have always been looked at as the source of significant and lasting human achievement. To step into the future, you have to shift your weight to the opposite foot and look at things from a new perspective. In the future, the source of human achievement will not be extraordinary individuals, but extraordinary *combinations* of people—in business, science, politics, and the arts. An extraordinary combination of people may be comprised of people who are already extraordinary in different professions or disciplines yet who see an exciting, new possibility and who have the desire to make it a reality, perhaps without knowing that they themselves and their occupations may be forever changed by it. Or this combination might come from ordinary people who discover their own capacity to be extraordinary in the process of collaborating with others who acknowledge their talents and gifts.

To be sure, creative collaboration is an idea that is on everyone's lips today. In some cases, people are talking about collaboration as what is happening (or needs to happen). In other cases, it articulates what has been a vague notion of what is missing in the individual's life that will make a difference. Thus, when you mention creative collaboration, it speaks volumes. What we discovered in speaking to scientists, business people, educators, and others in researching this book was that, if we would merely mention the word "collaboration" once in a conversation, it would, in the course of the ensuing dialogue, be repeated back two, three, or more times. People would launch into their own personal stories of collaboration with passion and zeal. "Collaboration is an incredibly useful term to describe what's happening in particle physics," said Harvard professor Peter Galison, winner of the MacArthur Award or "genius award" in science. "Collaboration is the key to reinventing government," said Senator John McCain of Arizona. And there were more. "Collaboration is big, big, big," said Bill Gates of Microsoft. "I love the idea of collaborating, whatever that means," quipped shock-jock Howard Stern.

It was interesting to note that when people talked of their own experiences of collaboration, however they defined it, they became very inspired, animated, and enlivened. Everyone we talked to in writing this book told us that they found an "aesthetic," "uplifting," "alchemical" quality to creative collaboration that allowed them to transcend the mundane aspect of daily affairs. "There were moments of recognition when I saw for the first time who I was and what I was magnificently capable of as an individual," said one collaborator. Others referred to "when I saw I was part of a living community or system," and "when I was able to reach up and touch the web."

What Is Creative Collaboration?

It is a proven fact that a flock of birds flying together
in a V formation has the lifting power
to carry twice the distance of a
single bird flying alone.

Discovering the Elements of Creative Collaboration

Whether you are a scientist, elected official, business leader, or artist, being creative (or generative) means taking something that perhaps you believed would never come to pass, declaring it possible, and then working to make it a reality. This could lead to a new scientific theory, a pioneering legislative action, an innovative product, or even a unique art form. "Collaboration" implies doing something together, and that is exactly what it is. It is the desire or need to create or discover something new, while thinking and working with others, that distinguishes the action. The Wright Brothers aspired to be first in flight; Watson and Crick searched for the secret of life; Picasso and Braque experimented with a new art form called Cubism. When Jobs and Wozniak collaborated to create the first Apple personal computer in a garage, they joined this list of classic examples. Creative collaboration involves: (1) different views and perspectives, (2) shared goals, (3) building new shared understandings, and (4) the creation of new value. It can be applied to reaching goals, solving problems, or resolving seemingly impossible conflicts.

Collaboration is extraordinary combinations of people.

Collaboration is the act (or process) of "shared creation" or discovery. Collaborative people are those who identify a possibility and recognize that their own view, perspective, or talent is not enough to make it a reality. They need other views, perspectives, and talents. Collaborative people see others not as creatures who force them to compromise, but as colleagues who can help them amplify their talents and skills. In World War II, for example, physicists and scientists who barely understood one another's work came up with the idea of radar. Former President Jimmy Carter brought Menachem Begin and Anwar Sadat together and produced the Camp David Accords. Walt Disney spent hundreds of hours in the 1950s talking to people who designed movie sets and amusement parks, and came up with the idea of Disneyland—Tomorrowland, Pirates of the Caribbean, and Mr. Toad's Wild Ride.

Collaboration is shared "understood" goals.

Creative collaboration not only involves bringing people together but also enabling them to work together around a purpose larger than themselves. Michael Schrage, author of *No More Teams,* writes that one of the primary tasks of management in the years ahead is to be able to frame goals and problems in a way that inspires people to collaborate as opposed to doing their own thing or defending their own turf.[2] Creating shared understood goals allows smart people with big egos to subordinate their egos while contributing to something significant and lasting. It also creates a clearing that pulls people across different professional fields and allows them to create a common language. We refer to this clearing as a "trading zone." For people to collaborate, they must see the goal as significant and as something they cannot achieve on their own. The Beatles had a shared goal of writing and performing great music. Carter, Begin, and Sadat had the goal of peace in the Middle East.

Collaboration is building* new *shared understandings that lead to something new. The different views and perspectives in a collaboration are essential to help people better understand each other and light the spark of creativity. Each of us sees reaching a goal, solving a problem, or resolving a conflict through our own worldview. Often, we are completely unaware of how arbitrary our thinking and understanding might be. Thus, in every collaboration, there is a need for open, honest dialogue in which people construct a shared understanding of: (1) the problem, (2) its root causes, (3) the solution, and (4) actions to take. This shared understanding can lead to new ideas, fresh approaches, and innovative solutions.

A prime example is the Camp David Accords. In 1976, President Carter wanted to do something to encourage peace in the Middle East. He invited Menachem Begin and Anwar Sadat to attend a meeting at Camp David. As the story goes, Carter asked Sadat, "Why is this land important to you?" Sadat answered, "It's been part of Egypt for thousands of years." He then asked Begin, "Why is this land important to you?" Begin replied, "Because we don't want tanks ten miles from our border." This shared understanding led to something new: The land would be returned to Egypt, but a new "demilitarized zone" would be created along the border.

Collaboration is an act of shared creation. Arthur Koestler has written in his epic tome, *The Art of Creation,* that most people usually think and work along the lines of a single frame of reference.[1] Creativity occurs when people are able to connect different frames of reference in ways that result in creating or discovering something new. Think of Mahatma Gandhi, who combined protest and pacifism to come up with his concept of "militant nonviolence." Think of the Internet, a combination of the computer and the telephone. Think of the nonstick iron that combines the technology of the conventional iron with that of the nonstick frying pan. Koestler thought in terms of creativity as a matter of extraordinary individuals with great minds, like Gandhi or Bell, who had an "aha!" experience. Yet think about how much greater the possibility for creative, high-leverage, catalytic ideas exists when many minds, or an extraordinary combination of people, are brought together through the shared context of a dialogue around a common goal or problem.

Collaboration can take a myriad of forms. We are often asked the difference between creative collaboration and teamwork. The answer is this: While all collaborations involve teamwork, not all teams are collaborative. Collaborations involve the creation of new value by doing something radically new or different—scientific breakthroughs, landmark legislation, new products. Most teams are focused on routine work and doing the same thing better—like the more efficient linking and coordinating of tasks. In the same sense, successful collaborative groups are made up of strange brews, of nascent combinations of people. Most teams, even multidisciplinary teams, tend to be fairly homogeneous.

A collaboration can take the form of a semipermanent network of twenty-five to thirty medical researchers seeking a cure for HIV; a multidisciplinary team of ten department heads (process owners) for a Fortune 500 company charged with reinventing an organization by shifting its emphasis from isolated tasks to integrated processes so as to deliver higher-quality products and services; a five- to seven-person coalition of elected officials who pass a piece of breakthrough legislation; or a fleeting team of two or three elementary school teachers who design an interdisciplinary study project on ancient Rome.

Creative Collaboration Is an Idea Whose Time Has Come

Ideas have the power to change the face of things.
—*MACHIAVELLI*

An Expanded View of What It Means to Be a Human Being

When we look up in the sky at night, space becomes time, for the stars that we are seeing do not show the light of the present moment, but light of the past—radiations of the celestial present that are light-years away from the Earth will not reach us until the future. Similarly, when most people look out at what seems to be happening in the world around them, they do not see the present, they see the past. In other words, we see what fits our worldview. We admire golfer Tiger Woods marching up the 18th green in Augusta at the Masters Tournament because we see in him images from our own mind of the 1930s world of DC Comics: action heroes like Superman and Wonder Woman who singlehandedly accomplished feats that most of us would find difficult or impossible.

If we could pull a gestalt switch and see things from a different perspective, we would see something light-years away from Tiger Woods—an apostle of our religion of the superhero. We would see that whenever anything of significance is being accomplished in the world today, it is being accomplished by people collaborating across professional and cultural frontiers.

We would see that the future belongs not just to stars, heroes, or technical wizards who think and work in isolation, but to collaborative people who think and work together. It is not just the individual or technology on which the future of the world rests, but an expanding concept of what it is to be a human being.

An Age of Hierarchy and Specialization Is Colliding with an Age of Complexity

To deal with the complex problems we face, we elect a new president every four years, search for charismatic CEOs, and seek out other strong leaders for our university—or even our symphony orchestra. This is because we still see images of the strong leader on top of the pyramidal organization—the pharaoh or king at the top with different levels and specialized departments— even as we sit amongst its tumbled-down ruins and try to figure out what to do. Again, if we were to pull a gestalt switch and would see things in a new way, we would see that an age of hierarchy and specialization is colliding with an age of complexity. All too often, the bothersome issues and problems we face fall between the cracks of the organization chart.

For example, exhaust emissions from cars in Los Angeles are rising in the atmosphere in great concentrations and are entering into the food chain of the Eskimo in the Antarctic. A CEO in New York wonders what, if anything, he can do so that the smart people he has hired with six-figure salaries can learn to think and interact better with colleagues or customers. Scientists in particle physics no longer carry out bubble chamber experiments in a lab in the woods but in labs that are half a city block long and contain hundreds (indeed thousands) of people from distinct occupations and cultures—physicists, engineers, computer programmers, and administrators.

Top-down leadership and narrow specialization were, and still are, sound strategies for relatively simple problems and times, yet a new *lateral leadership* model is emerging, based on stimulating creative collaboration between specialists who see and respond to the world differently. These specialists can be people thousands of miles apart who communicate through phone, fax, modem, and invent new pidgin or Creole languages to communicate across occupational boundaries.

From Civilization to Planetization

We also see images of the past when we attempt to come up with creative solutions to problems that exist in world affairs. We see resolution of the Palestinian and Israeli settlement in terms of a nation-state for the Israelis and a nation-state for the Palestinians. This is because in our minds, we see the world through images of the past—nation-states, armies, and religious differences. In so doing, we miss the shift from civilization to what Teilhard de Chardin called "the planetization of mankind," or the many forces bringing us all closer together.

This new planetization is revolutionizing the world as we see it. Examples of new ideas that we now accept as mainstream are: (1) the global economy, (2) the shift from hierarchies to networks, (3) the democratization of technology, and (4) the knowledge society. The reality is that, despite all the things both players in the Middle East conflict do to pull apart from each other—the six-day wars, terrorist bombings, and imprisonments—they increasingly interpenetrate on a day-to-day basis. Historian William Irwin Thompson has suggested that Jerusalem might become a city-state, one analogous to the Vatican—not the military state of Benjamin Netanyahu or Yassar Arafat, but a cultural zone governed by an ecumenical counsel as the Earth's first planetary city—a cultural shrine of the three "Abrahamic religions."[3] The world has had enough nation-states and armies. It now needs places to experience itself as a world.

Today, as the Middle East peace process slows and government contacts dry up, a scattered but increasingly lush network of people-to-people contact is materializing. Some view it as a shadow peace process. According to a recent *Boston Globe* article, joint studies amongst Israeli and Palestinian specialists on the environment are taking place with the principle that "nature has no borders." Palestinian and Israeli doctors from the Gaza Strip live for months together, training at Israel's medical facilities, treating patients from both sides by day and going out to bars together at night. Contacts between lawyers, tax specialists, and customs officials are taking place every day. Palestinian and Israeli artists show and tour together. Teenagers from both sides learn more about each other through school and sports programs.

Recently, when an Israeli businessman and a Palestinian engineer tried to cross a border at Cairo together, the Israeli was let through, but the Palestinian with a valid visa was roughed up by the Egyptian guards who said they would send him back on the next plane. Malki, the Israeli, said, "Let him through or I will go back too." The guards let both through. Kinche, the Palestinian, said, "He put himself on the line for me. At that moment, I forgot his history and saw his humanity." "There are fanatics on both sides," Malki said. "We each have to give up little to learn to live together."[4]

The Great Man Theory of History Is Reaching Its Limits

History is not just made up of facts and events but is largely based on interpretations. We choose our interpretation of what happens to us based on our beliefs and assumptions, which are often arbitrary. This becomes our "his" or "her" story. For centuries, our story has been based on the Great Man theory or individualistic model. Our mental model acts like a filter. It filters in information that fits it and filters out information that doesn't. In many cases, our individualistic model has blinded us to the real source of creativity and effectiveness. Today, there is a profound shift taking place from the individualistic to the collaborative model due to many factors, such as change and complexity. Thus, people are beginning to reinterpret much of what has gone on before in a new light.

For example, it has been commonly thought that the Declaration of Independence was written by Thomas Jefferson before he reached the age of thirty-three. While this would have been a stupendous feat for anyone, only recently have historians begun to look at the drafting of the document in a new way. Massachusetts Institute of Technology (MIT) historian, Pauline Maier, has done important research revealing that the Declaration is not just a product of one extraordinary mind but is more a collective intelligence of ordinary people throughout the thirteen colonies.

As a matter of fact, there were over ninety "public statements" of Independence that were adopted by various towns, counties, and states between April and July 1776. These not only explained the reasons the citizenry had come to favor independence, but were essential in forwarding the Indepenence vote. As for the Declaration of Independence itself, a drafting committee of five outlined the articles to be included. From the group, Thomas Jefferson was chosen to be the draftsman. (As John Adams concluded, "You write ten times better than I do.")[5]

According to Maier, the drafting committee had a substantial role in its creation, far more than Jefferson recalled in the 1820s (although his accounts of that time are frequently cited and often accepted at face value). Congress's editing of the document, over a two-day period, substantially improved the committee's version, and reflected more exactly the conviction of the Congressmen's constituents, as revealed in the "other" declarations.

Music is another field where great works are viewed as the triumph of a single maestro. Recent evidence from scholars, however, shows proof that Mozart often collaborated on many pieces during the period of time he wrote *The Magic Flute*. Scholars believe he was involved in many Broadway- or Hollywood-style collaborations. Recently they came across two such operas. *The Philosophers Stone,* written in 1790, includes the names of those who contributed to various sections of the opera. Written above each section was the name of the composer in an unknown hand. Mozart's name not only appears above a duet but also is inscribed above substantial portions of the finale. The same applies to another opera, *The Magnificent Dervish,* and scholars suspect it applies to many other pieces, as well.

Of course, collaboration requires competence and knowing who not to work with. Mozart was once criticized by his patron, the Emperor of Austria, for having too many notes in his music. The Emperor suggested that a few notes could be cut. Mozart responded, "Which few did you have in mind?"

In science, there are many historic examples of creative collaborations that are largely unknown. For example, when Charles Darwin read "An Essay on Population" by Thomas Malthus in 1838, he was thunderstruck by Malthus's idea that population multiplies faster than food. If that were true, Darwin concurred, then animals and plants must compete to survive, forming new species from the survivors. It was the creative combination of the ideas of the naturalist, Darwin, and the economist, Malthus, that led to the theory of the survival of the fittest or "natural selection." More recently, Albert Einstein, renowned as the great genius who worked alone, once told a young girl who asked him about his experiments that he never conducted any. He said his work relied heavily on the experiments of other people.

Collaboration Is Here and Now

When authorities in basic fields like history, science, business, the arts, politics, and economics start to see the world in a fundamentally new way and act accordingly, it is a sign of a cultural transformation. Cultural transformations are not news events that can be seen like the explosion of the atom bomb at Hiroshima, or tanks crushing protesters in Tiananmen Square, or a peaceful picture of the Earth sent back by Apollo astronauts from the moon. In the middle of a cultural change, most of us cannot see what is really going on. Cultural transformations are more like deep, swift undercurrents that affect our passages about Earth, like a tide that sweeps us up from one beach to another without us hardly realizing it. Nonetheless, when a cultural transformation occurs, there are many signs of a shift in the climate of the times.

The Crystal Palace Exposition, put on at the 1895 London World's Fair, was not only the consummate symbol of the Industrial Revolution but also of management surrounding human culture and nature. Thomas Watson, founder of IBM, believed that there would never be a market for more than about a thousand computers worldwide and that those would be sold to the world's big industrial companies. Thus, we could say that the dawn of the Information Age occurred when IBM introduced its PC in the early 1980s with an ad during the

Super Bowl broadcast that showed Charlie Chaplin running a conventional factory as he did in his classic, *Modern Times,* with an IBM PC—the image of a machine worker being transformed into a machine programmer. The next era, called the age of biology, may make its presence known in vague ways through something that could have only come about as a result of a collaboration—biotech drugs. Yet, if we take a longer and deeper view, the next age may not be so much characterized by a breakthrough in technology, but by a breakthrough in the way we think and work.

Many Small Signs Show a Shift in the Wind

Oftentimes there are many signs of cultural change all around us, although we are not aware of them when they are occurring. Like an ant crawling on Picasso's *Guernica,* the figure-and-ground relationship is such that we are largely blinded to the full-scale cultural distortion that is taking place. Yet, it still affects the way we see and respond to the world, the way we think and work, and the way we make our daily bread. In writing this book, we saw many such small signs that indicated a profound cultural transformation, one that would alter the way each of us sees and responds to the world. These signs have led us to conclude that collaboration is an idea whose time has come.

We have found hundreds of instances of collaboration through cursory glances in daily newspapers and professional journals, as well as through serendipitous conversations with friends and colleagues. These articles spanned a broad range of fields—from government to molecular biology, from teacher education to hospital administration, from professional sports to the arts. They show a profound shift in the way people think and operate in their professional lives—from being an individual who asks, "What can I create?" to being a collaborative person who asks, "What can we create together?"; from thinking and working in isolation to thinking and working together; from the primacy of the parts to the primacy of the whole.

The same trend evident in our professional lives is affecting our personal lives. As both parents share the role of breadwinner, and children participate in more activities outside the home, family life can present a complex planning and logistical dilemma. Here's an anecdote about just how much creative collaboration is coming into play. Before the U.S. House and Senate leaders asked for family-friendly schedules, many legislators' children rarely saw their parents. When Dan Quayle was a senator from Indiana, his daughter Corrine was determined to get him to come to a school play in which she was performing. At the age of seven, Corrine had already learned where power lies in the Senate. She wrote a note to Bob Dole, then Majority Leader, asking him not to schedule any votes on the night of the play. He complied.

The Good News

Everywhere we look there are anecdotal examples that signal the arrival of an era of collaboration. Here are some of our favorites.

- *The Clinton administration has declared a national dialogue to eliminate racial prejudice. The dialogue was framed to root out not only prejudices between blacks and whites but also prejudices blacks and other minorities had about themselves. "It's hard to see yourself as an empowered person when you identify with ancestors who have been slaves, or brothers and sisters in jail."*

- *Management guru Peter Drucker has written that the single most important shift in the way business and work are being done today is from "ownership" to "partnership," and "from individual tasks" to "collaboration." In 1996, there were over 10,000 strategic alliances, joint ventures, and mergers that took place. That is one an hour, around the clock, every day.*

- *The judiciary from the state of Florida, reeling from a huge case load and fed up with adversarial lawyers, took a stand to refer all civil cases to mediation, or alternate dispute resolution, before a case can be heard in court. The results are extraordinary.*

- *A peasant boy broke his hip while playing at school in Istanbul, Turkey. The local doctors, suspicious that he was suffering more than a broken hip, sent X-ray images to doctors at the Massachusetts General Hospital in Boston via the Internet, where they diagnosed a benign tumor. The use of the Internet to transmit X-ray images is a clinical first. The child was flown to Massachusetts General for surgery and is expected to do well.*

The Bad News

When a new era is dawning, there are often signs that the old era, whose days are moribund, is still in its ascendancy. This is what cultural historians call the "sunset effect." As one era prepares to rise in the sky, another goes out in a blaze of glory. So just as there are signs of lateral leadership, collaborative communication, and cross-disciplinary learning, there are still many more signs to the contrary. These signs include indications of a search for charismatic leaders, of adversarial communication, and of fragmenting and specializing knowledge to such a degree that people from different departments in science, biology, and anthropology barely understand each other.

For instance, every three-and-a-half years, we get passionately involved in electing a new president—even though people don't really believe that this makes much difference—because we still believe in the "great man" theory of history. People in government still debate across the aisle, each staking our their position and holding on to it for dear life, even though it leads to government gridlock. Or they stick to their own specialty or position and ignore the subtleties of issues. For example, the Democrats believe in Pro Choice but rarely debate what happens to the soul of the aborted child or the spirit of the mother or other delicate issues. The Republicans believe in the Right to Life but do not pay much attention to how the child will be fed, clothed, and sheltered after it is born. That's a different department.

It is easy to stay centered in your old view of the world, to protect your noble certainties and ways of doing things when there is a lot of evidence to support it and not much in the winds of change. Yet when a new idea is born and the climate of the times shifts, people are brought to the edge of their old views and practices and begin to feel uncomfortable. When this happens, there are always those who will resist a new idea rather than care and feed it. There are also many signs of resistance to its proponents and of rejection by the existing culture.

For example:

- *One day after newspapers ran the story about the Clinton dialogue on race, authorities quoted in newspaper articles from the around the country said, "It can't be done," that Clinton's proposed apology for slavery would never be a meaningful act, but a mere gesture. Two weeks later, another article ran that said that the debate was doomed to failure because whites, blacks, and others lacked a common language that would allow them to understand each other.*

- *In spite of putting people on teams, processes, and joint ventures, the real barriers to collaboration and communication remain in people's heads, says Peter Senge, author of* The Fifth Discipline.

- *A United Airlines plane circled an airport while the three members of the crew struggled with a landing-gear problem. The cockpit voice recorder showed that both the copilot and flight engineer knew their fuel shortage was becoming urgent, but they never directly told the Captain, whose mind was on the landing equipment. The plane ran out of gas, the engine shut down, and a crash ensued.*

To be sure, whenever there is darkness, there is scattered light. There were many more examples we found in our research into this book that encouraged rather than discouraged us.

Creative Collaboration Is Spreading in All Fields Independently

There is a story told about monkeys in the islands of the South Pacific. It happens that for time immemorial, monkeys in this region would dig up potatoes in the bush, rub them a few times with their hands, and eat them fresh out of the ground. Then one day it was observed that one of the monkeys took his potatoes down to the beach and started washing them in the ocean. The other monkeys on the island just watched at first. Then after about a week or so, they started washing their potatoes in the ocean too. The story shows how a good idea spreads. But the story gets even more interesting. It turns out, according to the anthropologists, that after about six weeks all the monkeys in all the islands for 250 miles around started washing their potatoes too, without any obvious contact with the monkeys from the original island.

In doing research on creative collaboration in various fields, we noticed a very similar phenomenon. There are some leaders who have moved away from hierarchy and specialization and are using a collaborative approach in various domains as a result of seeing others "wash their potatoes." We have all heard the same gurus and read the same articles that are part of a shared information pool that includes terms like "skilled facilitation," "teams," and "integrated processes." At the same time, one of the most exciting aspects of researching this book is that we found people saying very similar kinds of things about collaboration in very different kinds of fields that having little or no contact with each other.

For example, AMC Thorndike, a famous particle physicist, writes, "Who is the 'experimenter'? Rarely, if ever, is he a single individual." The "experimenter" may be a group of astronomers banded together to carry out their work with no clear internal hierarchy. They may be a group of young physicists or engineers working on the Hubble telescope or on a passengered journey to Mars. They may be a group of physicians and biologists working on a new wonder drug. One thing the "experimenter" certainly is not: the traditional image of the cloistered scientist, working in isolation at the laboratory bench.

Let's turn to business and think about the words of David Kelly of David Kelly Designs, an award-winning industrial design company in Palo Alto, California. "The age of the genius designer is long past. We are all very smart people. But today, given the complexity of the design process, creative 'genius' comes from the minds of lots of smart designers working together rather than just one of them," says Kelly, whose company came up with the Apple mouse, the Crest toothpaste tube, and the design for the Motorola flip phone. "A true genius wouldn't be very happy here. I don't know if one exists."[6]

How about the arts? An article we read on jazz entitled, "What

We Haven't Done Before" says that most jazz greats are "cats who walk alone," yet they realize that no music is more fraternal than jazz. Greatness comes not from one man but from all exchanging ideas in a spirit of mutual support or friendly competition, often uniting them in a collaborative effort to raise the level of their art.

In education, law enforcement, and health care we noticed the same trends emerging time after time, convincing us that, today and in the future, significant and lasting accomplishment will not come from extraordinary people but from extraordinary combinations of people who learn how to think and work together. The following is intended to provide insight into how creative collaboration is showing up in diverse professions and disciplinary fields.

Creative Collaboration Is Transforming Science, Medicine, and Technology

Standing on the terra firma of Mars, the atmosphere is the color of salmon, and the Earth looks like a iridescent blue sphere in the evening sky. When the Pathfinder spacecraft landed on the ancient planet with its octagonal shock cushions protecting the Rover that would wander the surface, it may have marked the beginning of a new era in both science and management. According to geologist Bob Anderson, "Pathfinder is blazing new trails in technology, but it is also a pathfinder with respect to how people from different fields think and work together."[7] According to project manager, Donna Shirley, "Not one piece on the Rover vehicle was the product of an individual mind, but was from creative teamwork amongst scientists, engineers, and bureaucrats like me." Shirley says that "the key is enough space for the brilliant people on a project like this to be creative, while maintaining enough focus and teamwork to make sure the project is brought in on time and within budget."[8]

In Genetics Institute in Cambridge, Massachusetts, molecular biologists, physicians, manufacturers, and FDA (U.S. Food and Drug Administration) testing experts are creating designer drugs through biotechnology to cure certain kinds of cancers, heart disease, arthritis, and other illnesses. The different people all come from fields that may sound alike but are often, in reality, operating worlds apart, and, according to vice president, Ed Fritsch, collaborative conversation plays an important role in bridging differences. The often difficult process, through conversation, of learning to understand what different fields of expertise bring to a project ultimately pays off increasing yield, quality, and speed.

When we landed on the surface of the moon, it was a breakthrough in technology, but we lost the management technology that made it possible. One of the groups that is making sure this won't happen again involves a far-flung collaboration of scientists researching the Earth's upper atmosphere. Robert Claur, a space scientist at the University of Michigan, and others are testing ideas about the relationship of solar wind and the Earth's magnetic fields through a computer conferencing system called the Collaboratory. It is part of a multidisciplined project that not only includes space scientists, engineers, and computer experts but also behavioral scientists. The psychologists have permission to snoop on what's going on, in order to better understand how scientists are learning to collaborate.

"The days of the single scientist are over," Claur told me. "We use five instruments stationed in remote places like the Arctic Circle to record complex events. It used to be that a scientist was an expert on only one instrument, which would blind them. Now through cross instrumentation, we can see things from new angles. It used to be that, with one instrument, we were looking at the universe through a small peephole. With five, it is like we're looking through a mail slot." The data come in live on the left side of a big computer white board. On the right side, there's a space (chat board) for the scientists to discuss how they interpret the data. Says Claur, "The more eyes on the data, the more likely a Eureka event!"[9]

Here are some other examples:

- *By combining their observations made from the mighty Keck Telescope in Hawaii and the Hubble space telescope, astronomers have discovered the most distant object ever seen, a galaxy some thirteen billion light-years from the Earth.*

- *A study by Kellogg School of Management shows that in intensive care units, more open communication and collaborative problem solving between doctors, nurses, and technicians facilitated superior individual contribution, group performance of complex tasks, and a higher level of patient care and survival.*

- *A publication identifying a strong candidate for the gene determining susceptibility to breast and ovarian cancer featured 45 co-authors drawn from a biotech firm, a U.S. medical school, a Canadian medical school, an established pharmaceutical company, and a government research lab.*

Collaborative Attitudes Are Shifting Government Gridlock to Bipartisan Cooperation

It was a cold Sunday in January and black smoke from the ferry blew straight up in great gusts. The passengers had unknowingly taken the ferry to see the Statue of Liberty. When they arrived on Liberty Island, they saw the sign "closed for the day." The same Sunday visitors who had made a family pilgrimage to the nation's capitol were not allowed into the Smithsonian museums. The following day, workers would find out that they weren't going to receive their paychecks, having been deemed "nonessential." To be sure, we had no scarcity of strong, smart leaders in Washington—Clinton, Dole, Gingrich. What showed up as missing were leaders who could collaborate enough to pass a budget and keep the government open.

After this fiasco and the 1994 elections when the voters expressed their displeasure against Democrats and Republicans respectively, our national leaders moved beyond this climate of political acrimony and passed a bipartisan bill to balance the national budget by the year 2002. Other bipartisan efforts also began to show. A dozen times each day in Congress, a chairman leaves a committee hearing and passes off the gavel to another party member. But one morning in May of 1997, Senator John McCain, a Republican from Arizona and chairman of the Senate Finance Committee, did something different: He passed the gavel to Ernest Hollings, a Democrat.

According to a *New York Times* article by Michael Lewis, "A look of alarm passed Hollings' face. He and McCain exchanged words. Then McCain moved quickly away and was gone before Hollings could adjust." Later, Senator McCain called one of the lowest-ranking Democratic senators, Russell Feingold of New York, and asked him to collaborate on a bill for campaign finance reform. "What are the odds that a Republican senator (Republicans depend on PAC money) will come anywhere near my vision—public financing of elections? Why should he jeopardize his authority?" Feingold asked. McCain responded, "You are a Democrat and we disagree on many things, but there are others [areas] where we see the world in the same way. Let's take a first step." It was one man saying to the other, party politics are fine, but they only cut so deep around our real commitments. Since that time they have taken many steps, among them the McCain-Feingold Bill for Campaign Financing Reform.[10]

There are more incidents showing up like this every day, not just in Washington but in local statehouses. Donna Sytek, Speaker of the House of the New York State Legislature, says, "Collaboration is a much better approach to getting landmark legislation passed than conflict. We like to see a committee report getting landmark legislation passed than conflict. We like to see a committee report come out close to unanimous. For example, a 17 to 3 vote on a controversial bill is good. That means you have 17 people from diverse backgrounds agreeing—people from all parts of the state, different agencies, genders, parties, you name it—unless the committee is made up of too many like-minded people. But we try to have a diversity of opinion. The larger the group, the more likely you are to have a cross-section of opinion. If you get a 9 to 8 vote, that means to me that it is a particularly vexing issue or that people have not done enough work on it. I do not like 9 to 8 votes from a committee.

The most successful legislative products have come from a process where all points of view are represented. This means gathering all the different stakeholders and getting all the different sides aired, as well as the thinking process behind them. Finally, it involves coming up with a creative, constructive solution.[11]

- *A July 31, 1997,* Wall Street Journal *survey said that "the President and Congress are being blessed by the American public for collaborating." Fifty-eight percent of the electorate would reelect the Democrat, Clinton, for how he worked with the Congress on the economy and budget, 48 percent would reelect the Republican Congress.*

- *In India, Kocheril Narayanan, the first untouchable, was named president. Being born in the untouchable class taught him skills necessary for "coalition building, namely diplomacy, forbearance, and the willingness to listen to the concerns of the common man."*

- *Compelled by the passionate calls of the late Princess Diana, representatives from over 100 nations, on every continent, are meeting to work together to end the deadly scourge of land-mine use that has killed and maimed hundreds of thousands of innocents.*

In Business, the Competitive Edge Will Come from the Collaborative Advantage

"I know of few Fortune 500 CEOs who would say they are in control of such a complex organization with so many variables," says one executive at a conference. "I don't want to create an organization with ladders and mechanistic functions," says Juan Rada, former head of planning for Digital Equipment Corporation (DEC), "I want to create a tribe." "Why not think of an organization as an "enterprise web of different specialists and companies for meeting customer needs?" says former U.S. Labor Secretary Robert Reich. "My vision is that of a radically decentralized *chaordic* organization where tolerance of chaos generates order as in nature," says Dee Hoch, former Chairman of Visa International. "Why not think of an organization as a living being?" asks Arie DeGuess, former head of planning, Royal Dutch Shell. What all these voices and metaphors are telling us is that the traditional corporation based on top-down leadership and separate functions is over.

The collaborative corporation. A new era of collaborative organizations characterized by lateral leadership and virtual teams is emerging. These companies will be more concerned with nurturing creative people with a view toward creating resources that never existed before than they will be with reducing head counts or linking and coordinating tasks in order to cut costs. Their focus will be on engaging customers in a dialogue about their goals and problems. The main question will be "What's missing in the way of innovative products and services?", not "How do we improve what we are already offering you through existing products and services?" Instead of asking, "How do we break down this complexity into small parts and delegate them?", managers will ask, "What new patterns of relationship and interaction do we need to create to solve this complex customer problem?"

Sourcing an environment that nurtures creative people.
"Our vision was to build products that would help enrich people's use of the PC," says Andy Grove of Intel. "Yet, we purposely left it broad and flexible to encourage personal creativity and group collaboration." Over the last ten years, many big companies have tried to unleash the human spirit, yet most have been less successful than Intel. In the years ahead, the many people of the "E" or *entrepreneurial generation* will ditch the big corporation with its restrictive controls and boundaries to pursue their passions and emerging marketing opportunities. They will follow role models like Steven Jobs or Bill Gates, who paid attention to what was missing, built it in collaboration with other firms, and wowed their customers.

Interconnectedness. Ten years ago, Michael Porter wrote that strategic success was based on "core competence." Yet today, just being good at one or two things may not be enough. Companies are increasingly discovering that they must also develop a "collaborative advantage" that involves the capacity to integrate your company's culture, competencies, and processes with those of other enterprises to create a superior product or service for customers. Asks analyst Michael Schrage, "Do you think that Bill Gates could have developed Microsoft Windows without collaborating with Intel? No. Do you think that Andy Grove of Intel could have developed the Pentium chip without collaborating with Microsoft? No again." Collaborative advantage often involves creating new ways to think and work with others that presently may not exist, not just simply combining two technologies like ingredients in an omelet.

Demonstrating the power of collaborative action in projects. Big companies and small alike are throwing out the traditional model of organizations and replacing it with a project model. They will go out of their way to invent a creative, productive, friendly, informal environment where work is fun. "I try to foster an attitude of collaboration," says David Kelly, of award-winning David Kelly Designs, "by juxtaposing multiple ideas and talents in a zoo-like, carnival-like environment. People are constantly making things, talking about things, collaborating on things, and the key is to get the whole project in one room. As there are many projects happening simultaneously, the place has the look of a three-ring circus with lots of great stuff lying around just waiting to be put together in some surprising fashion. Zany personal design projects abound—a crazy lamp that can see around corners will lie next to a half-finished model of a blood analyzer and a new-fangled design for a fishing rod."[12]

- *General Motors has about 560,000 employees and a market capitalization of $47 billion. Microsoft has merely 20,500 employees and a capitalization of $168.5 billion.*

- *The Big Three automakers have collaborated to make a breakthrough in battery technology and to build the first electric car with the range of speed and distance that drivers are accustomed to.*

- *The National Bike company in Kokubu, Japan, builds made-to-order bikes on an assembly line. The bikes are fitted to each customer's measurements and are delivered within two weeks after an order is placed.*

Globalization, Technology, and Cross-Disciplinary Approaches to Complex Problems Lead to Collaborative Learning

We live in a "one-world culture" says Polish head of state and philosopher, Victor Klavel. We are enveloped by a planetary consciousness that Teilhard de Chardin called the "Noosphere" or "shared information pool." As CNN put up a latticework of communication satellites that surround the Earth with technology, we all began to draw our identity from the same images—the same-instant history where someone like Benjamin Netanyahu can be a CNN commentator one day during the Iraqi war and Prime Minister of Israel the next; the same international business culture where all the traditional tribes have been found and photographed and made part of the market economy; the same myths through books like Thomas Moore's *Care of the Soul*. While CNN teaches people all over the globe to speak with American accents, Americans are being exposed to "foreign ideas," dissolving small-town identities and cultural barriers. When the Dalai Lama goes to Washington and talks to President Clinton about Tibet, it is not just a local story about Buddhistic freedom, it is a morality tale that people throughout the planet participate in together.

As we become part of Marshall McLuhan's "global village," we learn from our differences as each of us becomes more educated and more specialized, with access to a shared information pool. The World Wide Web and Netscape have miniaturized the immense—making it possible for large numbers of "experts" from different fields in remote locations to think, interact, and learn from each other on any complex issue or problem. During the week when Pathfinder landed on Mars, staff scientist Bob Anderson, recorded tens of thousands of e-mails daily from scientists and laypeople all over the world who wanted to participate in the experiments. Just as doctors from the United States learn how to use the Internet X-ray hookup to repair the broken hip of a child, children in all parts of the world are doing their biology or math homework together through groupware.

We are learning collaboratively, not just through technology but through increasing face-to-face contact at countless professional conferences each year, made more accessible and affordable by jet travel. Walk through an airport in Zurich and you will see politicians, CEOs, and gurus hurrying off to attend the World Economic

Conference in Davos where different ideas intersect and new ideas are formed—such as the "one party, two systems" of China or the "new volunteerism" of Colin Powell. At the same airport, you will see doctors from Boston, Madrid, or Stockholm on their way to attend a medical conference on gene theory, or blue-haired grandmothers from Iowa off on an educational tour to Poland. People often report at these meetings that they learn more from building relationships and through talking to each other informally about common problems than they do from the noted speakers.

Thus, the idea of collaborative inquiry, where many different specialists think and work on a problem together, becomes a trend. MIT has set up a learning collaborative based on Peter Senge's idea of the "learning organization." Some thirty groups, including corporations like Ford as well as the Peel Police Department in Canada and local school boards, are learning from each other.

One of the areas where collaborative learning is increasingly showing up is in local secondary schools. Score, an organization dedicated to helping students deal with the school-to-work transition through a collaboration of teens, teachers, and school boards, is revolutionizing education in many communities. The approach, which has been used with thousands of students in more than three hundred schools, is successful because it starts with helping students verbalize their goals and aspirations and shows them how to design a plan for moving from where they are academically to where they want to be professionally. Instead of viewing learning as a solitary activity, students often work with each other in joint study projects. Other collaborative success examples include:

- *In Indonesia "globalutionaries" or activists groups made up of MBAs, entrepreneurs, and human-rights activists are pulling shenanigans to plug the repressive country into the global system, believing that if more people are exposed to uncensored news, multinational firms, and the women's movement, more pressure will be generated on leaders that will transform the country.*

- *The U.S. is looking at an apartheid economy in the future that will consist of a top tier of technical jobs, while the rest of the nation will be unskilled laborers, unless we reinvent*

*our education system, in partnership with industry, to pro-
vide creative thinking and competitive skills."—Speech by
Amar Bose, founder of Bose Corp.*

- *Union City, N.J. schools and Bell Atlantic found that they
  could improve poor student test scores dramatically by linking teachers with parents and students in a tutoring system
  via computer e-mail. Many poor students have now risen to
  the honors track.*

Choosing Collaboration and Communication Over Litigation and Confrontation

Ruini Guinier, Professor at Penn State Law School, has written that most lawyers are trained to be gladiators, to do battle in court rather than solve problems. It looks like the public, the judiciary, and now finally lawyers themselves are finding themselves loathing the traditional Socratic, quick-witted, winner-take-all approach to resolving disputes. Many are turning to alternative dispute resolution (ADR). We've already mentioned how the judiciary of the state of Florida is sending all civil cases to mediation before allowing them to be heard in court. Massachusetts, New York State, and Connecticut are beginning to follow suit. Hundreds of lawyers are taking mediation courses all over the country to find more collaborative, less contentious ways of dealing with divorces, real estate disagreements, and business issues.

This hot new school of mediation is called "transformative mediation." According to Robert Bush and Joe Folger, authors of *The Promise of Mediation,* most people have sincere and honest intentions, but when they get caught in conflict they often get stuck in the role of either "victim" or "oppressor," which is not the way they want to see themselves. "Return people back to their true selves," say Bush and Folger, "by encouraging moments of *empowerment* and *recognition.*" This helps people transform their relationship to themselves and each other, rather than finding a better way to divide up the pie. It strengthens individuals by helping them see that they have choices, and that they can learn compassion for others. Once this transition occurs, people feel better about themselves and each other, and are more likely to find a creative solution.[13]

In other cases, people may find that there is no win-win solution. Instead of *getting to yes,* à la Roger Fisher and Bill Ury, people have to *live with no.* Bush and Folger help people shift from a *individualistic* to a *relational* model by helping them see that, even though they cannot always get what they want, there is something in the relationship worth preserving. "It's those moments of empowerment and recognition, when a person dares to ask for what they want or when someone who 'just doesn't get it' shows that they understand, that makes the difference," says Sharon Press of the Dispute Resolution Center in Florida. Of the thousands of cases that are mediated in Florida and other places, over 80 percent of them are resolved in one meeting. In some divorce cases, people even decide to get back together. In real estate, the process of resolving conflicts and getting deals done has been speeded up considerably.[14]

On the criminal side of the law, collaboration is at the heart of a powerful new approach to police work called "community-based policing." In Ottawa, Canadian police are trained to be neighborhood team leaders who can engage the community in dialogue and get to the fundamental causes and solutions rather than just reacting to crime by stepping out of their squad car with a nightstick and flashlight. According to staff sergeant Rick Murphy, "We had a neighborhood where people complained every night about noise. We would patrol the area and occasionally arrest a few drunks and disorderlies, but we'd be called back again the next night. So instead, we had a community meeting and asked the neighbors to tell us what the source of the problem was, as well as how they believe it could be resolved. It turned out that most of the noise was from a bar that, at closing time, would leave its doors open. People would congregate around the door and pound on a mailbox outside the door, as well as a few newspaper vending machines. We did some creative brainstorming with the group which led to a viable solution. It simply involved asking the bar owner to shut the back door five minutes after closing and to remove the mailbox and newspaper machines."

Several other examples reveal the same kind of community-based learning and action pattern. Murphy goes on to say, "Hintonburg was a neighborhood that became a hang-out for prostitutes. Again, the neighbors called repeatedly to complain of the hookers, cars driving by, and syringes and needles lying about. We increased our patrols and arrests, but this was a lot like spitting against the wind. We called another neighborhood meeting to assess together what could be done. We invited the local neighbors, the police, the social service agencies, the health department, and even some teachers from the local school district. The idea we came up with had to do with giving the prostitutes counseling. Another idea involved passing legislation that required the apprehended Johns (customers) to attend "Johns school" for a week where they would learn the far-reaching consequences of their actions. Prostitution dropped significantly. The same approach has been used to dramatically reduce juvenile crime, as well as spousal and child abuse in this area."[15] Here are more examples of successful collaborations:

> • *In 1997, Attorney General Janet Reno directed all Justice Department lawyers to put collaboration ahead of litigation. She earmarked one million dollars in the agency's budget for outsider mediators to settle intractable federal cases.*

> • *In Boston, rates of teenage deaths from handguns dropped to zero from an all-time high two years ago. City Commissioner Paul Evans attributes it to one word—collaboration—between the police, schools, neighborhood outreach groups, and private citizens.*

> • *Authorities in Zurich, Switzerland, faced with a burgeoning crisis of drug users and pushers on the streets, collaborated with police, drug rehab centers, and citizen groups to reduce the overall drug use and related crime. They developed a comprehensive approach aimed at getting first-time and repeat offenders into treatment, streamlining laws and court processing, and introducing educational awareness in schools.*

Creative Collaboration Is Giving People the Opportunity to Make a Difference

In May 1997, Diane White, a twenty-five-year-old resident of Everett, Massachusetts, missed Colin Powell's call to volunteerism at Philadelphia's Cradle of Liberty. She was too swept up in *volunteering.*

She staffs a hotline at New England's largest shelter for abused women. For White, a customer-service representative for Citizens Bank, the desire to give something back wasn't lacking—time and opportunity were. What made the difference was hearing about the community service sabbaticals offered by her employer. CEO Laurence Fish initiated the program in partnership with local government leaders and nonprofit social service organizations and nicknamed it *strategic philanthropy* to emphasize a public/private partnership. To make this real, Fish offered Citizen employees the opportunity to take three-month community service sabbaticals and receive their full pay and benefits with a guarantee that their jobs would be waiting for them upon their return. "I didn't do it to be altruistic," Fish says. "Community service makes better employees." This innovative program shows that people want to make a difference and, when given the opportunity, they will.

There are other signs of a more collaborative approach among organizations that deal with environmental issues like land use. In Gunnerston, Wyoming, ranchers and environmental volunteer groups were traditionally at odds with each other, and stereotypes prevailed. The environmentalists tended to label ranchers with a condescending "All you care about is profit." The ranchers tended to look at the environmentalists as "the Commies coming over the next hill." Then the real estate developers moved into the beautiful, lush,green valley and begin eating up the range with condominiums, and both sides realized that they had something at stake that was more important than their stereotypes. Some dialogue and brainstorming sessions occurred that included all three groups building a relationship through face-to-face contact and then collaborating on how they could save the range. They came up with the idea of putting the land in trust so it could never be sold. The developers agreed to use only certain lands and devote profits from their developments to environmental nonprofit groups.

The same shift in approaches is occurring on the international scene with issues like hunger, poverty, and disease. In Kivu Province, Congo, a white Land Rover, bearing the red totem of "Doctors Without Borders" churns through the muck and mire that passes for a road in the rainy season, gears grinding, tires spinning as they seek to grip something solid. The agency was formed a few years back when French doctors were angered by the Red Cross's refusal to allow doctors to work in the rebel-controlled Nigerian state of Biafra. These doctors were also fed up with relief agencies that were overly specialized—one would do surgery, another would handle food and water, and another flood relief. This approach made it hard to deal with the problems that were interdependent.

Doctors Without Borders regularly recruits top physicians, nurses, and other volunteers from all over the world. The objective is not to prove how great they are in their own specialty, but to eliminate suffering—whether it takes the form of a cleft lip and palate in need of surgery, a hungry child, or a burned village with people in need of new shelter.[16] Other groups, like International Relief Teams (IRT), not only send in emergency surgical teams to war-torn or poor areas that lack specialists in cardiology, orthopedics, and eye care but also teams who teach local medical people and hospitals the latest techniques. The doctors are often top professionals who are tired of the fact that medicine has become a business and are willing to devote one or two weeks to a good cause without having to give up their practice. In 1996, IRT sent over a dozen teaching teams to train twenty-five to fifty local medical workers in countries like Latvia, Lithuania, and Armenia which lack adequate skills in cardiac resuscitation, infant medical care, and traumatic medicine. These groups of twenty-five would in turn train twenty-five others, eventually impacting thousands. Collaboration is contributing to making differences in many ways, including:

- *A twenty-worker team in Xerox's main plant in Webster, New York, has asked management to turn up the production line. They wanted to free-up one day a month to teach kids in an inner-city grade school. Xerox workers say it is altruism, not masochism.*

- *Hans Peter Hartman, a DC10 pilot for Swiss Air, did a breakthrough project after a leadership seminar in Europe. It involved pilots and crew organizing themselves to collect unused prescription medicine from people's medicine chests, and flying them to India. The project helped thousands.*

- *Michael Kremer, winner of the MacArthur Award and professor at MIT, decided to take a break during graduate school and teach a year in Africa. After his time in there, he needed a replacement and placed an ad on the MIT bulletin board. Deluged with applicants, he created a foundation called World Teach that sends hundred of teachers to undeveloped countries throughout the world.*

Artists Are *Intertwining* Across Disciplines to Create New Spontaneous Expressions

Ezra Pound once wrote, "Artists are the antennae of the human race," the sensing point for small signals that point to a future the rest of us are not yet aware of. Thus, the arts have long been a field where people have worked in a collaborative manner. Michelangelo created outlines of frescoes in renaissance Florence, and his students filled them in using their own imagination to interpret the colors. Some scholars see the masterpieces of Shakespeare not as the work of one person, but as the result of a committee who worked with him under his direction. In this century, novelists and painters who gathered in 1920s Paris—people like Fitzgerald, Hemingway, and Gertrude Stein—inspired and challenged each other artistically.

As F. M. Ford reminisced about his collaboration with Joseph Conrad, "We would write for whole days, for half nights, for half the day or all the night. We would jot down passages on scraps of paper or on the margins of books, handing them one to the other or exchanging them. We would roar with laughter over passages that would have struck no other soul as humorous. And we would almost sigh over others that no other soul perhaps would have found as bad as we did."[17]

Today, what we see in the modern movie theater—films like *Raiders of the Lost Ark, Jurassic Park, Toy Story*—are powerful demonstrations of creativity and teamwork. As magicians from the Hollywood movie set—directors, screenwriters, actors, makeup, sound and light people—increasingly come into contact with mechanists of the world of technology to do spectacular special effects and computer animation, something is created that allows all of us to transcend the humdrum aspects of daily life. "We not only collaborate to create movies," says Steven Spielberg, "we create collaborative teams that can work together and give the audience something special." The capacity of highly talented people with big egos to come together from different fields, build relationships, and create a movie like *Close Encounters of the Third Kind, Schindler's List,* or *Braveheart,* with constraints of time and budget, is something truly extraordinary.

One of the new trends in the visual arts is collaborations between professional artists and students, aimed at getting younger people involved. Jonathan Borofsky renowned for his paintings and his thirty-foot-tall sculptures, like the *Hammering Man* in Frankfurt, Seattle, and Tokyo, was asked to be a guest artist at Brandeis University for something called the "God Project." The project was supposed to be a collaboration between a world-renowned artist, the school museum, and the students. The museum ordered one hundred canvases and told Borofsky to fill them up as a way of getting more people participating in the arts. For ten days and upwards, nine hours a day, Borofsky welcomed any student for what he calls his "two-minute painting lesson." Not only did the art students involved in the God Project come into the museum to work on the art, but so did their roommates who were majoring in political science, engineering, and history. The project went on until the canvasses the museum provided ran out.

In music, one of the most popular recordings of recent years was "The Three Tenors." Luciano Pavarotti, Jose Carreras, and Placido Domingo performed together for the first time, singing classic arias and popular songs in a way not only based on their own particular talents and gifts but also harmonized so as to create a surprisingly new and powerful effect. Here are a few other examples:

- *Director Mike Leigh brings together a group of actors who improvise and develop their roles as they collaborate on writing a movie script. The result? Secrets and Lies, which is nominated for Best Picture for the 1997 Academy Awards.*

- *When a Wall Street investment firm wanted artwork for all of the offices in their new headquarters, they gave 35 mm cameras to employees and told them to "capture their world." What resulted was a rich collection of images that revealed a multitude of ideas, perspectives, cultures, backgrounds, and religions.*

- *When the Seattle Symphony Orchestra announced that they wanted to build a new concert hall but were tight on funds, they turned to the Boeing Corporation who offered to lend them a seasoned project manager and construction manger at no cost. Seattle now boasts a beautiful, world-class facility for its orchestra.*

The Recipe

Can a small group of people who see and respond differently to the world make a difference? Indeed, history shows it is the only thing that ever has.
—Margaret Mead

Is There a Recipe for Creative Collaboration?

In our work at The Institute for Collaboration—an organization devoted to the study and practice of lateral leadership, creative collaboration, and coaching—people frequently ask us for a recipe. One response we give is: We can give you a recipe, but, given your level of consciousness, none of the recipes will work. In many cases, mastering these disciplines requires not just a recipe, but reflection on deep beliefs and assumptions. At the same time, we recognize that people today often do not have the time or inclination to reflect. What we are offering you in this book is something as simple to follow as a recipe, but that also has the power of a methodology that is carefully thought out and structured. The power of this recipe comes from an appreciation of the complexity, not from oversimplification of it. Here are some simple, powerful things you can do to make sure that creative collaboration happens. (These will be revisited in Chapter Three in more detail.)

STEP 1.

Make a declaration of impossibility (something you want to accomplish).

Breakthroughs don't just happen. They often start by an individual taking something that her or she—and others—didn't believe in and declaring it possible. Jonas Salk declared the possibility of curing polio by inventing a vaccine. Jimmy Carter declared the possibility of peace in the Middle East. Steven Jobs declared the possibility of changing the world with personal computers.

Declaring the impossible, possible and committing yourself to making it a reality does not give you a guarantee. It does, however, force you to think outside the box and take extraordinary action. For example, you may have to shift your thinking from "What can I create based on my particular point of view and background" to "What can I create together with others who have different views and backgrounds."

The first step in our recipe for collaboration is for you (or your group) to make a declaration of impossibility. These questions may help: What's a breakthrough goal that you would like to achieve? What's a complex problem you would like to solve? What's an intractable conflict you would like to resolve? What would you like to create or discover that never existed before?

> • *Once you have considered these things, complete this sentence: I (we) designate that [the idea] is possible and I commit myself to transforming it into a reality.*

STEP 2.

Bring extraordinary combinations of people together who can make the impossible a reality.

Once you make your declaration of impossibility, the next step is to bring together a creative, "unique " combination of people that can help to make it a reality. Juxtaposing multiple ideas and talents is a powerful way to dramatically increase the odds for accomplishing something that is exceptional and out of the ordinary.

The Apollo Moon Project brought together physicists, engineers, geologists, software people, and bureaucrats. Roger Fisher, who co-authored Getting to Yes, brought Chilean soldiers and Ecuadorian guerrillas, sworn to kill each other, together for a year to negotiate. Remember, Walt Disney collaborated with carnival people and movie studio folks. It is often unlikely combinations of people that lead to the most innovative ideas.

Keep in mind that people are inspired to collaborate when they imagine a goal or complex problem that is deeply meaningful to them, and they recognize that they can't accomplish it alone. Often, they are more likely to collaborate when their interaction is grounded in a shared activity, like solving a customer problem. It is often problem solving that pulls people across the usual boundaries and enables them to think and work together.

In designing your own creative collaboration, think in terms of an extraordinary combination of people. Challenge yourself to include creative, yet purposeful combinations that wouldn't ordinarily come to mind. It is also important to think in terms of people who are competent in their fields and who can add value to the project. Who are the stakeholders that you would like to get in one room? Who could bring a fresh view or perspective? Who has key skills and capabilities that you need?

- *What would be an extraordinary combination of people to bring together in this project?*

STEP 3.

Build a shared understood goal that transforms the possibility into a live project.

Now that you have declared a new possibility and brought together an extraordinary combination of people to realize it, your next step is to build shared understanding around what you want to create together. Creating a shared understood goal transforms a possibility from something intangible to a specific project that everyone involved can get to work on. After Russia launched the Sputnik Satellite in the 1950s, the desire to be the leader in space exploration represented a declaration of impossibility for the United States. Deciding to put a man on the Moon resulted in men on the Moon.

Setting goals requires everyone's participation and that the goal mean the same thing to all involved. It is essential that these goals embody both the personal and collective aspirations that have brought these people together. It is also important that the shared understood goal be something that is grounded in practical problem-solving that transforms a mere possibility into a concrete project.

The goal in larger projects must provide the basis for different subgoals, telling each person or group what their role is, and serving to prioritize what really needs to be done. In a collaboration, a project leader has a special responsibility to make sure that the different people and groups interact in a coordinated way—optimizing the whole group, not just the parts.

- *What is a shared understood goal the collaboration will accomplish (in weeks, months)? What are the major milestones and priorities?*

STEP 4.

Do a "what's so" about what you want to achieve.

The next step in a collaborative process is to perform a complete factual analysis that shows the contrast between what we want to create together and "what's so" right now in the collaborative process. This includes taking an inventory of the strengths and weaknesses, everything that is working and not working, as well as listing the factors pulling for it and factors pulling against it. This is important to discern what energy and input is needed and wanted for the project to be a success, as well as to stimulate people's creativity and imagination.

It is important to do this in a way that is empowering by sticking to the facts and by avoiding disempowering interpretations such as "It can't be done." For example, when the Apollo Moon project started, it was a fact that the United States had some of the world's top aerospace scientists. It was also a fact that we didn't have the right rocket fuels or metals for a manned flight to the moon. That some people said, "It couldn't be done," was an interpretation. In a similar sense, before the Camp David Accords, we knew for a fact that people on both sides were killing each other in the Middle East. Who's at fault was left up to interpretation.

It is very important in doing a "what's so" analysis to be willing to honestly acknowledge all breakdowns, to provide vital information as to what's necessary for the project to succeed. To be able to do this, we need to view breakdowns as an opportunity to learn rather than a reason to give up.

- *"What's so" about where you stand? What are the strengths, and weaknesses? What's working and not working? What's pulling for it and pulling against it?*

STEP 5.

Identify what's missing that, if provided, could produce a breakthrough.

Once people have reviewed their goals (milestones) along with current reality, they are in a better position to look at what needs to be created. Gather the whole group together and brainstorm around the questions, "What's missing that, if provided, would produce a breakthrough?" For example, a new rocket fuel, a creative win-win solution like the demilitarized zone in the Sinai, or a breakthrough product like Netscape Navigator that allows people to find what they want on the Internet.

Asking the question, "What's missing?" is a different from asking ,"What's wrong?" or "What isn't working?" The first question leads to being creative and generative, the latter leads to analysis-paralysis and blame. The answers to "What's missing" often combine ideas and talents in an unconventional way.

For example, when it was recognized that people were starving in a district in India, the Hunger Project gathered the stakeholders together and asked, "What's missing that, if provided, could make a difference?" In answer to this question, they created a collaboration in the village between a nutritionist, who found out what was wrong in people's diets, and a horticulturist, who taught people how to grow the right grains and vegetables.

Once you identify what's missing, commit yourself to specific actions steps that will provide it. A sketch, scale model, or prototype that will test your ideas is an excellent way to demonstrate the power of collaborative action. For example, Picasso and Braque constantly sketched together in the process of creating cubism. Watson and Crick worked together on metal models of the DNA double helix. Everything changes. (Note: Periodically repeat steps 3, 4, and 5 until the project is complete).

- *What new idea, fresh approach, or innovative solution will help us overcome difficult facts and circumstances and help us reach the next milestone in the project?*

The Mars Pathfinder Mission

Glowing like a meteor as it whirled through the salmon-colored sky, a half-ton, tetrahedron-shaped spaceship sprouted a forty-foot parachute only seven miles short of Mars' rocky surface, its destination after a seven-month, 310-million mile journey from the blue morning star called Earth. Now 200 feet above the Red Planet, the ship's retrorockets fired for two seconds. Another two seconds and the parachute, rockets, and back shell were cast off. Finally, the Pathfinder, enclosed in a cocoon of giant air bags, slammed into the surface of jagged lava rocks at twenty-two miles per hour and bounced, like some mischievous giant's beach ball. It ascended fifty feet before falling back for a second bounce, then a third, then rolled over for ninety-two seconds before it came to rest—proving luck is an interplanetary force—in an upright position.

Slowly its air bags, sewed and mended for so many test landings on Earth by Eleanor Foraker (a modern-day Betsy Ross, noted for her work on Neil Armstrong's spacesuit), deflated, and revealed the lander inside. Designed by a team of scientists and engineers headed by chief engineer Rob Manning, the lander unfolded its three petal-shaped solar panels, impeded slightly by one air bag that did not entirely deflate. Safe inside the landing vehicle was the Sojourner, also known as "the Rover," a six-wheeled solar-powered vehicle the size of a microwave oven, equipped to transmit photos and gather and analyze soil samples. As the Rover began to send data to NASA's Jet Propulsion Laboratory (JPL) in Southern California, confirming the success of the landing, the scores of scientists, engineers, bureaucrats, and technicians who made it happen hugged each other, unable to contain their happiness. "The little engine that could—did," exclaimed Manning.

Pathfinder project scientists in collaboration with scientists from around the world will painstakingly analyze the data coming back from

Mars, seeking to answer questions like "What is the large rock 'Yogi' made of?" and "What are the surface qualities of the Mermaid dune?" But I interviewed the members of this incredible team with entirely different questions in mind. I asked them, "How did you work together?" "Did you build a shared understanding?" "What happened when disagreements cropped up?" After all, building and landing an unmanned spaceship is perhaps the most integrated and complex undertaking our species ever attempts—it must take collaboration to the outer limits.[1]

Back in the early 1960s, President John F. Kennedy declared that our nation would put a man on the moon by the end of the decade, and bold statement of possibility was realized. Putting a man on the moon was a great feat in terms of technology, yet it was an equally great feat in terms of humans thinking and working together. However, most of that so-called "soft" technology was lost. This Mars mission, I reasoned, should be different. As geologist Bob Anderson said, "Pathfinder is set up as a new way of doing things—the engineering demonstration on the plant, the way we are handling the science and science teams, as well as setting up an Internet site. We have done everything as a 'pathfinder.' " The things we learned about working together from blazing a new trail to the Red Planet should inform and infuse our earthbound journeys, too.

A Bold New Possibility

The Pathfinder mission is one project under the umbrella of the "Mars Exploration Program" (MEP), a series of missions over the next ten years that will integrate the robotic exploration of Mars with investigations by spacecraft designed specifically to orbit the Red Planet. These missions are meant to lay the groundwork for a human mission to Mars as early as 2018.

Like most far-reaching collaborative ventures, the MEP started with an outlandish declaration of possibility: We will pioneer a series of missions to Mars over at least the next ten years to better understand its life, climate, and resources; to provide a first step in the search for life beyond Earth; to better understand the solar system; and to pave the way for the human exploration of Mars. As if that were not enough, the mission was to be accomplished by developing a long-term industrial partnership for spacecraft development, continuously infusing new technology, and doing it all "better, faster, and cheaper" than the Viking 1 and 2, the last mission to orbit and land on Mars—twenty years ago.

MEP's costs are one-third of the $3 billion spent on the Viking missions. Each mission will cost about the same as a major motion picture, and the total cost of ten missions to Mars is about the same as one major military aircraft. Because the new Mars exploration missions are to be conducted at only a fraction of the cost of previous missions, the program designers decided that they needed to approach the whole endeavor in a different way—planning for the program as though it were a business—a major paradigm shift for NASA missions. Says Donna Shirley, MEP manager: "We have never had a program like this at NASA before. I had to figure out how to put a lot of projects together to make an overall program—one that can actually go and explore Mars in pieces but make it all hang together so that there is a lot of synergy between the projects that will result in cost savings."

Their first step was to create a strategic plan that was based on identifying current and future businesses. They specified five businesses: knowledge generation, exploration, education, inspiration, and technology development/transfer. They then selected which businesses should be their primary focus and which should be carried out by "partner" organizations. To accomplish the goals laid out by their strategic plan, JPL had to forge alliances with several industry enterprises, like Lockheed Martin, other NASA labs, international space agencies, various universities, and several high-tech businesses, including Motorola, Silicon Graphics, America OnLine, and DEC.

As we spoke to scientists, engineers, geologists, technicians, and project managers for the Pathfinder mission, one of the first projects in the Mars Exploration Program, we were impressed that not only were they collaborating with individuals and organizations outside of JPL, but that these extraordinary people were operating day to day in a highly collaborative way to create something that never existed before. What follows outlines the many new ways of doing business at NASA.

Pathfinder: Breaking New Ground

Pathfinder is the first robotic spacecraft NASA has sent to Mars since Viking 1 and 2 landers touched down in 1976. Those landers sent back 52,000 pictures until they fell silent in 1982. Pathfinder's primary purpose is to further investigate composition and diversity of rocks on the Red Planet's surface. "If you eventually want to put humans on Mars," explains chief scientist Matt Golombek, "you had better understand what is there."

Because the Viking landers had been built by contractors, NASA had little in-house knowledge regarding how to design and construct the Pathfinder. "We knew how to build a spacecraft that can fly to another planet and go into orbit, or fly past the planet," says Manning. "But to transform something from a flying-friendly spacecraft to a surface station with a little car that can drive around on the surface—that kind of transformation takes a lot of imagination. It involved a lot of new things that we had to develop that we didn't know anything about before we started. It was all new stuff."

Manning noted that Pathfinder's collaborative effort began with the building of the craft, which usually involves only engineers. This time scientists contributed from the start. "Normally, project scientists worry about what the spacecraft is going to do once it gets there. They don't usually worry too much about how it gets built or who builds it," Manning explains. "Being such a small team, we needed the expertise of Matt [Golombek, chief project scientist] and some of the other scientists and geologists to help us get to the surface of Mars. As a result, the scientists became very appreciative of the challenges of the engineering side. At the same time, because the scientists gave freely of their knowledge of Mars, we engineers became amateur Mars scientists ourselves. It really made the mission all that more joyful for all of us to know what it is we are doing and why we are going there."

Extraordinary Combinations of Experts

Putting the Pathfinder team together involved assembling a group of diverse specialists. "We do not have all of the skills necessary to do everything individually anymore," admits Shirley. The key to managing this diverse group, Shirley found, was flexibility: planning with a willingness to rewrite the plan as necessary, and overseeing without domination. "I mostly stayed out of the way when they worked together," she says. "If you really want to have a creative team, you can't try to dominate them, or they are not going to be creative." As the work unfolded, "there were no individual exploits, everything was a team effort and each member of the team contributed individual creativity, brilliance, and hard work," she says.

At the beginning of the project, Shirley fostered a team atmosphere by convening the different members into a series of meetings so that when the products were developed "they would belong to everybody. Everybody would feel invested in them." She drew a circular organizational chart, rather than a hierarchical one, "with people doing the work on the inside, doing the work together, and the managers on the outside acting like cell walls of bacteria, so that you make the nutrients come in—like the money— and keep out the disease, the bad stuff, like excessive interference from upper management."

Sometimes the cultures working on the mission clashed. "The scientists want to bring as much science out of the project as possible. The engineers want to use the best technology that they can. They think it is really cool to do neat new things, like encase the vehicle in air bags. The bureaucrats want to be able to satisfy the political objectives, like balancing the expectations of the public and Congress with the abilities of the team, and how to raise enough money to pull it off," Shirley explained. There even were divisions within each so-called culture. The engineers, for example, broke down into different specialties—computer, mechanical, electrical.

Building a shared mind between these diverse groups required lots of dialogue, and an honest exchange of views and information, until a satisfactory solution was hammered out. The scientists wanted to send all sorts of instruments on the Rover, for instance, but their wish list bumped up against the constraints of the spacecraft detailed by the engineers, such as the weight Sojourner could handle and the amount of power she could produce.

Similar discussions occurred over money, such as how much of the budget should be devoted to the Rover. First Shirley negotiated with NASA headquarters, then took the total she was given and broke it down among the various departments. "Of course they each came back with, 'Oh, we can't do it for that!'" By discussing the budget in a series of sometimes-heated conversations, "we arrived at what we all believed was a feasible solution." Then we had to descope the Rover to meet this price. Again she went back and negotiated with NASA for more money, finally settling on $25 million.

Science Operations Groups:
The Benefits of Cross-Fertilization

Crossing "instrument boundaries" was another first for NASA, where scientists are used to mulling over galactic data in the privacy of their home office. This project was too fast-paced for that kind of individual pursuit. Instead, scientists and engineers formed "Science Operations Groups," which were in close touch as they jointly made decisions on where the Rover would roam next—based on a shared understanding of where the scientists wanted it to go and what they wanted it to do and what the engineers said was possible. "All of this has to be worked through and there has to be a lot of respect and a lot of communication between engineers and scientists," says Anderson.

Cross-communication also increased the opportunities for scientific insight. Anderson, for instance, was intrigued by "the weather guys" who were focusing on the movement of dust. "When we look at a rock now we look at the dust covering it, which is not normally something I would pay attention to."

Communication between the different disciplines sometimes involved one scientist explaining the basics of his field to a colleague who was in unfamiliar territory. It usually turned out that all the scientists, engineers, and technicians gained something from the effort. "The Rover guy came up to me and asked, 'Can you explain something to me about the geology?' For the information to be useful, you have to make sure you explain the basic principles in words they can understand. Sometimes in the process of doing that, you reach a new understanding yourself because some of the best questions come from people who don't understand, and sometimes exciting, off-the-wall ideas come up," says Anderson. He also has a more generous attitude toward team workers than when he started out. "I haven't changed the basic way I do geology, but I do have more of an appreciation for the engineers or the guys at the computer."

Air Bags: Prototypes, Trial and Error

One of the big challenges of the project was ensuring a safe landing. "Our starting point was to come up with a cheaper, faster, better way of landing something on Mars," says Tom Rivellini, a member of the four-person "Tiger Team" assigned to generate initial ideas. One novel idea: envelop the spacecraft in air bags. According to Manning, "Since this was totally new to us, we quickly realized that no amount of analysis or brainpower could come up with a bright solution, and that the process that many of us knew of—top-down engineering—basically did not work. We realized that we had to come up with a process where we could put forward ideas, implement as much as we needed, try them out by testing, and if it did not work, throw it away and start over, or modify the design."

That is exactly what they did. After determining how the air bags might look, Rivellini assembled a team of fabric experts and engineers to make and test them under extraordinary conditions. First, Sandia National Labs was hired to help pattern and construct a small-scale air bag. Mission accomplished, Rivellini brought the design to ILC Dover to put a larger one together for testing. With a small team of engineers and technicians, they collaborated on every detail of the air bag, with a second team working on a testing effort to make sure the bags would survive on impact, which would involve hitting rocks on Mars' surface. Says Rivellini, "It was a tight group of engineers, so team members from each group helped out with parts that the other group was working on. There was a lot of mixing."

Testing their concept meant doing the equivalent of dropping a Volkswagen from one-hundred feet high at sixty miles an hour and making sure it didn't bump. The Lander weighed 800 pounds. And the air bags added another 200. The entire devise had to be propelled off a platform sixty feet long and forty feet wide that hiked to a sixty-degree angle— steeper than a hill that even the most experienced skiers would want to attempt. To make sure the air bags would fall fast enough, they had to be attached to bungee cords that would pull them down with at least 2,000 pounds of force.

When Rivellini presented their test requirements to scientists at NASA's Plum Brook Station outside Cleveland, Ohio, which has a gigantic vacuum chamber, they responded by saying, 'Holy Cow!' You want to do what? Slowly, my colleagues and I talked them into it and told them it was feasible. One day they finally bought into the idea and we went full force designing every detail and testing it. Then we were in each other's faces all of the time, making changes, calling each other, and faxing each other as we worked out the precise details of the testing site set up."

The two key questions the engineers and scientists asked were "How hard should we hit the bags, and what kind of rocks should we use?" "Eventually we got a system that the NASA folks were happy from a 'this thing is going to work' standpoint. We were happy from a 'this is going to match our needs' standpoint,'" says Rivellini.

In the meantime, another group of engineers and scientists was brainstorming about how to get these huge air bags to work. "Probably the most important reason that our efforts succeeded is because we asked the question 'What if?' thousands of times. 'What if we do this?' 'What if we change that?'" Rivellini says. "Ninety percent of the what ifs you come up with you wind up putting aside, but they get you to that 10 percent that make the thing ultimately work."

Using a big white dry-erase board, the designs quickly began to evolve into ideas worth testing. According to Rivellini, "We started in one corner. One person would sketch something and then the next person sketched something next to it, and the next person, again and again, and at the other end you wind up with, 'Wow, this thing is going to work.'"

But, like in most collaborations, their initial models proved their designs needed further adjustment. When the team first began to test the air bags, for instance, the air bags failed, ripping open. The scientists had to keep reworking the design so that it was light and yet strong enough to survive a sixty-mile-an-hour hit against knee-high jagged lava rocks. That raised the question of money: How to get the most bang for their testing buck? Part of the solution they came up with was to create test bags that were made from a combination of different fabrics and designs so that several possibilities could be tested at once. They equipped the platform with several cameras, giving them still even more data. Yet, none of the air bags held up. So they went back to the white board to dream up new designs, trying to figure out what went wrong and how to fix it. That process was repeated over and over until, at last, they arrived at a design that worked.

Close Quarters: Power-Sharing, Mutual Respect, and an Action-Orientation

Another new concept was one of "co-location." The Pathfinder team lived in the same residence hall and worked in the same building, allowing for almost constant, direct interaction that enhanced the team's efficiency and feelings of closeness. "When you actually house people together, not separated by distance or time, the interaction is easier and more personal. And we humans tend to like personal interaction," says Golombek. "It was a lot of fun," says Manning. "It was a very social experience. We spent very little time documenting, and a lot of time exploring different ideas with each other in the hallways, in front of the coffee pot, then going back to our offices to work some more."

The close quarters also led to decisions being made and acted on almost immediately. Golombek observes: "We did not have rigid rules of writing things down, so we did not have long paper trails. If you had something to talk to a cognitive engineer about, that engineer was empowered to make decisions about what that topic was, and you could just go talk to him. If we agreed, it was done."

Leadership was fluid, depending on who was most appropriate for each particular task. "You very quickly realize who the leader is in any part of the design," Rivellini says. "The leader could be the one who is in charge of that part, or the one who came up with it." Manning, who had the title of chief engineer, agrees: "Some people might think my title means 'my job is to tell people what to do.' No way. That would be the biggest mistake I could possibly make. The only thing that the chief engineer should do is to find out what is going on and figure out what is not being done and what is being overlooked. One of the great things for me about having this title was that it gave me carte blanche to go out and ask anybody anywhere any question about this mission." And Manning quickly realized that this type of questioning had to be done by lots of people. "For something as complex as this," he continues, "you need everyone to think at the highest level. We have a group of people here at JPL that we normally call systems engineers. But I needed everybody to be a systems engineer. Everybody cannot be thinking about their own little widgets. They need to think about how each little widget fits into the bigger picture."

Harmony between team members was enhanced by the limitations of time and money, which kept everyone overloaded with work, and encouraged whatever sharing was possible to get things done quickly. "If you are swamped and you realize that everyone else is swamped, when you don't get something right away, you don't go and get pissed off at the other person, you see what you can do to help them," says Anderson.

When the group was discussing whether to use cheaper silicon solar cells or the more efficient gallium arsenate solar cells, the debate went back and forth. Do you try to scrimp and save money, or do you go out and get the extra power? The flight system manager, Brian Muirhead, who would have opted for the more powerful option, simply did not have the extra money to pay for it. Up stepped the ground data system manager, Al Sacks, who had no need or responsibility for the solar cells, and whose job would be made more difficult by the additional data. He offered to pay the difference out of his budget, because, says Golombek, "it looked to him like the right thing to do."

Bringing the World Together

The Pathfinder scientists, engineers, and bureaucrats are passionate about their work not only because of the possibilities for scientific breakthroughs but also because of a new connection they are building between their work and the rest of the world. Together with a consortium of businesses and government agencies, they have created a Website and complex network of mirrors that allows the team to share their discoveries as they unfold with hundreds of millions of people.

"On my desktop I have 3,000 e-mails from people all over the world, thanking us, complaining that their service does not work, and asking why we don't put out more information," enthuses geologist Anderson. "I have notes from more than 1,000 people who have told me that this is the best way that American tax dollars have ever been spent. We have opened the frontiers of Mars to every person in this world who has access to a computer, and over 400 million people have visited our site. We have done what nobody in this world has done before. I think we are bringing the world together."

Chapter Two

How to Become a Collaborative Person

*When people **think** differently,*
*they automatically **act** differently.*

B
egin right now! From this moment on think of yourself differently. Think of yourself as a visionary leader, a creator, a tinkerer,
and a generative force in the universe instead of thinking of yourself as an employee, a direct reporter, research assistant, a knowledge
worker, a benefit recipient, a consumer, or a couch potato.

Envision yourself and the next step in your career in terms of
being *an organizing maestro.* See yourself as someone who can bring an
extraordinary combination of people together and create some real
value instead of thinking of yourself as a manager, a director, a staffer,
or an administrator whose next career step depends on being able to
crawl up a ladder over a pile of bodies.

Envision yourself as working for a small skunkworks on something you are really passionate about instead of thinking of yourself as
working for a big corporation like AT&T, or a large nonprofit agency, or
a government bureaucrat in a job where you may spend the rest of
your life as a kind of indentured servant with little opportunity.

Envision yourself as being a great team player and a supportive
colleague, incredibly curious about who other people are and their

particular perspectives, instead of envisioning yourself as an individual performer (specialist) who is incredibly certain and who tends to presume how others see and respond to the world.

Envision yourself in terms of "I am part of a living network" or system where even my smallest action can spread out and have far-reaching consequences instead of envisioning yourself in terms of "I am my position" or someone who works on something and throws it over the cubicle to the next department.

Finally, envision yourself as actually creating something together with other people within an immutable timetable and budget—a rapid mock-up of a Nike shoe, a scale model of the Mars Rover, or a prototype of a bread machine instead of envisioning yourself as someone who is supposed to make elaborate plans and preparations before trying anything.

* * * * *

One of the things that envisioning yourself differently will accomplish is freeing you up from all of the conditioning you have had in the past, so that you can be more of a collaborative person. As you begin to envision yourself differently, you will begin to act differently. It doesn't matter (in a sense) if you stay in your job at a big company or if you leave it. I guarantee that as soon as you begin to think and operate from a different personal mindset, you will begin to see your own possibilities for visionary leadership, creativity, and collaborative action.

Characteristics of Collaborative People

Collaborative people tend to be *leaders* with a vision of a possibility they want to realize. They know that collaborations don't just happen by chance; it takes someone who is passionate about a possibility or opportunity to make it happen. Masters at building relationships, collaborative people have a loud, exuberant conversation about what they want to create in the world versus a silent (or suppressed) one. They tend to give people the gift of their presence, listening with a high quality of attention. They often prove to be organizing maestros (not just a virtuoso in one instrument) in bringing people from divergent opinions and backgrounds together with a view toward identifying opportunities, solving problems, or creating value.

The collaborative person could be a chief negotiator, like Harold Holbrook of the U.S. State Department, a strategic broker of joint ventures, or the head of multidisciplined team made up of people brought together, not based on title and rank but on the distinctive contribution(s) they can make. These individuals form networks of communication, commitment, and support that are much more effective than traditional structures, no matter how decluttered and delayered. In a sense, the "Rolodex" of a collaborative person constitutes a large informal organization all its own, with people whose skills may be combined in certain ways for some projects and recombined in different ways for others.

Collaborative people tend to see where their own views, perspectives, or experiences are limited and have a basic attitude of learning and a beginner's mind. Darla Hastings at Fidelity Investments once talked to me about Fidelity's chairman, Ned Johnson. "Ned was curious about absolutely everyone and everything"—the stock-market, Zen, antiques. Once Mr. Johnson traveled to England just to get a different perspective about stock market investing than he could get from people in Boston or on Wall Street. At Fidelity, they hire people who are passionate and creative, and the company is quick to sponsor teams who have zany ideas to try. The company was the first to use toll-free numbers to sell stocks over the phone rather than making people go into a broker's office, the first to offer check cashing on mutual funds, and the first to pay fund managers to learn from each other.

Collaborative People Awards (Role Models)

Positive role models exist in all walks of business. The following trailblazing collaborators are prime examples. See how these individuals used the power of collaborative thinking to accomplish the near impossible.

Government and International Affairs: *Terje Larsen.*
Larsen represents an extraordinary example of what a lateral leader can do to inspire people to collaborate and, as a result, produce a

breakthrough. In 1992, Larsen, a private citizen of Norway who was engaged in a social research project in Israel, had the opportunity to talk to leaders close to Yitzhak Rabin and Shimon Peres who were frustrated with the breakdown of official talks between Israelis and Palestinians in Washington. Larsen, whose wife worked for the Norwegian Foreign Ministry, offered to provide a negotiating back channel in Norway for direct talks between the two polarized groups. According to diplomatic journalist David Makovsky, Larsen's personal commitment and creativity played a crucial role in making the talks happen, as well as in the talks being upgraded from an unofficial "academic conference" to an official level that would alter the course of history. This back channel led to the breakthrough that resulted in the Oslo Accords that afforded mutual recognition of Israel and the PLO and allowed other issues to be resolved.[1] (See the Interlude, Passionate Diplomacy, following this chapter.)

Business: *Steve Jobs*. When Steve Jobs announced at the 1997 *MacWorld* trade show in Boston that Apple would enter into a joint venture with Bill Gates and Microsoft that would include a $150 million investment, some Apple aficionados booed and cynical critics scoffed, "that amount is a drop in the bucket." What they overlooked was Jobs's skill as a collaborative person, first to return to the company he sourced and, second, to bring together such an extraordinary combination of people to turn the tide of its falling fortunes. What was interesting about the collaboration is that not only did Jobs heal old wounds with former enemies Bill Gates and Microsoft, who were engaged in a copyright dispute with Apple over Windows 95 software, but he also created a board with other people who were rivals to Gates, such as Larry Ellison, head of Oracle software. The group also included Bill Campbell, president of Intuit, and Jerry York, the brilliant finance executive who helped to turn around IBM. As Gates said of these moves, "We're all going to have fun helping Apple."

Science: *Matt Golombek*. Golombek is the chief scientist of the Mars Project. Usually during a spaceflight, the scientists go to work, set up their instruments, conduct their experiments, and have little time or attention for the engineers who design the spacecraft. Golombek, however, was cut from a different cloth. According to chief engineer

Rob Manning, "Normally, chief scientists work in their own area. They worry about what the spacecraft is going to do once it gets there. They don't worry about who builds it or how it gets built, or how much it costs, as long as it gets there and does what they want it to do. The big difference with being such a small team working on Pathfinder is that we needed the expertise of Matt to get to the surface of Mars. He and the whole science team generously got involved for the whole duration of the project with the engineering part of the job in a way that actually allowed us to land."[2]

The Arts: *Harrison Ford.* Ford appeared on *Larry King Live* after his film *Air Force One.* When Larry asked Ford about his role in the success of the movie, he said, "I'm just the product, something that's needed to sell movies, marquee posters, and popcorn." Ford went on to say that there were lots of stars in movies that failed. The real success of his films, like *Raiders of the Lost Ark, Air Force One,* and *Patriot Games,* came not from the star's presence but from the creativity and collaboration of the director, producer, special-effects people, and many others. Ford is known for taking responsibility for the success of all parts of the movie, not just his role, without stepping on toes. When he saw the outtakes of *Air Force One,* he was so grateful to the director that he went over and hugged him. Ford likes to think of himself as one of the team, and he's been know to kick off his shoes after a hard day on the set and drink a beer with the rest of the crew.

Sports: *Grant Hill.* Hill, a forward for the Detroit Pistons, "is a very creative player," says NBA spokesperson Jeff Fire. Although he is a forward (traditionally forwards hang around at the basket), he has reinvented the position and plays like a guard, passing the ball to the rest of the team, slashing to the basket and jamming, or taking up rebounding or pivot move duties. "I just think of myself as a creator—someone who makes things happen on both ends of the court. I like to go and create out there for myself and my teammates," says Hill. As a result, he averaged 21 points per game on offense last year, but is known by his teammates as a quintessential team player. On defense, his teammates call him "Rimbrant," averaging 9 rebounds and converting to 7.3 assists. Says Hill, "Sometimes being a creator means scoring a lot. Other times it means dishing off and not scoring at all."[3]

The Rules of Success in a Hierarchical World Are Different from Those of a Collaborative World

Have you ever asked yourself, why is it that so many successful people, who sincerely want to collaborate, have such a difficult time doing so? We are talking about people in high-powered leadership positions, who are highly educated and highly paid. Perhaps the reason has something to do with the fact that the rules for succeeding in a hierarchical world are different than those in a collaborative world, and so many successful people grew up in the former one.

Think about what the rules of success have been since World War II. First, "Get into a top college and major in a specialty like business administration, law, medicine, engineering." Second, "Get a job in a big organization, like Stanford University, IBM, or the federal government." Then, "Get to the top of a pile of bodies on the hierarchical ladder with the title of manager, head of neurosurgery, chief engineer, trading off your intellectual discipline or specialty."

Other rules for success are: "Just do your job, and when it's done, throw it over the cubicle to the people in the next department." "In meetings and teams situations, become a very powerful advocate of your positions in order to win, while discouraging inquiry into them." "When there are problems, fiddle with the strategy or structure, but do not self-reflect or make your behavior subject to other people's scrutiny or examination." "Focus on the boss, reading the political tea leaves versus focusing on the customer or the average person."

An individual following these rules in the past may well have been very successful. Today, a person who blindly follows these same rules may find that they backfire.

- *Being an expert in your field may lead you to develop a know-it-all attitude that prevents you from thinking or working with others.*

- *Reaching a level of authority may allow you to make arbitrary decisions but does not guarantee that these decisions will be implemented.*

- *Pursuing your own agenda can often result in your overlooking the big picture and leave you sorry in the end.*

- *Using force of argument or pressure to get others to accept your views often makes capturing the collective intelligence of the group impossible.*

Below are three examples of high-powered, "successful" people still following the hierarchical rules of the past and who have not yet recognized that it is a collaborative world. It will be interesting to see what their fate is in years to come.

Bob Crandall. The combative and highly successful chairman of American Airlines, Crandall was the architect of a two-tiered salary system for pilots, which he hoped would pit the high-priced, more experienced pilots against the lesser compensated, newer ones. Instead, Crandall became the universal object of their shared dislike and distrust. He further soured the pilots by deriding them in public and threatening to ground the airline unless the union agreed to further concessions. In March 1997, the pilots voted to strike. (The strike was averted by President Clinton, who signed an executive order requiring the airline to remain in operation during a cooling-off period.)

Jesse Helms. When Bill Clinton announced that he was going to appoint Governor William Weld of Massachusetts as ambassador to Mexico, Helms, chairman of the Foreign Relations Committee, responded by saying that he didn't consider Weld "ambassador material." Later Helms further defined his position by saying that he didn't approve of Weld's record on drug traffic. Yet, Helms refused to allow inquiry into his position, by himself or others, by holding a fair hearing, saying he would stick to his position until "hell freezes over." In effect, Helms held the president, the whole Congress, and the country hostage. What's interesting is that the other senators were presented with a dilemma: "Speak up" and reap the chairman's wrath, or "be silent" and make the issue undiscussable, which in effect was colluding with the chairman's self-sealing, nonlearning, anticollaborative behavior. To his credit, however, Weld was willing to discuss the undiscussable, even if undiplomatically, which exposed Helm's (and other's) defensive routines and raised Weld's status as presidential timber.

Jean-Pascal Delamuraz. Billionaire Edgar Bronfman, president of the World Jewish Congress, went to Zurich to discuss the secret bank accounts of Holocaust victims in response to hundreds of complaints by the heirs. Delamuraz, president of Switzerland and the chairman of the three largest banks, lead Bronfman into a cold dark room with no chairs or tables. When Delamuraz suggested that perhaps a small compensation fund would be set if accurate records could be found, Bronfman, who was stunned by their "very uncooperative attitude," said he favored "the creation of a process" that would address his constituents' concerns. Delamuraz later dismissed the request for his country to establish a compensation fund for Jews and other Holocaust survivors, saying "this is nothing but blackmail," a plot by people in Washington, D.C., and London "who could not be trusted" to compromise Switzerland as a financial center. He added that Switzerland would correct any mistakes based on historical proof, not attempts at "extortion." Shortly thereafter, a security guard at Union Bank of Switzerland discovered the extensive wartime records of Jewish bank accounts on their way to the shredder.[4]

The Rules of Success
in a Collaborative World

When we say that it is a collaborative world, we do not mean that the individual has no place in it. To the contrary. People see that they have more choices as individuals than ever before to pursue what they passionately care about—even within the big institutions that, in the past, have turned people into grist for the mill. At the same time, while this is an age of individual choices, most of the really important choices we make as individuals can only be realized by collaborating with others in projects or groups. The same applies to organizations. Success in the future will increasingly depend on organizations that have a particular core competence yet realize that, in a collaborative world, the company that stands alone will have a difficult time surviving. It no longer makes sense to vanquish your competitors, as they may be your next collaborators in a problem-solving project for the customer.

The following discussion provides a set of rules for succeeding in a collaborative world, with a view toward the individual reader as a person, not an organization. Keep in mind, however, that it is one thing to learn new rules, but quite another to unlearn old ones.

RULE 1.

Create or find a project that makes a difference.

In the past, the first rule of success was that you were only as good as your position on the hierarchical ladder. In the future, the first rule of success will be "you are only as good as your last (next) project," with your reputation depending on your ability to bring a diverse team together to create something of real value. In a collaborative world, those who will be the most successful are those who have an eye for identifying powerful new opportunities. People who have put their finger on such opportunities and transformed them into collaborative projects include Fred Smith of Federal Express, Ross James of Netscape, and William Beverly of Starbucks Coffee. Creating or finding a project that's new and makes a difference can come about in three main ways:

1. Unearth what you are passionate about and what you intuitively feel is an emerging opportunity.

2. Engage constituents, customers, and colleagues in an authentic conversation about the bothersome issues they face.

3. Poke around. Collaborative people are great networkers who excel at knowing what is going on and at making themselves known.

RULE 2.

Be a great collaborative team player and colleague.

Stop thinking of yourself as a "manager"—an obsolete term. Instead, think of yourself as being an "effective team person." As the people on the Mars Project told us, being a great colleague means offering to help out others who have their hands full. Start by bringing together a diverse team (scientists, artists, engineers, anthropologists) and engage in a deep dialogue on a customer's problem: for example, how to surf the Net without becoming discombobulated, how to custom-publish a book for a college professor, how to sell printer drivers to your top competitor, Hewlett Packard.

Providing an opportunity for this kind of problem-solving

dialogue tends to ground people from different communities of practice in something real and allows them to think and work together. In some cases, being a great team person involves expressing your interpretation (or side) with authenticity and vulnerability. In other cases, it may mean stepping back and actively listening to the interpretation of another team member who see things from a different angle. This process is like passing a ball of energy back and forth until a creative or "shared" interpretation emerges, the very goal of effective collaborative action.

RULE 3.

Be an extraordinary expert in a distinct area that creates solid value.

Tom Peters, business writer, makes the suggestion to people who want to be successful in the future: Be the CEO of your own company or creator of "your own brand." If you want to be invited into a collaborative project, it is important that people know who you are and what knowledge and skills you have to contribute. Forget about your status and rank, and ask yourself, "What do I know how to do that is distinctly different?" or "Where have I achieved an excellent result that I am proud of?" or "What real distinctive value can I bring to the table in this project?" Though we live in an age of complexity, it takes different kinds of leaders and experts for creative collaboration. A healthy pride in your accomplishments will serve better than false humility. Throw out your résumé with its static jobs and dates and create your own marketing brochure based on accomplishments, especially in groups and creative teams. Publicize what you can do to add value or team zest to the next project. Get on five CEO's Rolodexes, other people's "Whose Who," or their preferred e-mail list.

Runners-up to the Collaborative People Awards (additional examples)

Government: *George Bush* for the brilliant job of international leadership and collaboration with the United Nations and leaders of other countries during the Gulf War.

Business: *Jay Abrahams,* a self-proclaimed "Marketing Wizard," for creating countless entrepreneurial joint ventures.

Science: *Tim Berners-Lee* for inventing the technology of the World Wide Web (without regard to personal profit), which allows people to collaborate independent of time and space.

Sports: *Scottie Pippen,* of the Chicago Bulls, for the critical role he played in winning four NBA championships, a superstar who subordinated his ego to a team goal, without concern as to whether Michael Jordan got more media attention.

The Arts: *John Updike* for sponsoring a contest to write a novel collaboratively in 1998. Updike will create a story line, choose five winners, integrate their pieces, and then write the last chapter.

Empowerment Is Overrated

Imagine that you are an executive in a big company, sitting in a high-powered meeting about a shared strategy or a complex problem. The meeting continues without resolution while you and others try to convince and persuade each other toward reaching a conclusion. Sooner or later, you throw your hands up and realize that the problem is not that there is a lack of vision or an absence of available solutions; rather, there aren't enough collaborative people in the meeting to take one of the solutions and make it work. You go home that night and meet your wife in the driveway, a doctor who wants to devote her time to practicing quality medicine but instead is spending most of it dealing with HMOs and other insurance people who just don't cooperate. Later that evening, you have a conversation about who will take Johnny to the soccer game and Rebecca to the birthday party. The discussion escalates into an argument because both of you want to have a free day. "My God," you say to yourself, "is this all there is?"

Like the people in the example above, you may be discovering that the people in your world are hitting a kind of wall. You'll know you've hit a wall when you realize that no matter how sincere or well intended you are, or how much you truly desire to produce results, you have reached an impasse. You'll realize this when all of your charm, knowledge, and skills are not enough to help you solve the problems you face. You'll know it when, in spite of the fact that you have been empowered by your boss, it is hard to feel empowered unless you are in collaboration and communication with others. You'll know it when the power that propelled you to where you are will not get you past this breakdown place. You have reached the limits of your power, as based on the "paradigm of the individual."

To some of us, this walls occur on a daily basis. It can happen when you run up against difficult superiors, uncooperative team players, economic constraints, or the very real limits of your own intellectual power, athletic prowess, or ability to influence others. And you'd better get used to these obstacles, because from now on, and in the future, they will occur more and more frequently. Ever more complex and numerous social problems, ever-changing government regulations, ever-growing interest groups, ever-expanding economic forces, and ever-confusing international influences are already—and will continue to be—more than a match for our individual talents. Think of these obstacles as a series of hurdles that can only be surmounted with stepladders where other human beings join hands to form the rungs.

When you hit the wall, you can continue to either charge or finesse your way ahead alone (until your limited inner resources sputter and absolutely give out), or you can try to put together a human ladder and be lifted up by a potentially unlimited new source of ideas and possibilities. Choosing to continue to battle alone may still work in some instances, but that solitary route may come at great, and unnecessary, cost.

The Power to Be a Collaborative Person Is Here, Now, and Accessible to Everyone

Wanted, an Impresario to preside over a workshop of wizards.
—HELP WANTED SIGN, APPLE COMPUTER, EARLY DAYS

Discovering the power to be a collaborative person presents a new opening for possibility and action. This power gives you the ability to take something that you believed you could never achieve on an individual basis and achieve it by expanding your ability to think and work together with others. Collaborative power completely different from the types of power we use in traditional groups where we rely on our position in the pecking order. As mentioned in Chapter One, this power has no relationship to authority, whether or not you have a corner office six inches bigger than the next person or the ability to make things happen by compelling people to comply with your wishes. It has little to do with your particular area of knowledge or competence.

The beauty of collaborative power is that it is accessible to everyone, no matter your rank, area of expertise, gender, race, nationality, or age. For those of us who have been "going individual," as they say in sports, and operating on overwhelm, this power can be exhilarating. In our consulting work, I've seen so many committed, talented, visionary, yet isolated CEOs get little done because they are unable to build creative and productive relationships. Then, when they learn how to expand their personality to include others, their horizon of possibility opens and their effectiveness expands dramatically.

In business, for example, gurus are discovering that it is not the big leader who makes things happen, but ordinary staff and line people who operate discreetly behind the scenes in networks that connect people and translate the vision into a market reality. In government, we read in the newspaper about presidents and senators and congressman, but, in reality, most of the real work gets done by staff people who prepare speeches, set up important meetings, and smooth the way for their bosses to be able to think and work together. This occurs in every sector of business.

How Do I Become a Collaborative Person?

In her book, *The Last Word on Power,* Tracy Goss suggests that when most leaders and managers think about reinventing the corporation, they think in terms of strategies, structures, and culture.[5] What they often forget is that the strategies, structures, and culture they are trying to change are rooted in their own minds. Thus, they overlook the need for executive reinvention as a first step toward real and fundamental change. As we have seen, executive reinvention starts with learning to become a collaborative person, not just with introducing others to collaborative strategies or infrastructures. This is a source of a whole new dynamic mindset, and a whole new kind of power.

Learning how to tap into your power to be a collaborative person doesn't happen automatically. It involves transforming who you are not only in your professional life but also in your personal life. This involves the way you think and interact with others and your daily practices. Like learning to play golf or tennis for the first time, it can be a bit awkward and counterintuitive at first, and it takes time. Becoming a collaborative person involves not only takes learning new habits but, of course, unlearning old ones.

The kind of learning that can serve to help people transform who they are and the way they think and interact is called *transformational learning*. This is different from *transactional learning* which is about acquiring information. It involves reflecting on the particular perspective, beliefs, and assumptions that shape who we are in the world, and the professional beliefs and assumptions that determine the way we think and interact with other people in the workplace.

Learning occurs when people are able to detect and correct error (which, if uninterrupted, would lead to failure) and are able to produce desired results. In my previous book, I spoke about *triple-loop learning*. In brief, triple-loop learning involves altering the particular perspective, underlying beliefs, and assumptions (or old rules) that shape *who we are* as a human being—what we identify with. Figure 2.1 illustrates this. *Double-loop learning* (similar to triple-loop) involves altering the rules or underlying patterns of thinking that determine the way we think, interact, and solve problems. *Single-loop learning* involves trying to do the same thing better or gaining some transactional tips and techniques.

Successful people tend to be good at single-loop learning—for example, they know a lot about succeeding as traditional leaders by virtue of their position or by altering structures and strategy. When there is a problem, they tend to respond to it by doing something about altering the structure and strategy. They are less successful at triple- and double-loop learning precisely because it involves looking into the mirror and surfacing, questioning, and revising assumptions. (In Chapter Six, we will look at triple-loop learning as it applies to becoming skillful in each of the five phases of a collaborative conversation.)

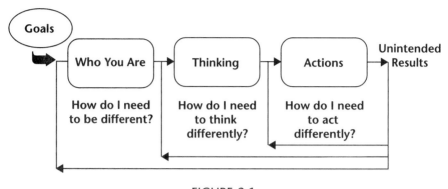

FIGURE 2.1
Triple-Loop Learning

The following steps will help you become more of a collaborative person. It starts with shifting who you are, your thinking and behavior, and then adjusting your actions and behavior to be consistent with this thinking.

STEP 1.

Resolve "to be" a collaborative person.

What is it that you dream of? What are your real aspirations? What big goals, complex problems, or conflicts would you like to be able to impact? Are these breakthrough results something that you can achieve on your own, or will they require a corresponding breakthrough for yourself as a human being—to become a collaborative person? If achieving this breakthrough requires becoming the latter, of this you can be certain. Breakthroughs start with a declaration of commitment on your part.

The declaration doesn't guarantee that the breakthrough will occur, but it tells you that you will be open to whatever is necessary to make it happen—to learn powerful lessons in personal change. It tells you that you will be willing to study, practice, and ask yourself tough questions: What is the thinking that allowed me to succeed as an individual? What is the thinking I need to succeed as a collaborative person?

The method that we subscribe to here for becoming a collaborative person is based on a transformational learning approach (not the

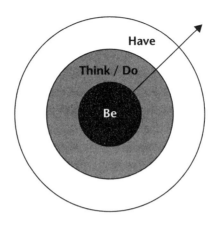

FIGURE 2.2
Be-Do-Have or "Inside-Out" Model

transactional one). It proceeds from what my colleagues and I call the "BE, DO, HAVE" or *inside-out* model. This is shown in Figure 2.2. Results are generated from the inside out. First, you must ask and answer for yourself, "Who do I have to *be* in the matter?" Next comes, "What do I have to *do* to *have* the results I want?"

The story metaphor. Where is the self? To paraphrase Jerome Brunner, the answer is "nowhere," because the self is *not* a "thing." It is a point of view that unifies the flow of experience into a coherent narrative or story, a narrative looking to connect with other narratives. We can operate from two views of self: one based on "apartness" or the separate self sense of the individual and the other that is based on "a part of -ness" or the community nature of the self. Collaborative people draw their identity from both their individuality and the community at the same time. To become a collaborative person, you do not have to give up your individuality or desire for success, instead, you need to expand who you are to include a community nature of the self and make that real through action. This is a process of transformation that perhaps the following story metaphor will help to facilitate.

Who you "are" is shaped by your story. Each of us has an inner conversation or story that shapes who we are, limits our thinking, and defines our behavior. The story is not based on facts, but on an interpretation of things that have happened to us. For example, we may have a story about ourselves that says we have to be Numero Uno, to score a lot of points at meetings by having the right answers, to be strong and not ask others for help, or to protect our mistakes rather than correct them. These stories often reflect the decisions we make about ourselves or others based on our childhood conditioning, education, and careers. Nonetheless, they shape our way of being, leading to all manner of thinking and behavior. The result of these stories is that they tend to be self-protective and anticollaborative.

While our stories may have been okay when we were children or teens, in the early stages of our career, or appropriate for the climate of the times in our organizations, they often reach a point where they get old or become "rut stories," that is, stories that keep us stuck. We often come to a place where who we are—as shaped by these stories—limits "who we can be in the world." When this happens, we have a choice: We can either pull the wool over our eyes and go on as we have, or we can give up the old "rut stories." To do this we have to reflect on and inquire into what the old rut stories are, their payoffs, and their costs. This is the beginning of transforming our "rut story" into a "river story," that moves us forward.[6]

While our stories may have allowed us to succeed as an executive in a hierarchical company or in a specialized department, they may prevent us from showing who we really are or doing what we really want with all of our passion, commitment, and zeal. Although we may have a story about the importance of wresting power and control over others, or being careful about what we say to the boss, we may, in fact, have a deeper inner need for authentic communication and to be part of a real team. We must also understand that while this scenario may have worked for us in the past, it has outlived its usefulness. As a person in one of our workshops said, "I know my story is something that I made up, but I hang on to it as if it were real."

STEP 2.

Clarify the story that has limited who you are as an individual and as a collaborator.

Keep in mind that what we call "our story" here represents a network of deep beliefs and assumptions that need to be examined and questioned for transformational learning to occur (that is, triple- and double-loop learning). The first step in giving up your old story—and the childish, socially conditioned ways of thinking and the behaviors that go along with it—is to label what your old story is. The idea is to bring it from the background of your mind into the foreground. The second step is to see the areas in your life where you are producing unintended results and try to connect them to your story.

This action has a powerful effect on being able to give up your existing story with the ways of being, thinking, and attitudes that go along with it. As one seminar leader I heard said, "What if I asked you to go back and find the clothes you wore when you started your career and wear them today?" Of course, they would be ill fitting and out of style. Yet we wear our old stories in the same way, even though they may no longer fit. Our stories are not something that are a part of our personality or that has weight and mass, like a part of our brain. They exist in words.

For example, you may have once made a decision, "I need other people's approval at all costs," whereupon your life became about getting the approvalof others, whether that meant getting elected to a particular position, having the right answers in class or at the big meeting, or withholding your real communication to avoid embarrassment or threat to yourself or others. Since our stories are expressed in words, please take time out and write one sentence that describes the old story that has limited who you are in some way or has prevented you from being a truly collaborative person. The following are some examples.

- *The results I am producing that are less than what's possible or that I do not like are . . .*

- *Write one sentence (or three to five words) that describes the story: Who have I been in the past that I need to let go of this?*

- *What specific attitudes and ways of being and thinking do I need to give up along with the story? (Figure 2.3 might be helpful in answering these questions.)*

Model 1 Collaborative (or Relational) Model	Model 2 Hierarchical (or Self-Oriented Model
• Designates new possibilities; shared understood goals; seeks creative, entrepreneurial results	• Presides over status quo; pursues own agenda; seeks predictable results
• Builds collaborative networks and new patterns of relationships and interactions; shows authenticity and vulnerability	• Relies on traditional structures of organization; view emotions as sign of weakness
• Attitude of learning; is a specialist and generalist; equates success with questions	• Acts like a "know-it-all"; is a specialist; equates success with knowing
• Balances advocacy of views with inquiry into own and other's thinking; listens to deeply understand others	• Passionately advocates views in order to win and discourages inquiry; listens as if "out to lunch" or reactively
• Empowers others on job by acknowledging talents and gifts; provides an enabling environment	• Controls others on job by diminishing their talents; takes care of others so they will submit

FIGURE 2.3
Collaborative Model vs. Hierarchical Model

STEP 3.

> *Transform your story by declaring a new possibility for yourself as a member of a community of commitment and then commit yourself.*

The next step in discovering your power as a collaborative person is to declare a new possibility for yourself. This becomes feasible the moment you distinguish the story that has defined you in the past and the predictable ways of thinking and behavior that go along with it. Again, words or language have the power to transform who you are and the way you think and interact. First, consider the power that language has had in shaping who you have been in the past, such as: "I have to be in control," "I have to look good," "I have to protect versus correct," "I have to be able to do things my way."

Then consider the power of language in reinventing yourself, both as an individual and as a collaborator. This involves not only seeing what's possible for you as an individual but also envisioning how that connects to others in a community of commitment. Transformational learning doesn't involve a new personality or three years with a psychiatrist, but rather an alteration in the master programs that shape, limit, and define who you are. To paraphrase Tracy Goss, this process starts with three declarations: (1) "I declare the possibility that what is possible is what I say is possible"; (2) "I declare the possibility that who I am is the possibility I declare for myself, 'e.g., be a collaborative person'"; and (3) "I declare that who I am is the stand (or commitment) that I take to . . . "[7] The commitment doesn't give you a guarantee, but it sets you on the course of doing whatever is necessary to make your declaration of possibility a reality.

It's important in declaring a new possibility for yourself to choose your own words (three to five) that express a new possibility for who you are as an individual and as a collaborator. The possibility should reflect who you are authentically as well as your passions and qualities of excellence—not the mass of pretenses and defenses you have designed out of your old story or things you did to please others (for example, being a lateral leader, a team player, or initiating innovative work). Also, think about the new ways of being, thinking, or behaving that you need to call forth to complement this new possibility. Here are a few examples.

- *What I passionately care about and want to create in the future through collaboration with others is . . .*

- *Write one sentence (of three to five words) that declares a new possibility for yourself as a successful individual and collaborator.*

- *What new ways of being, thinking, and behaving do I need to call forth?*

STEP 4.

Try on new roles and get coaching feedback about thinking and behavior.

Declaring new possibilities and reframing beliefs and assumptions cause people to view circumstances differently and to act differently. However, we as humans often fall back into old patterns under conditions of stress and pressure. People collaborate more effectively by having the right tools and methods that can help to reinforce a new mindset. As Buckminster Fuller once said, "If you want people to think differently, don't tell them how to think, give them a tool."

First, search out a role model of a collaborative person you can emulate. You can find people inside or outside your organization or through networking in your community. It's good to find role models who possess the particular skills or capabilities you admire. It may not be possible to find all of these qualities in one person, so scan the horizon for two or more role models who have a particular attitude or skill you can incorporate. Keep in mind that you don't have to copy your role models, but rather incorporate their strengths into your own personal style.

Once you figure out what roles your role models embody, try one of those on, whether or not you feel that it comes naturally to you. For example, if you are the person who has a silent conversation in a group about your goals and aspirations, then take on the role of being the kind of person who has a *loud* conversation where you express your passions with commitment and zeal. If you are the kind of person who tends to see things in terms of predictable goals and codified processes and procedures and does not encourage breakthrough-goals thinking or free-wheeling creativity, assume the role of challenging the group to stretch their goals, minds, and skills. Or, if you're a person who generally has to advocate your position in order to win and avoid losing and seldom inquire into your own or other's thinking, take on the role of an inquirer who attempts to deeply understand and who can simply listen without having to win.

Once you begin to try on these different roles, invite other people to approach you and give you coaching when they recognize that your behavior is inconsistent with your new intentions. Figure 2.3 may help you and your coach in identifying collaborative thinking and attitudes and the roles that accompany them.

STEP 5.

Practice, practice, practice.

As Ralph Waldo Emerson aptly observed, "Who you are speaks so loudly that it drowns out what you are saying." Tapping the power to become a collaborative person is not just a matter of acquiring the best ideas or employing the right techniques or methods. You can use all the jargon of collaboration and pay lip service to the best techniques in the world and still not act in a collaborative manner. In our consulting work, we've discovered that many people think they are acting one way when they are actually acting another. An open door does not call for friendly, informal, face-to-face communication unless you step out of it yourself and talk to people. Soliciting ideas from the team at meetings doesn't make a difference if everyone waits in silence to hear what you will think before they venture an opinion.

As Chris Argyris of Harvard University has pointed out, there is a difference between our *espoused theory* (what we preach) and our *theory in use* (our actual practice).[8] Often people start out with collaborative behavior and then, as we said, revert to form under stress and pressure. Often when this happens, people are unaware of it. Therefore, feedback is important as well as opportunities for practicing the skills of thinking together (listening reflectively), speaking together, and working together.

- *Use your reflective powers to examine your stance during every collaborative opportunity.*

- *Try to create new opportunities for renewed exploration and discovery on actions to take that promote collaboration.*

- *Do regularly invite open, honest feedback and receive it with humility.*

Peter Senge has discussed the difference between "practice fields" and "performance fields." It is important for all groups that want to collaborate to design practice fields where they can practice skills of collaborative conversations without the stress and pressure they find on the performance field. Paul Allaire, CEO of Xerox, does this through a process he calls "organization reflection and learning" that occurs in the course of three presidential reviews a year on a specific topic—such as "How do we move from customer satisfaction as our goal to creating customers that are extremely satisfied?" After the review, people in the organization find they think and interact differently when they're with customers. Ray Strata, CEO of Analog Devices, regularly meets with executives of other firms in something called "learning circles" to discuss such common problems as strategic planning, human motivation, or sales results.

Finally, it gets down to action. The best way to learn how to collaborate is to go out and actually collaborate on something—either with a specific purpose or for the sheer joy of collaborating. The next time you have a problem, ask people in your group to sketch out their ideas for the solution. Or go out and build a scale model or prototype of your latest brainchild. *Remember:* None of us is operating in a collaborative mode all of the time. By accepting this fact and using your own self-awareness as a resource to help you detect when you are being decidedly noncollaborative or cutting off potentially powerful possibilities, you are on your way to maximizing your creative potential.

Passionate Diplomacy in the Middle East

Yitzhak Rabin:

We have come from Jerusalem, the ancient and eternal capital of the Jewish people. We have come from an anguished and grieving land. We have come from a people, a home, a family that has not known a single year, not a single month in which mothers have not wept for their sons. We have come to try to put an end to hostilities, so that our children, and children's children, will no longer experience the painful cost of war, violence, and terror.

Let me say to you, the Palestinians—we are destined to live together on the same soil in the same land. We, the soldiers who have returned from the battle stained with blood; we, who have seen our relatives and friends killed before our eyes; we, who have attended their funerals and cannot look into the eyes of their parents; we, who have fought against you, the Palestinians, we say to you today in a loud clear voice—Enough!

We have no desire for revenge. We harbor no hatred toward you. We, like you, are people; people who want to build a home, to plant a tree to love, live side-by-side with you in dignity, in affinity, as human beings, as free men. We are today giving peace a chance and saying to you again, "Enough." [1]

Yasser Arafat:

Mr. Rabin, The signing of the Declaration of Principles marks a new era in the history of the Middle East. In firm conviction thereof, I would like to confirm the following Palestinian commitments: The PLO recognizes the right of Israel to exist in peace and security . . . and affirms any [previous commitments] we have made which are inconsistent with this, are now inoperative and no longer valid.

The PLO commits itself to the peace process, and to the peaceful resolution of the conflict between the two sides and declares that all outstanding issues relating to permanent status of a Palestinian homeland will be resolved through negotiation.

The PLO considers that the signing of the Declaration of Principles constitutes an historic event. . . . Accordingly, the PLO renounces the use of terrorism and other acts of violence and will assume responsibility over all PLO elements and personnel in order to assure their compliance, prevent violations, and discipline violators.[2]

It was perhaps the most photographed handshake in history. Guided gently toward each other by President Clinton's outstretched arms after they had signed the Declaration of Principles—a far-reaching peace accord—on the White House lawn, once bitter enemies Yitzhak Rabin, prime minister of Israel, and Yasser Arafat, head of the Palestinian Liberation Organization (PLO), seized the moment and touched each other for the first time ever, thereby touching the hearts and minds of people around the world.

Though the image of this event is familiar, the behind-the-scenes collaborative diplomacy that led up to the 1993 signing ceremony has rarely come into public view. It is a tale of countless handshakes, breakfast meetings, late-night calls, vociferous arguments, and humorous and heartfelt reconciliations among an extraordinary handful of ordinary citizens from three different nations who were bound together by their shared vision of peace. Intensive preparation through day-in, day-out "people-to-people" contacts and conversations built the confidence and trust to move beyond an age-old dispute of mind-boggling complexity—something that had not been accomplished by State Department heads, diplomatic sanctions, or even an arsenal of powerful weapons.

* * * * *

It is a story first of what an ordinary individual—Terje Larsen, a Norwegian social scientist—did by daring to heed the call of a possibility larger than himself, and to take the catalytic, high-leverage actions needed to make a difference.[3]

Larsen—as he is called in the Middle East—and his wife, Mona Juul, an employee of Norway's Foreign Ministry, drove through the wartorn, mean streets of Gaza, where graffiti, the color of blood, dripped from the walls, their senses filled with the sights and smells of rusted-out cars, burning tires, and great boulders of broken cement with steel rods in their path. Over the sound of the engine of their armored car, they heard Islamic Mullahs shouting cries about the death of Israel through crackling PA systems in nearby mosques.

All of a sudden, they were eye-witnesses to an incident, one of many such things that happened daily in Gaza, a decaying city of refugees that cramps more than a million people into its network of shanties near the Mediterranean. A unit of young Israeli soldiers and a Palestinian youth gang faced each other. The soldiers held weapons in their hands, the gang members rocks. Larsen looked around for a place to hide, but before he could find one, he heard bullets whizzing by and rocks crashing. As their driver, a colonel, jumped out of the car and tried to restrain the soldiers, Larsen had his eyes glued on the scene in front of them. What he and his wife observed possessed him for months to come.

It was one of the things that would move him to take a stand to do something, not only seemingly difficult, but downright impossible. In both the eyes of the Israeli soldiers and the eyes of the Palestinian youth gang members, who were the same age and looked so similar, he saw the same defiance and despair—and the same fear.

Later that night in the Gaza Strip United Nation's Club, Terje Larsen and Mona Juul talked at length about what they had witnessed, and about what they or anyone else could do to influence the situation. Larsen told me when I later interviewed him about his role in this international collaboration, that he just suddenly had this feeling that he could do something about this conflict. Larsen was in Israel as the head of FAFO, a research organization conducting a survey on living conditions in the Gaza Strip's occupied territories. Larsen and his colleagues surveyed hundreds of people, an extraordinary opportunity to talk to people at every level of society as well as political leaders. It also provided Larsen, an incredibly social man, an opportunity to build up an impressive network of relationships and to develop a deep interest in the region's problems. "Larsen told me that he felt that he understood the conflict better than the people who he was reading about in the newspapers and magazines. For one thing, Larsen believed that the problems could only be resolved by direct talks between the Israelis and the Palestinians.

Bilateral talks were already taking place in Washington, D.C., between three Israeli teams and three Arab delegations, none of which included representatives of the PLO, who were banned from the talks. Yet many Israeli leaders, including former Prime Minister Shimon Peres, believed that these delegations would not be able to reach a settlement without the involvement of Arafat, who was pulling the strings from exile in Tunis. Also, the talks tended to break down under the scrutinous eyes of the media. Diplomatic protocol led to much posturing, and considerable time was spent deciding who was going to sit where around the negotiating table.

Aware of the lack of progress, Larsen, as the head of FAFO and with contacts in the Norwegian Foreign Ministry through his wife, was driven to set up a more effective dialogue process, one that he felt would eventually have to include the PLO and be done more privately.

The articulation of this idea to a friend marked the beginning of Larsen's career in what he calls "passionate diplomacy." Such an effort stemmed not from position but from vision and the courage, as Larsen says, "to do what you believe in, and to believe in yourself." His next step was to recruit other people for his collaborative idea.

Setting Up the Back Channel

A friend of Larsen's suggested that he meet with Yossi Beilin, an Israeli official in whom he thought Larsen would find a kindred spirit, especially regarding the wisdom of direct talks. Beilin, a protégé of Shimon Peres who had served as his cabinet secretary and was a self-proclaimed "dove," now simply served as a member of the opposition party in the Israeli Knesset. "I understood since 1974 that we had to talk directly to the PLO and not find third-party partners," Beilin recalls. "Gradually, I got the courage to express my views. But after 1985, when the Likud Party and some Labor Party members passed a law banning any kind of official contact or communication with the PLO, I mixed my courage with caution.

"I never violated this law, but I was so angry," he continues. "It was sheer lunacy to pass such a law. It was malicious and beyond any reason to call such contacts treasonous. Yet in some way, this foolish law somehow provoked me and triggered in me a commitment toward some kind of reconciliation with the PLO. Slowly, I began to be more outgoing about the idea of supporting negotiations." His public statements brought him face-to-face with anger and ridicule.

Larsen first met Beilin for lunch in Tel Aviv. Larsen suggested, in light of what was happening with official negotiations on the "Washington track," that perhaps they could set up another dialogue. "We need a two-track system." Beilin agreed and went further to say that a two-state solution was inevitable. Larsen and Beilin discussed the idea of Israelis meeting with prominent Palestinians and that this could become the basis of a back channel that might resolve and clarify issues to move forward the talks in Washington. Larsen, having received backing from the Norwegian government, also promised Beilin that they would do everything they could to assist the process of creating the back channel, including financing.

Shortly before the Israeli elections in June 1992, Larsen and Beilin set up a meeting at the American Colony Hotel, a gracious but quiet hotel in East Jerusalem with an oasis-like atmosphere created by turquoise tiles, bubbling fountains, and a warm and gracious staff. Faisal Husseini, a prominent East Jerusalem Palestinian who, though not formally a member of the PLO, was considered the organization's leading representative in the occupied territories, also attended. They agreed to try to set up a second secret channel if the Labor Party won, and discussed how the Palestinians might help make that win happen.

Three days later, the Labor Party won the Israeli elections, and Rabin became prime minister. He appointed Shimon Peres foreign minister and Peres, in turn, appointed Beilin as his deputy minister. After the new government was in place, Larsen recontacted Beilin, this time bringing with him the authority of the Norwegian government. Jan Egeland, deputy foreign minister, was ready to lead a delegation to Israel to talk about setting up a secret back channel.

With Larsen's involvement in the FAFO survey and Beilin and Egeland as former academics, the idea occurred to them that they could set up a meeting in Norway under the cover of an academic conference that would discuss the results of the FAFO study on living conditions in the occupied territories.

The Palestinian Connection

Yasser Arafat, smarting from criticism of his backing of Saddam Hussein in the Gulf War—which cut Arab funding of the PLO in half—knew his luck would run out unless a solution was found. Despite his public posturing, he had known for years that the solution would require negotiating with the Israelis. His choice negotiator was Abu Ala, a key aide who ran Samed, the economic wing of the PLO. The financial brains and banker for the PLO, Abu Ala had a rare combination of charm and toughness, political insight, and street smarts. Furthermore, he had dared to speak out at the 1977 PLO National Conference advocating contacts with Israel, at a time when other Arafat's aides had disappeared from assassins' bullets. He also had written a paper on economic cooperation that had been taken seriously on both sides.

When Larsen and Abu Ala met, there was an instant click. Larsen told him about the proposed talks in Oslo. Abu Ala assured him that high PLO officials would be very interested and told him to assure the Israelis of the same.

Oslo: The Land of Gentle Giants

Instead of the triumphant statue of Lord Wellington on his horse in Trafalgar Square, commemorating his battle victories over Napoleon, or the statue of General Sherman, after trouncing the Confederates during the Civil War, in Oslo you will see Gustav Vigeland's statues of families: men and women embracing, a mother cradling her baby, children playing together, an old man holding his wife in a dying embrace. Throughout Norway, there is a community spirit apparent in even the most casual interactions. The word "solidarity" is frequently used in every village and business to make sure that all people of society—rich and poor, strong and weak, sick and healthy—are everyone's concern.

It is into this culture of peace and solidarity that Abu Ala; Maher El Kurd, an economist from Arafat's office; and Hassan Asfour, who had lived amidst the barbed-wire and war-torn streets of Gaza and was educated in Marxist doctrine in Moscow, arrived for the initial talks. After their driver was stopped by police, a chill went through their veins because they assumed they were being recalled to the Oslo airport because they were PLO members. To their relief, they found out this was only for a routine alcohol test of their Norwegian driver.

The three Palestinians were gentlemanly and sophisticated-looking, with an air of intelligence and worldliness. They stood in contrast to the two scholars that made up the Israeli delegation: Yair Hirschfeld, a professor of Middle East Affairs at Haifa University and a passionate believer in dialogue, and Ron Pundik, an expert on Jordan at Hebrew University's Truman Institute. Hirschfeld resembled an absentminded professor who had a youthful exuberance and enthusiasm but was permanently disheveled. Pundik had the look of a wiry, mad scientist with owlish eyes.

Preparation: Structure Influences Behavior

Former Norwegian Foreign Minister Holst's wife and co-developer of the FAFO survey, Marianne Heiberg, told me that Terje Larsen was one of the most charming, charismatic, creative, and entrepreneurial men she had ever met. "He is the greatest salesman Norway has ever produced." Asked why, she replied, "He not only sold the idea of the Oslo channel to leaders on both sides, he sold the individuals involved to each other." According to Heiberg, Larsen poured on the charm. "He got them to lighten up, he got them to relax, he established an atmosphere of joviality, of friendship, of fun, in addition to creating a setting for very serious negotiations."

Larsen's focus on building relationships between the men stood in sharp contrast to the U.S. State Department's efforts. None of the 400 State Department staff members working on the talks in Washington knew any of the fifty to sixty delegates from either the Israel or Arab sides in a deep personal way, and the fly-in, fly-out diplomatic efforts that had been employed had not worked. Because everything happened in front of the media spotlight, people felt they couldn't do anything more than put up a strong nationalist front.

"I believe you need deep trust and confidence for a complex process like this, with the conflicts and mutual distress as deep as it is," says Larsen. "You cannot be an effective intermediary unless you have vast amounts of time to build relationships that are real. Because of my work with the FAFO survey there, they could see me not just as a representative of a side, but as a human being. This, I believe, created the mutual trust and confidence for a small nation like Norway to be used as a diplomatic back channel. You cannot do this with in fly-in, fly-out diplomacy. You have to be here on the ground and build trust and confidence all the time. You have to have empathy for each side, understanding the minds and the hearts of the people, and treating everyone with dignity. You also have to know how to build bridges between two different cultures."

The Israelis tend to be more direct, more blunt. For the Palestinians, there has to be an enormous amount of small talk before you get to business. If two Bedouins meet in the desert, they can spend fifteen minutes just saying hello. They are testing each other, testing the dialect, understanding where their families are from—there is a latent function of building relationship that is more important than just saying hello. Also, the Israelis or Europeans may like to cross their legs. However, to a Palestinian, showing the souls of your shoe while crossing one leg over another would be a terrible insult. Larsen's knowledge of each culture and his rapport with each group helped him serve as a bridge between them.

Even more important than bridging cultural differences was Larsen's constant commitment to peace—unwavering at all times and under all circumstances. Describing the negotiating process as a roller-coaster ride, Larsen said you have to do this whether you are at the "peaks of breakthrough" or in the "valleys of stalemate or depression." Larsen adds, "You have to believe and do what is needed to make each party believe in the goodwill of the other side and believe in the idea that there is at least a possibility of a solution."

Larsen kept the negotiating teams small, isolated them from their peer groups back home, shielded them from the need to make official statements, and housed them side by side in a normal environment. Says Heiberg, "We did everything we could to create an intimate atmosphere. We arranged for them to eat breakfast together, lunch together, and dinner together." This was the opposite of what was happening in Washington, where the delegations ate alone with their own people and spent more time talking to people back home than "the enemy over on the other side of the table."

Another structural aspect of preparing for the talks was to create "intellectual space" by encouraging people to declare possibilities, make proposals, and brainstorm half-baked solutions (that might not have been welcomed at home), always allowing the freedom of complete retractability. This allowed for real quality of dialogue with each other.

The First Phase of the Talks: Spearheading the Breakthrough

Abu Ala was optimistic when he looked ahead. He realized that Israel would not negotiate directly with the PLO at this point, but his intuition told him that this academic exercise with Hirschfeld and Pundik could be transformed into something that could provide the spearhead for a breakthrough.

In a way he was right. Had the Israelis assigned a high-level official, the talks would have been about staking out positions and negotiating fine points almost from the start. Because Hirschfeld and Pundik were clearly associated with members of Israeli government but were not in Oslo in an official capacity, it allowed for building a shared understanding of Palestinian and Israeli thinking, which could later be turned into a shared strategy for solutions.

During the first evening of talks, Abu Ala made a formal speech that had a profound impact. The speech in Arabic rejected the idea of talking about historical grievances. "We have to deal directly with the issues," he said "and not go back to history—to repeat our history over and over again. We have our view—that Palestine is for the Palestinians. You have your point of view—that Israel is for the Jews. If we go back to history, we will spend years arguing—without any achievement. We must take what we can agree on and put it down and then go to where we have different points of view and find a way to deal with them. That's what we must do. We're not here to compete, to show who is the most clever or intelligent."[4]

Hirschfeld then gave an impromptu speech. They needed to focus on the issues that could be resolved, and distinguish those where flexibility was possible. Those issues on which agreement seemed impossible might be handled later. Hirschfeld made a brilliant proposal, saying that he was not there to negotiate but to build shared understanding which in turn might lead to successful negotiations later.

Abu Ala later came back with the idea of writing a Declaration of Principles (DOP) that was not an agreement but, as Hirschfeld implied, a shared understanding of each side's issues which, in turn, might lead to an agreement. Everyone felt that this was a masterful suggestion. The Palestinians and Israelis were both curious and interested in being able to distinguish between public posturing and each other's real thinking process around the issues that divided them. Beilin said he was less interested in what the Israeli academics said to the Palestinians than what he could learn from Abu Ala and his group. Hirschfeld considered the task before them as constructing a shared mental map or, as he referred to it, "the mapping of the Rubicon."

It was not long before they sketched the major building blocks of the DOP: Israeli withdrawal from Gaza and parts of the West Bank; postponement of difficult issues to be resolved through negotiations later; the concept of "graduality" or turning over of infrastructure such as seaports, electricity, water, schools, and hospitals to the Palestinians for interim self-rule over a five-year period; and tying the two people together through economic cooperation (interdependency). Though there would be many interactions over the coming months, this general outline stuck. There was a period of exuberance as people began to feel a sense of accomplishment at the same time as they were getting to know each other as human beings.

The Norwegians had decided before the meetings started that they would act as facilitators, not mediators, trying to influence the substance of the talks. Larsen declared at the first meeting when the delegates urged him to participate that he would only intervene "if it got into a fist-fight." Larsen's main role took place between meetings: evoking images of aspiration, or even fear, urging people back to the table when they got discouraged, as well as making it clear to both sides that he and the other Norwegians deeply understood how they felt. During lunch and dinner conversations, he avoided taking a position on controversial items, preferring instead to encourage moments of recognition by reframing what one side said to another, so they could hear it better. He and his wife were always ready to do what was necessary—offering encouragement to a despondent delegate ready to get on a plane to go home, making breakfast at 2 P.M., awake for coffee and chats at 1 A.M.—to keep the talks going.

"One of the best things we offered," says Larsen, "was a chance to talk about things unrelated to the negotiations. We would get them talking together about their aspirations, their families, their history, their friends, their hobbies. This provided a shared context for people to begin to see each other as people, not as demons."

Over time, the personal walls broke down. For instance, Hasan Asfour told us that, at the beginning, Israeli delegates approached him and asked, "Are you really Palestinians?" For his part, Abu Ala eventually abandoned his suspicions that certain Israeli delegates were spying for various Israeli leaders.

As the dialogue continued, each side reported to their home governments that momentum in Oslo was building. Both sides brought discussion papers regarding the DOP, prompting an all-night brainstorming session. The result was the Sarpsborg document, a melding of their views that was agreeable to both, and another trip home.

Shimon Peres, the Ultimate Creative Collaborator

Israeli Foreign Minister Shimon Peres, a longtime advocate for peace, had been informed about the proposed back channel in Oslo shortly after the first meetings back in early June. Peres, who had decades earlier proposed many of the solutions that wound up in the DOP, was cautiously optimistic. "We were always looking for Palestinians to have contacts with; the question was, who we could have contacts with that could deliver," he told me in an interview.

Over the past two decades, Peres has been the author of countless creative solutions to seemingly impassable problems, but only rarely had he found others with the same spirit of collaboration. "I tried my hand on many occasions, the most important one before Oslo was in London when I met King Hussein of Jordan and reached with him a full agreement in 1987," said Peres. "But this was rejected by the other party [the Likud]. I wanted this very much, because if we signed an agreement at that time, we would have saved a lot of blood and [avoided] the Intifada and other things." That agreement, which was very similar to Oslo in nature, was based on ceding a state to the Palestinians and included Peres's concept of "Gaza First," a gradual turning over of the Gaza Strip to the Palestinians for self-rule, to be followed by other disputed territory.

Even with the resistance, Peres continued to look for opportunities to build bridges that might lead to peace in the Middle East. "I also thought it was very important," he said, "to build a very trustworthy relationship with the Egyptians. Because without the Egyptians, we would never be able to sell it to the Palestinians." He told us that during Oslo talks, the Egyptians were "in the know the whole time"—even though only a few people on both sides were aware that the talks were occurring.

Abu Ala was an admirer of Peres's visionary and creative thinking, as well as his collaborative stance toward the Palestinians. He knew that he would get Peres's attention when he suggested the withdrawal from Gaza as the premise of the DOP, something the PLO had previously opposed.

Because Peres had heard that Abu Ala was a member of Arafat's "kitchen cabinet," he urged Prime Minister Rabin to take the Oslo developments seriously. Peres recalls, "Rabin tended to believe that the Washington talks would bear fruit, and I said to him, 'Look, nothing will come out of it.' There was too much formality and media attention. We had to find another channel. We had talked to other Palestinians in the past, but Abu Ala was a man who could deliver."

Upgrading the Talks to an Official Level

At the first round of talks following the Sarpsborg document, Abu Ala began to press for Israelis who could talk to him on an official basis. Hirschfeld reported this back to Beilin, who agreed in turn to ask Peres to speak to Rabin. With some skepticism, Rabin and Peres both agreed to send Uri Savir, a recently appointed head diplomat to Oslo, on a secret basis. By this time, the ban on official contacts with the PLO had been repealed, but the talks would still be held on a secret basis in order to avoid derailment the Washington negotiations.

At this point, Rabin and Peres had to overcome their own past political rivalry so they could work together to help move the peace talks forward. Again, direct contact and dialogue worked best. According to Peres, "In the beginning, Rabin did not believe in Oslo, but he let me do it. Then when it started to work, I suggested that nobody should be in the picture but him and me. Until we started to work just the two of us, I had a lot of troubles. When the two of us started to work, no troubles. All of the decisions were taken by the two of us without anybody being present, neither an aid nor a note-taker. And that helped to create a great deal of trust, because nothing was licked, nobody knew where we were heading."

When Uri Savir arrived in Oslo, Larsen urged him to treat Abu Ala, an older man, with deference and respect. In fact, he even made him rehearse his greeting on the way from the airport. Savir thought this amusing, and went along with it. Larsen also had done something similar with Abu Ala, asking him to show his charming, bright, compassionate side, not his austere formalities and tough PLO line. He wanted the two men to like each other and introduced the two delegations, "Here's your public enemy number one," with exaggerated bonhomie.

Larsen then asked Savir and Abu Ala to go into the conference room, loosen their ties, roll up their sleeves, and get down to work. Instead, they all sat stiffly in the conference room and Larsen left the room embarrassed, telling his wife he had made a terrible fool of himself. Uri Savir made some opening remarks and then started to talk tough. Abu Ala responded by saying that he was greatly pleased that an official of the Israeli government had come to speak with them. Later, when Larsen peeked in, mystified as to what was happening in the conference, peeked in, they all looked back at him with a sheepish look on their faces, their ties loosened and sleeves rolled up.

The two groups spent long hours hammering out an agreement over the course of the summer of 1993. They would often go for long walks in the woods together. Though the first draft of the DOP (the Sarpsborg document) was a good beginning document, many details needed to be worked out, and that required taking the shared under-standing to a much higher level, a much more difficult task. While Uri Savir, a calm intellectual, never seemed to get upset, Abu Ala in contrast, called on the full range of human emotions to make his points: anger, tears, joy, logic, intuition, depression, and laughter.

In addition, Joel Singer, an Israeli lawyer, was brought in to make sure all the i's were dotted and t's crossed, which made the discussions even more difficult. Yet the spirit of Oslo continued to triumph in spite of many disagreements and breakdowns.

More Creative Collaborators: Mrs. Heiberg and Her Son Edward

During the talks, delegates from both sides would visit and have talks with Norway's newly appointed Foreign Minister Johan Jorgen Holst and his wife Marianne Heiberg at their home near Oslo. They would discuss issues together informally and when the discussions would heat up, Marianne often stepped out for a moment to fetch their youngest son, Edward, who was four years old at the time. The child's presence, she had noticed, helped to cool down the discussion and remind the delegates of the underlying purpose of the talks: to achieve peace for their respective fam-ilies and children.

"I think the thing that had the greatest impact was the 'normal-ness' of the whole atmosphere," says Heiberg. "The house, family, and neighborhood was so safe and so normal, so stable and predictable that it stood in sharp contrast to their own lives, knowing that their own chil-dren would be raised in houses that could be affected by violence, at any moment, in neighborhoods of terror. I am speaking particularly of Uri Savir and Abu Ala realizing that there was something at stake here more important than the seemingly irresolvable issues that were separating them at the time."

Back at the Negotiating Table

Still it was not always smooth sailing. From one session to the next, there were major breakdowns. On one occasion, the Palestinians repeatedly took a moderate position, and then when the Israelis accepted, backed into a harder line, tempting the dog with the bone. Then the Israelis would follow the same tactic.

One day there was a breakdown over issues that concerned the status of Jerusalem for Palestinians and security for Israeli settlers, especially the right to patrol international border areas in and around Gaza.

Another time there was a surprising breakthrough. "If we hand over to you the Department of Education in the territories," asked Singer one day to Abu Ala, "will you be responsible for running the schools inside the settlements?"

"No," said Abu Ala.

"And your position is that you will be responsible for running the hospitals the Israelis will use?"

"No."

"So how about the Welfare Organization provision—will that be your responsibility?"

"No."

"So you're telling me you don't want to be responsible inside the settlements?'

"Right," said Abu Ala.[5] While this was a major concession to Israeli presence within the territories, Savir's way of speaking made Abu Ala uncomfortable.

Later, when Singer presented the group with his version of the Declaration of Principles, and Abu Ala became enraged. "You're trying to destroy everything we have built up in the last six months. You're living in the past and won't look to the future. This takes us back to square one." Abu Ala was depressed and Larsen consoled him, even though Abu Ala would often take out his anger and frustration on Larsen. "Maybe you're nothing but an Israeli spy," Abu Ala told him. "We took our beatings," admitted Larsen.

The toughest issues were eventually settled through an initiative of Savir who suggested that they split the sixteen remaining sticking points up. The Israelis would stand firm on the points that mattered most and give in on others, and vice versa. This led to a new solution called "Gaza

Plus," which covered Jericho and much of the West Bank. Palestinian acceptance of Israelis settlers and current borders were non-negotiable. Other issues would be handled by later negotiations.

The Spirit of Oslo

During the intervals between talks, Larsen acted as go-between with his cellular phone. At this time, the phone lines between Israel and Tunis were blocked, and Larsen was constantly on the phone with both sides. "Are the Israelis serious?" "Yes, I think so," said Larsen. "Is Arafat really ready to move?"

But Rabin and Peres had seen the historic opportunity in front of them and wanted to seal the deal with Arafat. The two collaborated on ways to reframe issues so that they would be acceptable to both sides. When Arafat expressed fear that "Gaza First" would come to mean "Gaza Only," Rabin and Peres authorized Savir and Singer to move on Peres's new articulation: "Gaza Plus."

Peres came up with many other creative solutions, like his idea to let Arafat return from Tunis to Israel. Says Peres, "I made a suggestion that a year earlier nobody would have believed. It turned out to be one of the toughest decisions Rabin and I had to make, and that was to invite Arafat to come from Tunis to Gaza. If Arafat would remain in Tunisia, he would remain there as the head of the PLO, who would always say 'no' to any agreement." Rabin eventually consented, and even went beyond it by authorizing the team in Norway to play their trump card, which was mutual recognition with the PLO. Arafat was being offered land and recognition of his leadership of the Palestinian people. Smarting from being snubbed by the United States in the Washington talks, they knew Yasser Arafat would find this offer hard to resist.

From Paris to Tunis and Israel

In the first week of September, just days before the signing in Washington, the talks moved to Paris for final details. After an all-night session at the Bristol Hotel, where there was much shouting, countless drafts being pounded out on the computer keyboard by Mrs. Heiberg, and numerous phone calls to Tunis and Israel, the two negotiating teams reached a final agreement on the DOP and on the wording of letters of mutual recognition and the rejection of terrorism to be signed by Rabin and Arafat.

After staying awake for twenty-four hours, Larsen, Mona Juul, the Norwegian Foreign Minister Holst, and Marianne flew immediately to Tunis with the letters for Arafat to sign. They would then deliver the letter to Jerusalem for Rabin's signature. Arafat's office was a picture of disorganization. "A few people came out to witness the signing, and the event itself was a very somber affair," Larsen recalls. "Arafat was very self-absorbed and reflective, although it was impossible to read what was on his mind." Nonetheless, he gave them the letter and they flew directly to Tel Aviv.

There the mood was completely different. Yitzhak Rabin and Shimon Peres were in attendance, along with a press delegation. A very jovial Rabin said, "I believe that you have a letter for me, and I believe that it is a letter that I will sign." Thus the stage was set for the dramatic document signing on the White House lawn.

Peace Will Triumph over Governments

Oslo is a story of many heroes, some famous and others unfamiliar, all of whom took great personal risks to move the peace process forward. Each one was extraordinary in his or her own way, but none alone had the power to achieve what they accomplished together: mutual recognition between Israel and the Palestinians.

Since the signing of the Oslo Accords, much has transpired. Yitzhak Rabin was assassinated by an Israeli, and the Labor Party lost the election to the Likud party under Benjamin Netanyahu, re-escalating the hostilities and triggering the extremists on both sides.

Still the participants in the Oslo back channel have been permanently transformed by their shared vision of peace, and the giant step they took toward achieving it. Says Hasan Asfour, "We suffer from war. The Israelis suffer from war. We learned from this suffering that we need peace. We ask about peace because we don't have any other choice. We must pursue the peace process we started in Oslo, if we want to be a normal people, if we want stability."

According to Beilin, "I see my role in mending the fences and ensuring that we have very close informal relationships with Arab countries and with the Palestinians, so that they will know that at least half of Israeli society would like to have peace and are willing to pay the price for peace."

He goes on to say, "I value the power of dialogue and people-to-people contacts in this, for it has proven itself so effective at Oslo. I will also try to create the future by refocusing my attention from the present context to the year 2020. By working together with Palestinian planners and Jordanian planners, we can plan a future of ensuring peace and prosperity, no matter what crisis we face now." Terje Larsen also insists on remaining optimistic: "The deeper the crisis, the greater the possibilities and opportunities."

Not surprisingly, Peres, too, is indefatigable. "Oslo will triumph in spite of all of the difficulties," he said. "I am not impressed by the difficulties. I think peace is stronger than governments."

Chapter Three

The Building Blocks of Creative Collaboration

"I t's one thing to have collaborative people," a healthy skeptic at one of our Collaborative Advantage seminars asked, "but how do you create groups (or organizations) where collaboration happens by design rather than by accident—especially in traditional organizations?" In thinking about the answer to that question, a statement from a friend, Bob Fritz, author of *Creating,* came to mind: "Structure influences behavior." Whether that is a formal structure like an organizational chart or an informal structure like the network of relationships through which people actually get things done, structure will automatically shape, limit, and define behavior. Thus, we have designated seven building blocks that are crucial for productive and creative collaborations.

To introduce you to the building blocks as shown in Figure 3.1, we will describe three ground-breaking collaborative projects and highlight their supportive role in each project. References to the seven building blocks will be noted in parentheses throughout (e.g., see Building Block #1). Later in the chapter, we will describe each building block in depth.

Three Collaborative Projects

1. Collaborate on creating a collaborative corporation.
How can you transform a traditional organization? Can you create a collaborative local government? A collaborative school system? A collaborative hospital?

1. Reinvent yourself as a lateral leader.
2. Seek out competent people and strategic partners.
3. Build a shared "understood" goal.
4. Designate clear roles and responsibilities, but not restrictive controls or boundaries.
5. Spend time in dialogue, grounded in real problems.
6. Create shared work spaces.
7. Load the project with "zest factors"

FIGURE 3.1
The Seven Building Blocks of Collaboration

We chose the collaborative corporation as an example because of its capacity to change its culture and to innovate new work practices, based on the need to compete, satisfy customers, and make a profit. In our view, the collaborative corporation or Enterprise Web will be such a world apart from the traditional corporation with its hierarchies and functions that it will be almost unrecognizable.

The collaborative corporation or Enterprise Web of the future will be made up of lateral leaders from different disciplines or fields who possess a particular core knowledge or technology skill, yet who also have the capacity to think and work together with others to create new opportunities or to solve customer problems. According to Roger Ackerman, CEO of Corning Incorporated, the Enterprise Web may include people who have somewhat different visions of success, but who remain grounded in their shared values.[1]

Examples of shared values may be: (1) openness to new relationships, (2) nurturing and supporting new ideas, (3) rigorous thinking that includes questioning deep beliefs and assumptions, and (4) operating with integrity. Cultivating these values will expand an individual's capacity to identify opportunities, solve problems, and generate real value for customers.

Let's say you are a leader of a traditional company and you want to transform your organization into this new model. Imagine further that you have already done some things in that direction. Now what? What do you need to do to reinvent yourself as a lateral leader? (see

Building Block #1). What extraordinary combination of people would you like to assemble to talk about building a more creative and collaborative organization (see Building Block #2)? What would you talk about? Would you ask: What is our shared vision of the future? Of new products and services that fall between the cracks of our business? of strategic joint ventures? Of making the teams we have set up embody our values? (See Building Block #3.)

One good way to begin building a collaborative organization is to have an authentic conversation in which each person around the table looks at how his or her own thinking and attitudes may inadvertently contribute to a noncollaborative organization (see Building Block #4). For example, when we consulted Adidas' chief of marketing, Rob Strasse, formerly of Nike and an inventor of the Nike "Swish," he decided that he wanted horizontal control of products from concept to market. This included control of the functions of Michel Perraudin, the production chief, who resisted the move. This conflict caused tremendous stress and tension in the company, but no one would own up to it. Strasse was a brilliant marketer and good at creating structure, yet very poor at self-reflection. It wasn't until after about a year, when Strasse died of a heart attack, that people began to acknowledge the destructive consequences of the conflict and implemented changes.

The heart of the collaborative business organization lies within people's ability to create a collaborative dialogue with their customers (or constituents). Consequently, one of the most powerful areas for creative collaboration is tapping the involvement of people who have the most frequent contact with real customers—salespeople, technical reps, and service reps. These people have a foot in two camps. They can become powerful consultants—or knowledge brokers—by interacting with both groups of people in their own and in their customer's business organization. Talk to customers about a business problem and then assemble a virtual team across different disciplines to engage in a dialogue about solving it (see Building Block #5).

Collaborative actions speak louder than words. Depending on your goals, see if you can put together a scale model of a new bubble jet printer, a mock-up of a new marketing brochure for a mutual funds firm that addresses the distinct needs of "Young and Actives" or "Senior Savers," or create a sample tray of things to taste from a menu for a new restaurant that specializes in gourmet Chinese and vegetarian cuisine.

2. Create a headhunter agency for collaborative people and teams. Robert Reich, former Clinton Labor Secretary, said in his book, *The Work of Nations,* that one of the growing job niches in the year 2020 will be the "Strategic Brokers"—people who can find out about a new business idea, attract investors, and bring an extraordinary combination of people together to make the vision a reality.[2] This creates a huge opportunity to go beyond the traditional headhunter paradigm to a team one, and collaborate on a Team Search agency that operates in one or more Collaborative Zones—such as aerospace, software design, a Hollywood movie set, or a courtroom trial. As we're living in a project world where people are increasingly doing things that have never been done before, standard staffing doesn't apply.

The people at Team Search will need to know how to ask questions that will elicit insights into what combination of engineers, consultants, anthropologists, or MIS specialists constitute just the right combination of people needed for a particular project. They will also have contacts in their Zone that the client would possibly never know about. Whether people stay in the same firm or move from place to place, Team Search will have relationships with them. The agency will be networking constantly to make itself known, to be aware of what is going on, and to make recommendations: "Who was involved in that project? Who (or what) made it a great team? What technical specialist did they use for specific parts of the project?"

If the idea interests you, how would you lead the way and customize it to make it your own? Who would you bring together on your collaborative team for your Headhunters group? Would they be futurists, venture capitalists, Fortune 500 strategic planners, industry experts, project leaders, university department heads? How would you introduce people to the idea (see Building Block #1)? Think of your job in terms of orchestrating a strategic alliance of people who have both value-added expertise to offer and a track record of being good collaborators (see Building Blocks #2 and #3). You might be able to earn additional consulting revenue by offering coaching sessions where you bring the team together to get objectives agreed upon and conflicts ironed out.

Still intrigued? What would your Team Hunters agency look like? For example, it could include a corporate human resources person who coaches, or a market manager who excels in bringing teams together to satisfy a particular customer need. It might look like a strategic philanthropic organization such as Doctors Without Borders, which assembles multidisciplinary teams to deal with disasters (see Building Block #5). It could also be a small search shop of three to five people or a network of affiliate "team hunters" agencies spread out around the world connected by "search" e-mail. Would you specialize in one market segment—like biotech, telecommunications, movie productions—or create a web of different segments by collaborating with different groups? What project could you immediately begin that would give you and your team a reference case to be able to brag about later on (see Building Blocks #6 and #7)?

3. Reinvent the liberal arts degree. Every year thousands of students graduate from colleges all over the country with BAs and BSs in history, biology, foreign languages, art history, anthropology, classics, and the like. Every year these students, who have been told that they must go to college to get a good job, wind up employed as receptionists, waiters, retail store clerks, part-time mail carriers, file clerks, or government "nonessential" employees. Their parents, who have shelled out upwards of forty to eighty thousand dollars—often their life savings—for these degrees, don't know what to say. We need to find a more compassionate approach.

It's one thing to say smugly that a liberal arts degree teaches you how to be a human being, not how to make a living, but tell that to the young man or woman who has read Spinoza, studied advanced microbiology, or wandered the Louvre, as they sit at the receptionist desk doing data entry in a big Manhattan bank! As Amar Bose said, "We are moving to an apartheid economy of rich and poor—a top tier of people with technical skills and the rest, even with college degrees, who do not have the skills to compete in the world's job market."[3] The result is that a growing number of people will be living as common laborers at subsistence wages. These aren't people who "messed up"; they are people that did everything the adult world told them to do.

If this problem interests you, imagine what leadership role you could play in bringing this to the national or local agenda, as well as what kind of creative collaborative you would bring together to engage in a deep dialogue about it—college deans, CEOs, parents, teachers, elected officials, and so forth. What kind of structure would you create for the group to work together? What would be the key questions to ask (see Building Blocks #1 and #2)? For example, you could ask, "What is the source of this problem: our educational paradigm, the hyperspecialization of everything (school and work), or the debate between viewing learning as based on abstract performance versus practical problem solving?"

What would be a fundamental solution? Reinventing the liberal arts degree so that it includes a balance of liberal arts and marketable job skills (at least one)? The solution could involve a serious collaborative analysis of our university curricula by leading university faculty members, business leaders, and government agencies that provide college loans that we all have to contribute to. Or perhaps setting up more internship programs like those at Northeastern University where, for example, a student spends a semester studying biology and anatomy and then a semester in the job market as an assistant physical therapist (see Building Block #3).

Another potential solution might involve more innovative use of interns by companies. John Seely Brown of Xerox's research institute told us that he hires bright young people as summer interns, watches them closely, and then hires the most creative, talented, and cooperative.[4] "JSB," as he calls himself, not only hires liberal arts graduates, like anthropologists, but also finds creative ways to use them to make sure his scientific and high-tech products, such as the Xerox live board or automatic repair manuals, are grounded in real work practices. This might include studying communities of practice such as executive meetings, or the work patterns and informal information sharing of service reps. Another example might involve donating sophisticated technical equipment to trade schools, like Bose did to local technical schools in Framingham, Massachusetts, so people who were already familiar with the equipment could be hired later as employees.[5]

What kind of short-term breakthroughs could be accomplished that would add momentum to these kinds of efforts (see Building Block #7)? A paper on a new model for education? A new curriculum offered at a top liberal-arts college that balanced liberal arts and job skills? A semester in a company program sponsored by organizations that want to find bright, young, creative talent? An accelerated graduate school program, like a three-month pre-executive MBA, to introduce people into being business executives with skills in accounting, marketing strategy, process management, and team building?

The Seven Building Blocks of Collaboration

BUILDING BLOCK #1.

Reinvent yourself as a lateral leader.

All of the lateral leaders in the collaborations we studied shared numerous characteristics that may be useful to keep in mind.[6] Each was to some degree charismatic, creative, and bold—not your standard committee member. They influence others less by their leadership positions than by being infused with a passion that has the capacity to ignite a shared vision. Rob Manning of the Mars Project said, "Most of the people here had childhood dreams about working on a mission to another planet."[7]

Each leader also had an appreciation of the big picture and the lateral relationships they needed to create among different specialists in order to deal with complex human problems. Joan Holmes of the Hunger Project told us, "Hunger is a nexus issue interrelated with poverty, health care, and civil unrest."[8] Each leader was a rigorous thinker yet, at the same time, bighearted and a bit of a rogue. Yossi Beilin, a key player in initiating dialogue between the Israelis and Palestinians, spoke with a Kissingerian pragmatism about fighting political battles with *fait accompli,* yet insisted on being called a "dove." A lateral leader not only makes decisions based on building a shared mind but steps out sometimes and acts as a tiebreaker.

The first thing to realize in striving to become a lateral leader is that the notion of the "all-powerful" U.S. President, CEO, or Chief (expert) is a thing of the past. It is a notion that is fitted to dealing with situations of minimum complexity, not the kind of maximum complexity that we see today. As Roger Ackerman said, "Instead of one man making a decision, we regularly engage in 'deep dives' or a rigorous dialogue about complex issues. These dialogues include people from every department and level of the organization together with experts from the outside and customers. The leader's role is to ask rigorous questions and to help elicit the collective intelligence of the group—not to tell people what to do." We found that as people in a collaboration communicate up and down levels and across departments, the traditional chain of command is displaced by a network of commitments, communication, and support.

The second point to realize in becoming a lateral leader is that, with globalization, technology, and human contact, the world is becoming increasingly interconnected and interdependent. This means that to accomplish goals and solve complex problems, a lateral leader must place emphasis on creating new patterns of relationship and interaction. As Joan Holmes points out, however, collaboration doesn't just happen, it takes leadership. This means being an organizing maestro who can bring people together who are normally off each other's radar screens to talk about goals or issues that are "unthinkable" or usually "undiscussable." It also means juxtaposing multiple talents and gifts to create new business schemes. This not only includes linking and coordinating tasks but also altering the ways we think and interact with each another on the most basic human level.

The third thing to realize in becoming a lateral leader is that you can create new (real) value by thinking outside of boxes. McGraw-Hill chairman Joseph Dionne was a schoolteacher in Long Island when Marshall McLuhan was writing about the electronic age shrinking the world into a "global village." As chairman of McGraw-Hill, Dionne, adapting to that vision, came up with a metaphor for a company as an "information turbine" that would take all the bits of knowledge "generated by our myriad writers, editors, and analysts," and produce an ever-changing matrix of new products to meet customers' needs. This process starts with liberating the knowledge from the functional stovepipes it has been trapped in and creating multidisciplinary teams where the knowledge could be shared or combined in new formats.

One result is the pioneering of a new field of custom publishing for the college market. "A professor can now call up their Primus unit and tell us that his class will cover these specific topics. Together we will design a book that matches his syllabus, drawing the chapters from a database that comprises a number of books, articles, and case studies, as well as the professor's class notes. Within a week, we can have the book printed and in that professor's college bookstore."[9]

BUILDING BLOCK #2.

Seek out competent people and strategic partners.

A collaboration between people who do not possess the basic competence in their particular discipline or task cannot be successful, no matter how well-intentioned people are or no matter how hard or intelligently they may try. The individuals in the collaboration don't have to be brilliant, but they have to be up to the particular problem they face. The Wright Brothers may have run a bicycle shop, but they were superb model builders and had the intelligence required to understand aerodynamic phenomena. The people who were involved in the Manhattan Project were all excellent in their respective fields—physics, engineering, explosives. The Beatles were all capable studio musicians.

It is important to keep in mind that the success of any collaboration relies on the competence of the strategic partners you choose, as well as the ability to think and interact together. It is a good idea to network in your area for the best players in the new collaborative zones that are opening up, so when the opportunity arises you can seize it. (Here's where our Team Search idea might help.)

"Think about it. The level of competence needed varies according to the collaborative opportunity," says Xerox's John Seely Brown. "If you were going to fly on the next Boeing 787, would you want that plane to be built by a collaboration of kids fresh out of aerospace or engineering school? No. Would you want to use a piece of software designed by a group of high-school kids from Silicon Valley? No again. Would you want to take a very important drug for a heart condition that was invented by a group of medical- and pharmaceutical-school students? Absolutely not!"

According to Roger Ackerman, "It is important to be very focused on your particular core competence or technologies, yet be a lateral thinker who sees new emerging opportunities and can form strategic partnerships to exploit them before a window of opportunity closes. We invented fiber optic technology, but we didn't have the cable or the distribution system to market it. We went to AT&T, but they were not interested. So we went with Siemens." Today, the $1.8 billion division is flourishing. It has doubled its size since Ackerman took over in 1996, and is expected to double its size twice again before the end of the century. "It is very important that the two strategic partners have strong, equal contributions to make to the venture if things are to work out," Ackerman adds. "You want to make sure that people have deep competence and knowledge in a particular area as well as lots at stake."

This is an interesting paradox, when you look at staffing a team of people for a collaboration. While you want to have people who are *specialists* in a particular area, people often have to learn to be *generalists*. According to Rob Manning, "It takes only a few years to become a specialist at electrical engineering. In reality, it takes years to become a generalist who can achieve something like a breakthrough on the order of a passengered mission to Mars."

One of the issues raised here is that it may be time to redefine what it means to be a competent professional. Traditionally, it has been someone who studies dry textbooks for a few years to find out everything that is known on a specialized subject, like aerospace or engineering, and is then conferred a degree, in a medieval ceremony, wearing ancient cap and gown, and then is presented with Latin honors. A new interpretation of the words *professional* or *competent* might be someone who can also collaborate, communicate, and create new knowledge in the process of solving a complex problem or completing a difficult project.

Things to Do:

- *Scan the horizon for the people who are strategically positioned to best help you seize and exploit opportunity.*

- *Make sure the people you invite to collaborate are competent.*

- *If you find yourself starting to resent others early on, ask them what they have at stake and whether they feel they have some value to add.*

BUILDING BLOCK #3.

Build a shared understood goal.

According to Michael Hammer, reengineering guru, a team is a group of people with a shared understood objective. In our investigation into the nature of collaboration, we have discovered that this statement echoes a simple and profound truth. In fact, a shared understood goal is the single most important building block in enabling a group of unlikely collaborators to come together. "In a way, what happened on July 4th when we landed on Mars wasn't the most significant event. It happened when we created the shared goal of landing there and our combined commitment to it," said Rob Manning of the Mars Project.

The shared understood goal is the most powerful antidote we have discovered for the human tendency to pursue one's own agenda, get stuck in arbitrary thinking, or defend one's turf. "This goal or mission brought out the best and the brightest in each person, of all ages, all disciplines, and all backgrounds. It allowed us to transcend individual stereotypes and defensive reactions," said Donna Shirley of the Mars Project.[10]

Collaborations often begin with a "declaration of impossibility" that has a powerful effect on inspiring people to collaborate, as well as helping people to transcend the political and intellectual differences that might otherwise separate them. The Mars Project set the goal of landing a lander and Rover in a fifty-square-meter area from fifteen million miles away, something equivalent to shooting a hole-in-one in golf. The Hunger Project set a goal of eliminating hunger and poverty by the year 2000 (something they won't reach, but has still had a significant impact). The Oslo Accords between the Israelis and Palestinians set a goal of breaking the stalemate and building shared understanding, which eventually lead to an accord on mutual recognition and security. According to Manning, "Regarding landing on Mars, the people in the project were not stopped by the possibility of failure because they wanted to succeed, and success was a possibility. In fact, they wanted to do something that was hard, where failure was also a possibility." The goal must be big enough and compelling enough for people to be able to subordinate their egos, as well as do something they feel they cannot achieve on their own.

Things to Do:

- *Ask your colleagues what they are passionate about.*

- *Identify a big problem that the group feels compelled to solve, or a goal people would give anything to achieve.*

- *Reconsider this: Is the shared purpose really something that could not be accomplished by an individual working alone?*

BUILDING BLOCK #4.

Designate clear roles and responsibilities, but not restrictive controls or boundaries.

In her book *Leadership and the New Science,* Margaret Wheatley points out that traditional management theorists believed in Newton's notion that the universe was like a big machine—a clock that had its different functions and a clock maker who, at some point, would leave the shop.[11] Based on this metaphor, their thinking was that a machine suffers from the law of entropy and therefore tends to run down and disintegrate into chaos. Therefore, while managers might believe in Marx's words "autonomy is good," in truth, they act like "control is better."

This led to a philosophy of management in organizations based on the command-and-control model, or bureaucratic models where there is a place for everyone and everyone in their place. Wheatley points out with simple but elegant logic that in the universe, in reality, no one is clearly in control—like a clockmaker in the shop—but, nonetheless, the universe is able to endlessly transform chaos into order. The myriad things in this world come into existence as a result of richly diverse environments, like the rainforest or the African bush, combining themselves in different ways to create new phenomenan. Whether we're talking about the life of a cell, a giant elephant with tusks, or distinct anthropological groups like the Bushmen, all of these creations took what physicist David Bohm called its own "implicate order." We can see this graphically expressed in the billowing but symmetrical shape of a passing cloud, the spiraling leaves of a cabbage, or the way water flows over our toes when we are standing in a summer stream.

There is an important lesson here for structuring collaborations: While people with different views and backgrounds may at first seem to degenerate into chaos without management control, the best collaborations seem to exist and seek their own natural order based on people who love what they are creating and share stretch goals along with an immutable timetable and budget. Though clear roles and responsibilities are often assigned, there is nevertheless a reluctance to impose restrictive controls and boundaries. Such projects basically follow the *principle of self-organization* based on what is being achieved, where the problems are emerging, and what the next milestone is on the horizon. "My only hierarchical prerogative as executive," says one biotech manager, "is to be able to go around and ask any questions I want." Collaborative people keep their antennae up so as to be aware of who is doing what, and what issues are surfacing that need to be resolved. There is a powerful, dynamic, fluid structure to this sense of reaching out to others and offering help, even if you're not a specialist in their particular area.

Rob Manning often observed people who were brilliant at one specialty or another and would stay within the comfort zone of things they were familiar with. He would then walk up to them and say "Joe, I hereby dub you 'systems engineer.'" According to Manning, "when I dubbed people systems engineer, I was giving them permission to be a generalist, and they needed that permission because they would often feel they were stepping on someone else's toes by offering assistance. I would say, 'Listen, there is so much work to do here and so few of us that there are gaps in between. There is no one competing for work. There is more work than people, and if you want to expand out and take a larger portion of it, please do so now.'"

Tom Rivellini, also an engineer on the Mars Project who worked on the air bags, told us, "We had as much engineering occur in front of the coffee machine as anywhere else. It was a hallway kind of work. People would walk down the hall and see a few people in someone's office working on a white board on a particular problem that may have nothing to do with their area, and they'd get involved. We spent little time documenting. We spend almost all our time running into our office, doing some work, running out to the hallway, talking to each other, running back into our offices, back and forth, back and forth."[12]

Things to Do:

- *Ask each person what they will be responsible for, in light of their talents and gifts, and what needs to be done.*

- *List what each member of the group has agreed to do and by when.*

- *Do everything you can to ensure frequent, informal, face-to-face communication like putting white boards in the halls, and coffeepots in places where there are tables and chairs.*

BUILDING BLOCK #5.

Spend lots of time in dialogue grounded in real problems.

Dialogue is important, not only in building a collaborative community around a project between people who don't know each other (well or even at all), but also in getting objectives agreed upon, learning to solve problems, ironing out conflicts, and creating a rallying momentum. Many collaborative or team efforts fail simply because people minimize the time they spend engaged in dialogue. This is a defensive routine used to suppress dilemmas, avoid conflicts or blow-ups, cover up mistakes, and then cover up the cover-ups. As Chris Argyris of Harvard University has pointed out, people in groups often exhibit defensive routines that involve doing whatever is necessary to avoid embarrassment or threat to themselves or others. One of the key strategies for this is avoidance.[13]

The best antidote is to ensure that the people or groups spend enough time in dialogue. Additionally, people should be given permission to engage in an authentic conversation about problems without feeling like they have to look good or have all the answers. Structurally, there are various ways to approach this, such as making sure there are regular, structured strategic or creative problem-solving meetings. Roger Ackerman says you can dive deep into a specific topic, as well as ensure enough time-out to get work done.

It also helps with diverse groups to ground the dialogue in nitty-gritty problems and persevere until there is a solution. For example, engineers at the Mars Project would have Wednesday afternoon meetings, where people would discuss whatever problems were coming up in the project. As Rob Manning tells it, "From one o'clock until the end of the day, Brian Muirfield, the project director, and I, and the rest of the team would go over what accomplishments there had been and what problems were arising. When a problem came up in other groups I have worked with in the past, people would say 'let's form a small group to solve it and report back to the big group next week.' In reality, we would not really solve anything, we would be having a meeting to decide on another meeting. Here, we were far too impatient for that. If a problem came up—I didn't care what was on the agenda—we were going to solve that problem right now, on the spot.

We broke a lot of management rules about making agendas and following them."

One of the keys to the success of this kind of dialogue is making sure that the right people are there. John Coonrod of the Hunger Project looks for the key opinion leaders, shapers, and noted experts in the field, as well as the conveners—the ones who can get other people and groups to sit down at the table. He also makes sure that he invites people who are passionate about the issue and are "ripe" to participate, especially if they have been excluded in the past.[14]

Collaboration happens in conversations. A collaborative person is likely to gather people together who can contribute to the effort and say, "Here's what I think. How do you see it differently?" In Chapter Five, we will provide you with a powerful, concise, step-by-step process called The Five Phases of a Collaborative Conversation.

Things to Do:

- *Create a structured meeting time, such as one day every month or every other week, devoted to one or two issues.*

- *Schedule a two-hour meeting with no agenda.*

- *Limit the meeting agenda to one or two topics.*

- *Discuss with the group how you will deal with honest disagreement, how you will deal with mistakes, and how you will handle praise and criticism.*

BUILDING BLOCK #6.

Create shared work spaces.

Collaboration is a process of shared creation. It requires a collaborative medium or, what Michael Schrage, author of *No More Teams,* calls a "shared workspace."[15] A conversation is a shared space. "It's not that we don't need conversation about what to do or how to do it," says Schrage. "It's that we need a medium of shared space to conduct the conversation so we can accelerate the creation of shared understanding" (for example, a napkin where two peace negotiators (or lawyers) casually sketch out various scenarios for a just settlement, a flip chart where an industrial design group collects and connects the best ideas, or a computer network and document sharing where scientists create shared interpretations of data, or a prototype for a new product or service). In fact, one of the best tests of whether a group is collaborating is to have an answer for the question, "Where's the shared space?" It's virtually impossible to collaborate without it.

It's also important to keep in mind that conversation can often lead to words that mean different things to different people—quality, service, innovation, and so on. We can talk about what these words mean to each of us, but to really make sure we understand each other, we have to put it to the test of physical reality. We have to move beyond words, or even collaborative tools that allow people to think and work together, and also provide shared spaces where people can build and test their brainchild. This could take the form of simple things like a preliminary budget proposal, a role-play of a sales pitch, or a school or orchestra rehearsal. Or, it could be more complex, like a ³/₈th scale model of the Rover for landing on Mars, a strawdog piece of health-care legislation, or a prototype of an innovative new product.

A scale model, prototype, or mock-up that takes the form of a small project is a good way to build shared understanding. For example, instead of designing planes by working in isolation and passing information between functional areas, Boeing Corporation aerospace, mechanical, and electrical engineers work on the design using the shared medium of computer-generated models. When one group has to make modifications to the design of the aircraft, engineers in other areas can immediately view the impact of these changes before they occur. This process of building a shared understanding of what works and what doesn't allows the engineers to design and "test fly" the aircraft before building a costly full-scale prototype. A two-year reduction in cycle time for design and testing has saved hundreds of million of dollars.

Traditionally managers have not thought of creating shared spaces for people because they have assumed that knowledge comes not from people thinking and interacting together, but from accumulating information. "In the future," says Schrage, "managers will increasingly look for shared spaces to be developed that can leverage people's process of building shared understandings that result in new innovations."

Things to Do:

• *Decide what will be used as shared space.*

• *Build a prototype to test shared notions.*

• *Appoint someone to be in charge of overseeing the shared space.*

BUILDING BLOCK #7.

Load the project with "zest factors."

In my 1996 book, *Masterful Coaching*, I mentioned something called the "Breakthrough Technique," which was influenced by the work of consultant Robert Schaffer, who identified zestful factors that elicit extraordinary performance in team situations.[16] Some "zest factors" we have discovered include a compelling challenge, asense of urgency, near and clear success, spirit of collaboration, self-organization, pride of achievement, fear of failure, experimentation, ignoring documentation, and taking action. What I and others have discovered in coaching many project groups is that loading a project with these zest factors has an enormous impact on transforming "great people" into a "great team" that overcomes organizational defensive routines and builds shared understanding, leading to breakthrough results. Here are some components of the breakthrough technique that will help you load your collaborative project with zest factors.

Enroll passionate people. An ad for Nike golf shoes shows a player walking down a beautiful fairway, with a series of captions—*I am the Nike Tour. (Pause). I am not afraid to do what I love for a living. (Pause) I am down to my last hundred dollars.* The moral of the story is that too many of us trade in our aliveness in order to earn a living at something we are not that crazy about. There's another message: People who are passionate produce far better than average results which, for instance, get them on the Nike Tour, even if you have to drive to every tournament. The same applies to the zest they bring to any project. Members of the Mars Project, the Hunger Project, and Fidelity Investments told us that one of the first things they looked for in hiring individuals or bringing them into a project is passionate people who think clearly and have good intuition. Giving passionate individuals a chance to shine can bring enormous zest to a team. In bringing these people on, ignore title and rank if possible, and instead think of passion, commitment, and zeal.

Create a breakthrough goal that can be achieved in weeks, not months, even if it is only part of your overall collaborative effort. Robert Schaffer says breakthrough goals that are challenging, but attainable, tend to inspire people. He also emphasizes that any goal that stretches out more than a few weeks or a month tends to fall off the radar screen of people's time and attention. In developing the software Microsoft Project, project leader John Reingold found that there were an unbelievable amount of software bugs and that this was discouraging the team. His first breakthrough goal was "zero old bugs" (bugs that already existed) within six weeks. Once that was achieved, he set a breakthrough goal to tackle new bugs. Having an achievable goal in a short time worked powerfully to remotivate the team and to accomplish something important.[17]

Focus on what's possible to do with existing resources, authority, and change readiness. In many groups, everything people say is an extension of their profound level of resignation. "The boss doesn't listen. It's not in the budget. It can't be done." One of the most potent ways to add zest is to refocus the group's attention on what they *can* do with existing readiness, resources, and authority. Matt Golombek of the Mars Project said that one of the most powerful forces for innovation was a non-negotiable breakthrough goal and an immutable timetable and budget. The people at the Hunger Project wanted to prove that the idea of the "Hunger Free Zone," based on the principle of self-reliance, could work and started the first one in Senegal where there was a great deal of existing readiness. Peter McKercher of Bell Canada wanted to create transformational training programs. To fulfill a company mandate for sales reps to shift from selling products to providing consulting services, he hired us to develop a "Collaborative Consulting Skills" course. Because of the readiness for change, rather than people saying "oh no, flavor of the month," they said, "this is what we've all been waiting for."

Get going and produce a result right now, immediately. The design of the breakthrough technique is to take goals that are too large and complex, with resources that are unattainable, and break them up so that they can be successfully attacked, one at a time. The idea is to bypass elaborate planning and preparations, and get going to produce an immediate result, a success, and then expand outwardly building on the scope of the original breakthrough, creating a widening circle of successes.

Things to Do:

- *Identify a performance opportunity or problem-solving project.*

- *Choose a team leader who will stand for the opportunity.*

- *Set breakthrough goals where success is near and clear.*

- *Create a written work plan.*

- *Jump into action.*

The Future of the Firm

The ideas I had come up with about lateral leadership and the collaborative corporation indicated a great deal about the future of the corporation that corresponded to what I was reading about in the business press. This included CEOs who talked about empowerment, strategic partnerships, and, of course, cross-functional teams and processes. Also, there had been a growing trend toward Internet and Intranet devices that gave everyone access to e-mail and made it possible through groupware to have "electronically distributed meetings" with people in different companies, locations, and times. This was pretty exciting.

Yet, in other ways, there seemed to be some disconnection between the ideas I and others were talking about and what I saw firsthand in many companies. I wondered if the typical Fortune 500 firm could really be a vehicle for taking advantage of the new management ideas and technological breakthroughs that had occurred, and if they were suitable forms for taking us into the next century. In 1980, Alvin Toffler wrote about "Second Wave" companies in a "Third Wave" world. It was now almost twenty years later, and many management leaders and gurus were asking themselves how much had really changed.

Due to a lack of organizational forms, there had been a hundred-year lag between the technological breakthroughs of the Industrial Revolution and the ability to transform technologies into economic fruits.[1] James Arkwright invented the water frame loom in 1760 and Eli Whitney invented the steam engine in 1769, but it wasn't until the mid-nineteenth century that the Industrial Revolution really took off in America. It was at this time that the notion of the "corporation" was founded as a way to bring together hard-to-find capital. After the Civil War, there were less than a million people nationwide working in factories. By 1910, in factories like the Ford Motor Company, there were tens of millions. Also, until that time, there was no such thing as "management"—the word at that time referred to the care and feeding of horses. Even in the early days of Ford, turnover was often as high as 70 percent a month.

Are we perhaps in another hundred-year lag where the technological breakthroughs of the Information Age cannot be realized because of a lack of organizational forms or appropriate management attitudes? It seems that, despite what was being written about Fortune 500's transformation in the business press, most firms are still very much the products of the same management "command-and-control" cultures as they were almost two decades ago.

Many times in my experience of working in different organizations, I had asked myself: Why are there so few CEOs and executives who dare to take a stand for ideas that are unpopular or controversial? Why did executives say one thing to me in private and then go to the big meeting and say something completely opposite—and then pretend that they didn't? Why, in spite of being empowered, did people still act like a canaries in a bird cage, afraid to come out and spread their wings? Were all the joint ventures I was hearing about just conglomerates designed to reduce administrative costs or were they really creating something new?

A Study of Roger Ackerman, CEO of the Corning Corporation

I began to search for people who could help me answer these questions, as well as for role models who could light the path toward the corporation of the future.[2] Which CEOs are good examples of lateral leadership, creating cultures of empowerment? What is a good example of an Enterprise Web? Where is radical innovation happening? I called John Seely Brown, chief scientist at Xerox, and asked him these questions (more on Brown later). He suggested that I speak with Roger Ackerman of the Corning Incorporated. The 150-year-old company was exploding with growth, almost doubling its business every year in fiber optics, photonics, and LCD-display technology. According to Ackerman, half the world is waiting to receive its first phone call, and, when they do, it will be on fiber optics.

Ackerman had an easy familiarity, like an old friend you had just gotten back in touch with. His ideas were simple but powerful ,and, at the same time, it was clear he had the attitudes and behaviors to go along with them, not just concepts in his head. I asked Ackerman about his management method and how the operational environment had contributed to astonishing business growth and financial success.

Deep Dives to Discuss Strategy and Management by Chaos

What is the strategic process by which this kind of innovative excellence occurs? "Maybe it is not a strategic process," Ackerman explains, "but rather management by chaos." For example, Corning doesn't have a strategic planning department. According to Ackerman, "Every eighteen to twenty-four months we go off for two or three days and basically dive deeply into whatever is going on in the business. All the strategic planing is done by senior management in collaboration with employees, other colleagues, and customers. Lots of outside consultants are used to stimulate thinking and looking at things in a new way. Random bits of new product or process knowledge are interjected into processes and products from a frenzy of bench-marking activity."

In effect, Corning is constantly creating an expanding, shared-information pool out of which diverse ideas in a fertile "environment brew" can light creative sparks. "There's a culture in the company that believes we have a unique strength in relatively focused, narrow areas— inorganic materials science—and should stay there." Ackerman continued, "We stay very narrowly focused on this and our core technologies. But besides that, we are open to new ideas and business—even those that haven't been invented yet."

Finding Strategic Partnerships Before the Window of Opportunity Closes

On strategic partnerships, Ackerman says, "We also have a tendency to think about joining up with other companies much quicker than a lot of other companies would. We do a lot of joint venturing, which helps because it gets you through the window of opportunity before it closes. We came up with something very new and innovative—one example being the optical fibers—but really didn't have any way of cabling it or the right distribution network to get it out there. Ackerman said that he quickly jumped to the conclusion that they had to have a partner—"You can make the fiber, but you have to put it in a cable and get it out to the phone company."

To make this kind of creative collaboration work, Ackerman emphasized, it takes a certain kind of leadership behavior: You have to be *open* (a key word in Corning lexicon) and not dance around too much with deal

113

making and attorneys. "We even talked to AT&T at one point, but they weren't interested so we *engaged* [another key word] Siemens. Ackerman and his team believe that "there has to be synergy, something each partner is bringing to the party, and it has to be roughly equal. There also has to be a cultural [workstyle] compatibility. "One side has to take the initiative in courting the other side," a role Corning often plays, "but both sides have to see the spark."

Personal Growth and Company Growth Are Interrelated

Ackerman feels that that this kind of growth-oriented environment must provide opportunities for people to grow. He and his group have worked hard to define the kind of leadership thinking and attitudes that could be embedded in practices, such as personal (organization) growth, strategic deep dives, focused creativity and invention, broad-range collaborative business partnerships, and teamwork. This involved the senior management of Corning spending over two years, four to eleven hours a month, grinding out a set of key behaviors. "Some of them are kind of interesting," says Ackerman, "like being open, engaging, enabling, rigorous. We didn't just want to have the list of the right behaviors—lots of companies have that kind of thing—we wanted the real attitude shift." Over two years, Ackerman and company spent a lot of time in thoughtful inquiry pondering questions like: What does it mean to be an open person? What does it mean to be an engaging person, or enabling?

Ackerman also emphasizes that personal and organization growth go hand in hand. Growing the company means providing a climate where people can grow, and where they can realize their dreams and aspirations. "If you are going to work at Corning, you are going to grow." It's part of what the values are all about. The company is one where the individual is cherished. Yet Ackerman points out, "We're not a 'me' society." People are asked to think in terms of what they can create together and how they can be part of a winning team. But it is not teamwork, with a capital "T", "group think," or 360-degree feedback instruments where everyone has to be the same. Diverse views and perspectives are fostered "perhaps to a crazy excess," with a high degree of tolerance for lopsided people.

Says Ackerman, "We have a tolerance for eccentric people who are creative. We honor them. It is one of the reasons why we have such breakthroughs in technology. If we are going to live off creativity and invention, we had better have an atmosphere that caters to people who are creative and inventive. We are not so concerned with who they report to or paperwork or administration. We try to make it really easy for these people to come to work every day."

Talking to John Seely Brown

It was both informative and interesting to talk with Roger Ackerman, yet I still had questions about the future of the corporation—especially the large company. These questions stemmed from the fact that as an executive leadership coach and management consultant, I had seen so many companies where the command-and-control model of management reigned, instead of what Chris Argyris and others called the "internal commitment model." In many ways, the old functional fiefdoms were still in place. Even though I saw examples of empowered people in companies, it was often the case that, six months later, these people would have the wind knocked out of their sails—sometimes by having their intentions thwarted, at other times by getting completely absorbed in internal power politics.

I had real questions about whether it would be better for people to get out of the corporation and find a different medium—such as entrepreneurship, self-organization networks, Enterprise Webs, etc. I had talked to John Seely Brown (or JSB as he calls himself), as well as Paul Allaire, CEO of Xerox, a few years earlier when I wrote my book on *Masterful Coaching*.[3] They created a strategy called Xerox 2000 through a very collaborative approach to strategic planning. Whereas most companies create a shared strategy (in words only) and then try to create enough of a shared understanding around it for it to be implemented, Xerox did something different. Allaire, Brown, and others spent eleven months creating a shared view of the world and Xerox's strengths and weaknesses with in it. This then became the basis of a shared strategy that was implemented with remarkable success.

I told Brown I wanted to speak to him for a number of reasons. First, he is warm and generous as a person, and someone who has a good understanding of big companies and how they are evolving. According to Roger Ackerman, who recruited Brown for Corning's board, "He is not only chief scientist but also a respected businessman."

Second, Brown is a fascinating, sometimes dazzling, leading-edge thinker, whose job is to run the Xerox Palo Alto Research Center (PARC), an organization that has an extraordinary track record for radical innovation. Years ago, PARC invented the first PCs, the Apple mouse, chunks of the Internet, and continues in that same vein today. Brown is a bit of a renaissance man. In addition to his scientific and business pursuits, a couple of years ago he produced an award-winning film called—•Art•Lunch• Internet• Dinner.

The Future of the Firm

Brown suggested that as background I might read a paper he and a colleague Paul Duguid had written, entitled "The Future of the Firm," to provide a kind of superstructure for our dialogue. I will summarize what Brown had to say about the future of the firm, and then introduce you to our fascinating conversation. I believe he chose the wording, "The Firm" for a particular reason—to emphasize that it was very much still needed and had a future in a cyberworld where little stood between Marshall McLuhan's "global village" and the empowered individual with a Web site who declares himself his own brand and sets up business over the Internet.

Brown takes the view that, while we may be suffering from many second-wave organizations in a third-wave world, it would be foolhardy to think that the firm wasn't needed at all—rather, it needed transforming. Brown agrees with many others that complex problem solving and radical innovation require a knowledge-creating company versus a production-creating company.[4] The future of the firm will be involved first and foremost in the production of knowledge, not the mass production of goods. Brown cites how Microsoft has a much greater market valuation, $187 billion, and only 20,000 employees compared to General Motors' $47 billion market valuation and over 500,000 employees.

One important distinction he draws to emphasize how important it is for our organizations to evolve involves the difference between the creation of new knowledge and information processing. Today's companies are often obsessed with smoother, faster, information processing (quantitative), almost to the exclusion of any emphasis on the creation of new knowledge. I cited earlier, for example, that one of PARC's inventions, the "Live Board" (computerized white board), failed in the marketplace, not because it wasn't an effective device for helping groups brainstorm new ideas and solve problems, but because these capacities were largely not even perceived by the customers. Instead of using the Live Board to help people think and work together, people used it, according to my interview with Tom Moran, for its graphic capabilities in making presentations—not an act of creative collaboration, but of information processing and distribution.[5]

Knowledge Ecologies

The onset of the Information Age has provided new technologies that have transformed not just features but whole landscapes into unstructured cyberspace. Brown believes that, although there is a place for the "E generation" of entrepreneurs (who have forsaken the corporation), the "free agent," and the amorphous self-organizing group, these people are likely to quickly bump up against serious limitations in what they can take on and deliver, especially in complex situations.

The primary reason is expressed in an insight Brown has that is key to how PARC works: "knowledge is a social activity." No one kind of specialist or group today has all the knowledge necessary for radical innovation or complex problem-solving projects. What this usually requires is gathering lots of people from different specialties who have local knowledge and then transforming it all into global knowledge.

In this scenario, the isolated entrepreneur, the free agent, and the amorphous self-organizing group, such as a pack of consultants without real accountability or alignment, are not likely to be very successful, unless they limit themselves to situations of minimum complexity. Thus, a lateral leader or "organizing maestro," as well as formal organizations, are needed to congeal the partial insights or knowledge of individuals and groups into "robust social knowledge."

While specialization, division of labor, and division of knowledge are needed and certain boundaries in formal and informal organizations are necessary, Brown feels the purpose of the firm is to make it easier for people to talk and exchange ideas and information across these divisions. Thus, organizations become powerful "knowledge ecologies." This not only lies in people identifying opportunities and being knowledge brokers who can bring the right team together but also in facilitating collaborative conversations about solving problems where people build new shared understandings that result in insights that no one had before.

The Organizing Maestro and His Enterprise Web

After I read Brown's article, I gave him another call and asked him to elaborate on various questions I had on my mind. It was a very intriguing, eye-opening conversation. Brown spoke in a low, (almost somber) voice and in a wandering, poetic style that reminded me of Allen Ginsberg, of the Beat Generation. Yet his insights were grounded in the practical reality of big business, as well as running a small shop known for radical innovation. The conversation served to confirm some of my own thoughts mentioned earlier in the book and, in other cases, answer a lot of questions.

What then, I asked Brown, was the future of the firm—how will it evolve? "The very likely evolution will be the extended enterprise model. What you are going to find are collaborative webs of corporations coming together for larger projects. The key to this extended enterprise model will be a CEO or leader that acts as a strategist and knowledge broker . . . in projects that require creativity and collaboration. Instead of managers communicating top down, to control different specialists, they will increasingly use communication to coordinate the activities of specialists."

I had read somewhere that at PARC, the public address system is not used to page people in the cafeteria or other places, as that might distract people from creative thought or dialogue. Instead, each person in the company has their own musical tone assigned to them that is sounded when they are being paged. I asked Brown, "How do you establish an environment that nurtures creative people? How do you ensure that these people recognize the possibilities and opportunities that become the basis for patenting breakthrough inventions? How do you foster creative people?"

"Here's the catch," he said, "we are a small research center—we only have 350 people—but we do everything from atoms to culture. We have physicists, mathematicians, computer scientists, and electrical engineers. Also, we have linguists, sociologists, anthropologists, and artists. We really have brought together an extraordinary combination of people. The way our folks think and work together starts with providing challenges" that appeal to different people's talents, interests, gifts, and in the process "they become attached to a problem. It is the problem that pulls us outside of our disciplines."

If the PARC groups are trying to build a new type of office system around engineering documents, for example, they will often send an anthropologist into a company or "community of practice" to see what work practices really need to be improved. Then, when some insights are gained, the anthropologist, together with computer scientists, engineers, industrial designers, and artists, all work together to invent tools that might be developed to assist in carrying out those practices. Right from the start, they look at questions like: If we build this, what will be the real value proposition to a customer? From what different angles do we need to look at the product? What will it take to produce a breakthrough?

Yet, bringing extraordinary combinations of people together and brainstorming are just part of building an environment that supports creativity and inventiveness. The real key in nurturing a creative environment, according to Brown, starts with the way he and others at PARC hire people. "We want people who are passionate, creative, and bold, but not just in la-la land. We want people who are able to ground these qualities in real experiences and real problems so that they really have an impact. The third property that we look for is people who have great intuition.

"How well the kids did (in terms of grade-point average) doesn't interest me. If they have a bunch of As and a bunch of Fs, that's fine with me. What kind of letter of recommendation they have, assuming I know the people writing the letter, is something I have a great deal of interest in. So I read these letters to get a sense of whether people have a passion for impact and boldness. I want people with a great intuition who can get things done. Many of the people that we hire today have been summer interns for one, two, or three years with us. So we've had a chance to work shoulder to shoulder with them. That's how we tell whether or not they have good intuition."

Lateral Leadership and Coaching

One of the areas that Brown emphasizes is coaching. I had mentioned to him that one of the observations I had made in consulting different companies was the prevalence of a climate of resignation in many firms, due to too much management control and not enough opportunities for people to realize their aspirations and grow, as well as organization defensive routines. How do you transform such a climate of resignation into a climate of possibility and opportunity? I asked.

Brown acknowledged all the things I had said, but then pondered. "What I find interesting is that a relatively small change can actually do a lot to transform this," he said. "First it involves transforming the attitudes of middle managers, from seeing themselves as controllers to seeing themselves as coaches, who can identify opportunities, act as knowledge brokers in bringing the right people together, and coach the process of helping people solve problems."

Second it involves coaching in the sense of shifting people's attention on an ongoing basis from focusing on power games and politics to focusing on the customer, as well as from shifting their focusing from their own psyche or the internal organization problems to being outwardly focused on customers. "Interacting with the marketplace is fun—it is motivating and energizing. Yet to do that, people have to be able to think and work together," Brown emphasized. "People want to collaborate and communicate, but often don't know how to come together."

"The whole notion of 'lateral' is incredibly important," said Brown, who sees the leader not as a top-down, authority figure who controls, but as someone coordinating specialists with talents and organizing knowledge. He sees the challenge of leadership as facilitating communication across the inevitable divisions that will arise in any organization. "If we think of most communication happening in organizations today, a huge portion of it flows the same way—cascading down the waterfall. This can only disseminate information, not result in creating new knowledge.

"However, real communication always happens laterally. For example, how do you share ideas amongst each other, if people are afraid the boss will resent it if it isn't his idea? How do you co-produce an understanding of what the strategy actually means? How do you foster the kind of communication that leads to creativity and invention?"

Creatively Exploring White Space

I asked Brown if he and his group looked for ideas that fall between the cracks of different disciplines and if this could be a source of the extraordinary innovations that happen at PARC. "We regularly bring people from different disciplines together in order to search for and explore white space." People are brought together and brainstorm around a problem—"always a problem." What will it really take to come up with new ideas or innovative solutions? "All the people involved will let things marinate in their minds over a course of a few hours, days, or weeks, while trying to crack it."

People may start the discussion from the framework of their particular discipline, but soon what happens is that they allow themselves to get pulled out of their disciplinary boundaries by collaborating with others around a real world problem. This allows people to take three or so differ-ent points of view and "triangulate" on how to see that problem. It allows them "to constantly re-see and reframe that problem until you get to the root of it and crack it wide open."

The Search for New Metaphors,
The Trading Zone, and "Pidgin" Languages

Brown had said that the challenge of leadership is to facilitate communi-cation and exchange of value across the various divisions of an organiza-tion, creating "knowledge ecologies in the process." Yet exactly how does this work? Each profession tends to have certain sacred assumptions, and their attitude is "Violate them at your peril." I can remember being asked a few times in my own work doing executive reinvention and culture change programs if we would work with others on, let's say, incorporating a reengi-neering project. As my field was transformation, I only wanted to work with people who had a transformational approach. Reengineering types, though good at structural transformation, never seemed to understand the impor-tance of transforming human attitudes.

I have heard many people in different professions speak the same way—CEOs, engineers, marketers. This often results in an exclusive atti-tude, such as "They're not our kind of people" or "How do I know I can trust them?" or "They don't speak our language." All others were "pagans," people to have a cup of coffee with but no more. Sometimes, I would hear people say, "It could work, but one of us will have to change our thinking and paradigms." Yet, there was the old joke from mental mod-els research that "people only changed their paradigms at their funeral."

Curiously enough, I had found very few answers to these ponder-ings. Around the same time I spoke to Brown about his knowledge ecolo-gies, I spoke to another scientist outside the business world, Peter Galison of Harvard University, who had just won the coveted MacArthur award (otherwise known as the "genius award") for his work on the history of modern physics.[6]

Galison had noted in his book, *Image & Logic,* how C. T. R. Wilson had invented the first bubble chamber: he blew the glass, forged the metal fittings, did the experiments, and recorded the results all on his own. Today, similar experiments are done in huge labs, half a block long, with barn-size bubble chambers, often with hundreds of participants all over the world, who communicate by phone, Internet, and fax. Galison noted that there are often many distinct branches of industries that do not speak each other's language at all—quantum physicists, mechanical engineers, computer people, software designers, administrators.

Galison wondered how these people from distinctly different professions, who spoke different occupational languages and often had incompatible opinions and assumptions, managed to think and work together at all. He stumbled across a metaphor by studying anthropologists who did work in "cultures at the boundary." He said that these people usually invented what he calls a "trading zone," where they could exchange information of value, without speaking the same language or understanding each other.

He found that scientists, engineers, and managers, in effect, did the same thing in the trading zone of problem-solving projects, citing the invention of radar as an example that involved physicists, radio engineers, and administrators. A conversation I had with some engineers and scientists at the Boston University's Photonics Center—a very collaborative organization that produces technologies that can be used profitably in industries—helped me to understand this.[7] (Photonics is used in fiber-optics systems and involves sending a phone call through modulating light.)

Jim Hubbard, chief engineer, told me that physicists like his colleague Bennett Goldberg, worry that the projects that they are working on represent the possibility of new scientific discoveries. They concern themselves about working on things that have already been discovered, considering them "absolutely irrelevant." Says Goldberg, "When I show some of them a measurement device and try to get them to give their input, their eyes roll up into their heads—it is not relevant." On the other hand, engineers worry about making sure that what they are working on has practical application.

Says Galison, "When physicists and engineers enter the trading zone, they drop some of their concerns and concentrate on the overlap. They don't have to agree on the same global or professional assumptions in order to exchange ideas and coordinate their actions in a local project." (One example of this collaborative activity, which we will discuss later in Chapter Six, has to do with the physicists and radio engineers who worked together before World War II on the invention of radar.)

Galison also points out that, when people who come from different cultures step into a trading zone, they often have language difficulties and have to find a way to communicate and exchange information. He points out that solving the language problem is often not just a simple matter of translation, as Brown mentioned several times, but actually involves creating a "pidgin" or "Creole" language, especially in complex problem-solving projects that require creating new knowledge that exists in neither of their fields rather than just sharing what they already know. The creation of the new language is coupled with being able to create the new knowledge. Galison cites an example: for physicists and engineers to invent radar, they had to invent a new language and calculational methods that were not in either of their respective fields. (See Chapter Six for a more detailed explanation.)

The point is that collaborators from different fields or institutions might find it useful to create a trading zone where they can talk and be of value to each other in a project, without having to convert each other's underlying opinions and assumptions. As Galison says, dropping some of what you worry about and focusing on the areas of overlap, is key. And as Brown pointed out, this new collaboration becomes a focused dialogue grounded in something solid, like a shared problem, that pulls people out of their professional stereotypes and occupational orthodoxies and not only allows them to coordinate their knowledge and skills but also to create new knowledge and skills.

The Role of Collaborative Conversations in an Enterprise Web or Knowledge Ecology

I asked John Seely Brown how he viewed the role of dialogue in ane Enterprise Web or knowledge ecology. Several times he came back to the idea that knowledge is a social activity and that conversation is the essential medium. "It starts when we are very young. For example, picking up a language is an interesting collaborative exercise with parents, kids, and others around us." As you move through school, the ability to talk through ideas with each other—about English, math, history—becomes a way to learn collaboratively as well. We all know that small, informal study groups are the best way to cement what a textbook has said. It's one thing to work on a problem by yourself, but it's even better to take a couple of people and talk through the problems. "My partial understanding is like a scaffold. Learning happens when I combine my scaffold of understanding with your scaffold of understanding and create a new scaffold of understanding on a higher level," Brown says. "With textbooks, all you have is the information. With a collaborative conversation, you create the opening to a moment of true insight."

Learning is not only enhanced by doing it together, notes Brown, but also when it involves the performance of real tasks versus abstract performance such as taking a test. "We have done a microanalysis of people studying such subjects as Newton's laws of physics, that have resultedin in-depth understanding, far superior to that of first-year MIT students who get As. This involved simulation games that allow for interacting with others, while trying to control the outcome. As the participants begin to try to solve the problem, they move beyond their own partial understanding of the situation and begin to co-construct insights, metaphors, and stories in this process as a result of their interaction, which leads to in-depth knowledge," says Brown. "This kind of learning is both creative and collaborative, and the amazing thing is that it happens without them even being aware of it."

Brown and others at PARC have taken these insights and applied them to many situations at Xerox's Research Center. Brown referred me to David Bell, head of the Eureka Project, who told me of an effort he and his colleagues were involved in to try to turn around the poor service record of Xerox France. The project involved sending an anthropologist to study how the repairmen fixed the machines. It was discovered that if the repairman relied on the 5,000-page repair manual, they got into trouble, but if they met with colleagues at the company cafeteria and swaped war stories and cheat sheets, then Eureka!, they often got a moment of true insight—and the next day the machine was fixed. This awareness resulted in the creation of a database accessible through a special phone system in France and some collaborative software tools.[8]

Authentic Communication

With all of this discussion about the importance of lateral leadership and cross-functional communication, I asked Brown what got in the way of Xerox collaborating to capitalize on their earlier inventions, like the PC and various ethernet inventions. Brown explained: "It's quite simple. In the early days, PARC was very much an 'us versus them' place. We were geniuses and the rest of the corporation were idiots. We had tremendous team spirit by being 'us versus them.' There was a sense of a common enemy, and the enemy were the people running the rest of the corporation.

"It's very easy to build a high-energy team when you define the opposition like that. It becomes a magical team, but it almost guarantees that team will end in failure, because when it came time to really interact with the rest of the corporation, the team can't have an honest conversation. By then, there is sufficient resentment built up, that even if you tried to have a authentic conversation, you can't." Many other organizations have sunk in the same mode.

One of the changes over the last ten years at PARC is the process of having ongoing dialogues with all parts of the corporation. According to Brown, "We carry it out by recognizing what parts of the corporation are most interested in the future. So you have a kind of co-evolutionary system. We have a dialogue with everyone in the strategy office. We address questions like: What does the Internet mean for copiers? What's happening with the printing game? How is color coming in?"

The success of these interactions depends on being able to have an authentic conversation. This not only requires the ability to treat each other as colleagues, surfacing rather than suppressing dilemmas that are potentially embarrassing or threatening, giving your honest opinion when asked, and openly disagreeing with anyone in the group.

Brown emphasizes that, while it's important for people to authentically disagree, he doesn't just mean people taking an arbitrary position in an argument and defending their noble certainties for dear life or "talking B.S." Rather, he's referring to people being grounded in their positions through rigorous thinking and facts. "For a collaborative conversation there also has to be a commitment from each person to move from his or her position and to co-construct the best guess (interpretation) on how to view something." It is not only important to be authentic but to be willing to be influenced. You notice in such conversations that both people's positions slightly change as they think and interact together. Some ideas and insight are created that just didn't exist before.

Generative Active Listening

Brown discussed a seminal event that happened in graduate school that taught him about how to ask questions and then how to listen. "I was walking home with this world-famous professor. We had just come from a seminar. I was really struck by how most professors at seminars ask killer questions to try to embarrass the student, and that this guy, Anatol

Rappaport, was different. During the seminar, I noticed that a student said something a little half-baked. Instead of the professor embarrassing the guy by asking him questions that exposed the errors in his thinking, he asked a set of leading questions that helped the presenter come to a better understanding of his own ideas and actually look better."

Brown recalls that as he was walking with the professor, he could no longer contain his curiosity. "I said, 'What's going on? You could have asked that person questions to make him see how foolish his thinking was, but you didn't.' He turned to me and said, 'John, those of us who are endowed with great intellectual capability should realize that it is trivial to tear people or their thinking down. The challenge is to generate and to build' . . . so that people get new insights or take their ideas to a higher level."

Brown referred to a fax I sent him, "What hit me in the note that you sent me is that for this type of really creative collaboration to happen, it takes not only stating your position and being open to other's ideas, but actively listening. I think people often underestimate the challenges involved. How do you listen to each another amid disagreement and reactive emotions? How do you go out of your way to actually make sense of what the other person is saying? How do you actively listen in a way that actually helps the other person express something he is struggling to articulate?" In effect, active listening not only requires giving people the gift of your presence but also suspending your position and putting a tremendous amount of energy into understanding their position. He repeated again, "The challenge is not to tear down, but to generate and to build."

Chapter Four

Close Encounters of the Creative Kind:

Launching Your Collaboration

"... a great hunger for community and collaboration existed everywhere,
despite profound mistrust,
alienation, and skepticism.
People wanted to come together.
They simply did not know how."

—EVA SCHINDLER-RAINMAN AND RONALD LIPPITT
BUILDING THE COLLABORATIVE COMMUNITY

Top executives at Chrysler were determined to build a prototype car that would derive its power from fuel cells that produce electricity, but they did not have all of the expertise needed on their own staff. So Christopher Borroni-Bird, advanced technologies specialist at Chrysler, assembled a team composed of people from both Chrysler and Delphi Automotive Systems (General Motors' parts division).

Disney-trained animator John Lasseter, vice president of creative development at Pixar Animation Studio, longed to make the first feature-length computer-animated film. He had a wonderful script in hand called Toy Story. *But to pull it off, he knew he would need to figure out a way to create characters who could exhibit human-like emotional expressions—a smile that was expressed in puffed cheeks, lifted lips, and crinkled eyes, or sadness that was reflected in droopy shoulders and hands, as well in facial expressions. So he enlisted the help of seven people with Ph.Ds in computer science, twenty-five traditional puppet, clay, and stop-motion animators, and twenty-two technical directors.*

* * * * *

Every Sunday evening, a writer on leave from a newsweekly magazine, who had been awarded a year-long fellowship at the University of Michigan, ran a salon out of her apartment. She invited fellow students, her professors and other professors she knew only by reputation, and interesting people she happened to meet in the community. "I supplied food and plenty to drink and the space was cramped, so we really got to know each other," she recalls. "Those were always among the most interesting discussions I had all week."

W hether you have a great idea you want to pursue with other people, an important assignment that requires help from experts in other fields, or you simply want to stage an informal get-together that introduces people from one side of the tracks in your community to those who live on the other side, gathering together a group of diverse individuals for the first time can be a daunting prospect. It is, after all, a new experience. Most of us tend to work closely with people in our own discipline but rarely get beyond superficial greetings with others. After work, we tend to socialize with our own kind—people of the same race, religion, ethnic group, class, even political party or profession.

But new products, ad campaigns, methods of conducting research, and solutions to age-old social problems cannot be discovered without first constructing connections between the diverse combinations of contributors you have gathered to collaborate with you. Your first encounter—whether a backyard barbecue, boardroom meeting, or conference—can be key to any collaboration's future success. In most instances, you will have people in your group who are unfamiliar with each other, many of whom may have misconceptions or even distrust of other group members. If you fail to knock down these barriers at the start, your creative concoction can explode, exacerbating the differences that already exist. If instead you attend to the complexities of bringing a diverse group together at the start, you can begin to lay the groundwork necessary for launching a highly successful collaborative venture.

The first step in your own mental preparation is to think about the type of collaboration you seek to achieve. In our experience, we have found that most collaborations fall into one of the following four categories:

1. **Mandated collaborations:** a group is formed to meet a challenge issued by superiors or a client, illustrated above by the collaboration between Chrysler and Delphi Automotive Systems.

2. **Self-initiated collaborations:** an individual (or small group or organization) calls others together to help pursue a dream or solve a problem that is too big for one person to handle. Lasseter's quest to develop a full-length computer-animated movie feature would fall into this category.

3. **Collaborations around a common concern:** people come together around a common social or organizational concern, such as developing a cure for cancer or addressing a community's rise in crime.

4. **Serendipitous collaborations:** people run into each other by accident, realize they have common or complementary goals, dreams, or problems and decide to work together. This type of collaboration often occurs after achance meeting, like the ones in the writer's weekly salons.

Mandated collaborations. Operating from a philosophy of *kyosei*, best defined as the spirit of cooperation in which individuals and organizations live and work together for the common good, executives at Canon in Japan created a mandate not only to cooperate internally among themselves and with customers and suppliers, but also to look for ways to cooperate with the competition. One such partnership agreement was made with Hewlett-Packard, who, when first approached, gave Canon executives the cold shoulder. But once Canon presented their patents and demonstrated their technological abilities, HP jumped on the opportunity. Engineers and designers from both companies got together and collaborated to build the fastest, highest-quality printers on the market. Using HP's edge in processing and Canon's edge in printer-engine design, both companies have catapulted to the top of the field of laser and ink-jet printers and have made obsolete those products manufactured by companies like Epson, once the undisputed leader in printing technology and market share.[1]

Self-initiated collaborations. Here the spark can be as simple as an individual with a dream. These dreamers are usually driven by the question, "What if?" but know they can't discover the answer alone. Usually their quest matches their talents and gifts, but they realize that they need other perspectives that won't come from their co-workers. Many people come from the position of fear, however, when approaching these collaborations. They are concerned that, in looking to others for help, their ideas will somehow be diminished. Remember Johnson Wax's "Mother, I'd rather do it myself" campaign? In fact, the opposite usually happens. Inviting others to participate with you often infuses your new colleagues with excitement, thereby amplifying your own power to realize your dreams.

Consider the case of Wilmer Ames, a reporter-researcher at *Time* magazine who had a vision of a news magazine aimed at a black audience. If he had kept his dream to himself, he would have spent the rest of his career reporting and fact-checking stories written by others. Instead, he sought out and brainstormed with designers, writers, editors, and potential investors and readers both inside and outside *Time's* headquarters. Enthused by his passion for the idea, magazine developers within the company helped him refine his vision. The result: Ames catapulted himself to the position of founding editor of *Emerge* (circulation 450,000), an award-winning monthly magazine, launched by Time, Inc. and subsequently bought by Black Entertainment Television Corporation.

On a smaller scale, a physician who wants to practice collaborative medicine might expand his practice with nonmedical or alternative practitioners like acupuncturists or nutritionists. Or a social worker may want to give his clients, artistically expressive teenagers, the opportunity to decorate the wall of his agency with a beautiful mural. Ruth Lande Shuman, formerly a project coordinator for the educational wing of the office furniture company, Steelcase and now known as "the Paint Lady," did something similar when she set up Publicolor, a nonprofit organization, to realize her dream of energizing the students in New York City's most poorly performing schools by painting over the drab walls with blazes of colors: lavender, chartreuse, kiwi, and tangerine. Fellow collaborators included the students, the Benjamin Moore paint company, the school chancellor, and corporate sponsors.

Collaborations around a common concern. Some social problems tug at people's hearts and minds—children without adequate food, elderly people without basic health care, deterioration of the environment. Finally an individual speaks up and says, "I'd like to do something about that." Their stand resonates with others who have long shared the same concerns, prompting them to join the cause.

When Bill Clinton initiated a "national dialogue on race," it was not just about holding big conferences or town meetings, but about creating a context for frequent, informal exchanges to occur. One exciting example of this kind of dialogue took place when the *New Orleans Times-Picayune* newspaper ran a series of articles about race relations entitled "Together Apart/The Myth of Race." The series generated scores of comments from readers, both in the form of telephone calls and letters to the editor. One reader, Rhoda Faust, a white woman who runs the Maple Street Book Shop, was so incensed by one Letter to the Editor that she submitted her own letter to the newspaper which read, in part:

> Thank you for tackling head-on such an important issue as race relations in New Orleans, despite the fact that the subject is so painful and therefore so unpopular with some of your readers. Your series "Together Apart" and the large space you are providing for responses is valuable in helping to solve a problem that is grounded in lack of communication.
>
> Some of the responses have come straight from the heart, and reading them has given me the feeling that I now know some of these people's feelings, and therefore them, a little better.

As a white person, I have been particularly interested in what your black respondents have to say because there are only a few black people whom I am very close to and talk intimately with.

While there have been a few ugly, hateful, ignorant, unforgiving, only-looking-for-the-bad-in-white-people responses from black people, mostly I have been encouraged. Most of your black respondents don't seem to have gone into complete despair.

And even though it's a little perverse, I was glad to read that some blacks practice skin-color discrimination against other blacks. This additional proof that there are black villains as well as white villains in the skin-color discrimination department means that it's not just a problem white people have to solve all by themselves. . . .

What will help black and white people come together? It comes back to language for me. Since most of us don't have many close friends of the other race and therefore don't have the ideal opportunity to speak easily and openly, we must find a way to let it be known that we're trying to be colorblind.

Even if we can't start having whole conversations right away, we can start getting messages to each other that show good will, friendliness, willingness to give the benefit of the doubt and basic love. All of us can think of situations that happen every day that might give us the opportunity to say a little something to let a person of the other race know we're on the same side.

Let's think of ways to let each other know that we love and respect one another as God's fellow creatures. We each have to do our best to reassure the other race of that fact. Once that message gets through, we can go from there.

RHODA K. FAUST

Faust's letter touched a responsive chord in Brenda Thompson, an African-American employee of the newspaper who also had been upset by some of the readers' responses to the series. She wrote directly to Faust:

Dear Ms. Faust,
I don't know if I'm violating some rule, but I felt I had to write to you. I am an employee at the *Times-Picayune* and I read your

letter as it was being edited for publication in the Letters to the Editor. I was touched by your caring and concern, and I wanted to let you know.

I am black and I just recently moved to New Orleans, and though I have friends here, I just find things quite different from the small town in Illinois where I was raised. We all live together there, we go to church together, we socialize together . . . there is very little we do that keeps us from mixing. There is a lot of interracial dating and not much of anyone pays attention to it. It is very different and I suppose I got used to things being open and honest between everyone. I knew when I moved down South that things would not be like that. I have lived in Florida in the past and noted the polarization between the races. I guess I naively thought that is because this is a big city and because things are rather easy here that it would not be as bad. It isn't. It's worse.

Since I have been working at the *Times,* I am privy to some of the things going on. I work near the girls who type and transcribe the tapes that come in over the telephone (you know, the twenty-four-hour line where people can call in and voice their thoughts on the "Together Apart" series) and I have heard some serious and some sickening things. I wonder what causes people to hate so much. . . .

But anyway, I wanted to let you know that some of us felt better after reading your letter. There is some measure of hope, after all. And I would be happy to get together with you and work out some sort of symbol, signal, something to let the world know that all of us aren't infected with hate and can find a way to work together. Are you interested? Maybe if others could see this, they could join in or get together and try to make things work. What do you think?

Sincerely,
BRENDA J. THOMPSON

Upon receiving the letter, Faust called Thompson and proposed that they meet. Together they formed a group, ERACE, which has held meetings twice a week since 1993 in an effort to erase racism by offering people the opportunity for focused conversations that encourage an open, critical exchange of ideas.[2]

Serendipitous collaborations. When two or more creative people rub up against each other unexpectedly, a new idea may erupt without warning—even if it takes years to be refined. Back in the 1800s, Sir William Gilbert, a lawyer who wrote comic verse in his spare time, was introduced to composer Arthur Sullivan when the latter was asked to write the music for his comic libretto, *Thespis*. The first Gilbert and Sullivan production flopped, but the two men were drawn to each other and continued to meet socially until 1875, when the manager of the Royalty Theatre in Soho suggested a second work. Their second collaboration, *Trial by Jury*, ran for a year and established the pattern for all of their subsequent works. Together they developed a new art form, the operetta.

Perhaps one of the silliest collaborations we have uncovered was sparked five years ago when members of the Berg family of Sturgeon Bay, Wisconsin, sat in the dark during a power failure. Jim Berg and numerous members of his family had gathered for a reunion on Christmas Day. Berg, a thirty-three-year-old kindergarten teacher, declared that he could fix the circuit breaker with duct tape. "Jim can fix anything with duct tape," Kelly, Jim's wife, told the gathering, sparking everyone else sitting in the dark to toss out ideas for using duct tape. Their ideas ranged from the practical ("patch old blue jeans") to the ridiculous ("bind submarine sandwiches for intact transportation"). Before long, Jim's brother-in-law, a writer from Roseville, Minnesota, added a creative spark of his own: "There's a book in here somewhere."

Once power was restored, Berg and his brother-in-law vowed to collect all the uses for duct tape they uncovered. The results: *The Duct Tape Book*, containing 162 tips, and a sequel, *The Duct Tape Book 2—Real Stories*, features uses from readers' letters written in response to the first book. A third book in the series, on the versatility of the aerosol lubricant, WD-40, is currently in the works.

Designing and Orchestrating the First Meeting of the Collaboration

Thus far we have talked about the idea of collaboration, developing yourself as a collaborative person, and the building blocks used to structure a collaborative project. Because collaboration involves bringing people together across boundaries to engage with each other, setting the stage for the first meeting, is vitally important. Our experience with the Israeli/Palestinian issues, the Hunger Project, and various business ventures like Fidelity Investments,designing and orchestrating this meeting beforehand is almost as important as the meeting itself. This follows four distinct stages: formulation, invitation, preparation, and facilitation (see Figure 4.1).

FIGURE 4.1
Setting the Stage for the First Meeting

I. Formulation

Think about the question,
"What do I (we) want to create together?"

In designing the first meeting, it is important to have a basic idea about what you or your group expects to create with the collaboration. A collaboration can be something visionary and deeply purposeful, like putting a man on the moon, eradicating HIV with a new biotech drug, or passing new legislation that provides for a sustainable environment. It could also be something that is designed to serve your particular interests in a business, such as creating a strategic partnership with another organization, setting up a multidisciplined team, or improving the quality of conversation over your team e-mail system. The collaboration could even involve something creative and entrepreneurial like a hybrid cuisine at a new restaurant, or artistic like two novelists writing a book, or something zany you do for the pure joy of creating and collaborating.

When most people think of collaborations, they tend to think in terms of *form,* such as what individuals or groups do to bring people together, as opposed to *essence,* the quality of the way people think and interact. For example, many managers today say they want to collaborate with their teams and not be so control-oriented. Yet, when people go to the team meeting and the boss asks a question, they aren't sure if he is really serious about all this team business, so they hold back and don't say anything until they're certain of his opinions or preferences. The boss views this as lack of ownership in the group and seizes the control back, which, in turn, reinforces the team members' prejudices. An idea for a collaboration might be to transform this vicious circle into a virtuous one by becoming aware of the pattern and consciously creating new behaviors.

Ponder on just who the right combination of people would be.

We can't overestimate how important it is to assemble a diverse, provocative, yet purposeful cast of characters for your collaboration. In their book *The 500 Year Delta,* futurists Watts Wacker and Jim Taylor put it well: "The problem with twenty white men making decisions in a conference room is . . . collectively, they have a low diversity IQ, a foreshortened ability to see the world through multiple perspectives."[3] "We try to get the whole project in one room," says Marvin Weisbord of Future Search, a community planning organization. "So the more diverse the attendees, the greater the potential will be for shared understanding, shared innovation, and implementation. We need people with ideas, people with authority to act, people we want to influence, people with special skills and creativity—all with a stake in the future search task."[4]

Design ponderables. According to Douglas Dayton of IDEO, it is important to think in terms of a "crazy, but catalytic group of people."[5] Start by thinking about the purpose of the collaboration. Then think about what would be just the right combination of people. Who are the different leaders, opinion shapers, and movers that can help to bring the various stakeholders to the table? Who is really passionate about this idea? What mix of people would represent the different views and perspectives that are needed? Who is competent in area XYZ? After you collect a list, reexamine it and ask yourself, "Who is missing?" When you think you have a fairly complete list, call a few of the most open-minded people on the list and ask for their suggestions.

Seek people who can bring a divergent view or perspective. L.L. Bean, the conservative, Maine-based clothing company, invited me to give a talk on collaboration. They were working on an reengineering effort that involved dramatically improving inventory tracking and reordering procedures so goods that customers wanted were always available. My first questions to a leader of the team were about crazy combinations of people: "Who can you invite to add a new perspective? What would make this a more unusual combination of people?" Prompted by these questions, the manager realized that they could invite some clerks from their retail stores and commented, "The clerks are really the only ones who can tell us what is hot at the moment. It could take us weeks or months to get that data statistically, but the store clerk can see firsthand what is going out the door fast."

Seek people who are not afraid to disagree or to give their honest opinion when asked. In the normal course of events, we tend to include people who think like us and agree with our views, often attributing to them qualities of intelligence. In the same sense, we normally exclude those who don't think like us or who disagree, often assuming that they are dumb or are not team players. Our experience shows that a key to a good quality of dialogue is often people who think differently and who are willing to openly disagree with anyone in the group. These disagreements often light the spark of creative collaboration. So when you are designing your collaboration, include people who are not afraid to disagree or give their honest opinion when asked. Also, make sure you have people in your group who are good listeners. Good listeners can often act as facilitators and help others recognize the truth within the words they disagree with, rather than treat others' words as the enemy.

Embrace your enemy. Talks between Nelson Mandela and F. W. DeKlerk brought about the end of the apartheid regime in South Africa and the threat of civil war. The idea of embracing your enemy starts in the heart and mind, whether your "enemy" is in a foreign country, or in the next office, or at home. It involves making an existential choice to look at your enemy with compassion and understanding rather than hatred. It involves seeing them and their past actions in terms of the pressures they were under and the circumstances they were in, rather than in terms of something they did against you. One of the most powerful things you can do to "Get to Peace" or to resolve a conflict is to embrace your enemy and include him or her in your group, or at least begin to share a meaningful dialogue about the problems you both face.

Think in the opposite direction by "including the excluded." If you are considering including older and experienced people, think also in the direction of including younger, less-experienced people who may be more in tune with the climate of the times. If you think men, include women, and so on. For example, a growing number of Silicon Valley companies are inventing new software and computer-graphic products by hiring bright people in their teens and early twenties to assist in the development efforts. "These people don't have to imagine the future like a forty-year-old engineer," says one executive, "they *are* the future." Another good principle is to include the excluded people. In Africa, breakthroughs in eliminating hunger began to occur when the talks began to incorporate women, who traditionally were left out of the discussions.

II. Invitation

Design invitations to collaborative meetings that excite and reassure people.

Designer Fred Holt replaces the receiver on his purple polka-dotted telephone. He had just gotten a call from Douglas Dayton, his boss at IDEO, inviting him to a brainstorming session. "Yes!" he shouts as he shoots a fist in the air. He'd been given the nod for the third time that month. These sessions are his favorite part of the job, and an invite meant the higher-ups are very pleased by his contributions.

How many people? Like the diversity of the mix, the number of people you invite must suit the purpose of the collaboration. In the Israeli/Palestinian talks, there was a large group of fifty to sixty people from each side that was sent to the Washington talks. While the Israeli team was represented officially, the leadership of the Palestinian group was not an official representative of the PLO but a mixture of people from various Arab countries. The two groups spent over a month discussing protocols such as who was going to sit where. Posturing and defensiveness were increased in the spotlight of the media. Meanwhile, the secret track of the Oslo group, represented not only direct talks but also a much more intimate setting with a combined negotiating team of three or four people.

Small group size is not always required. For example, CEOs of big companies are increasingly inviting over one hundred people to town meetings where they build shared vision and values, and ask questions about improving the company's future opportunities and present processes. Tackling a community social issue can sometimes be more productive by assembling a larger group. Future Search, for instance, typically invites sixty to seventy people to their conferences on tackling such community problems as the need for school improvement. Their goal is to get the "whole system" in the room. "We want to encourage the forming of as many new relationships as possible so people see the big picture and creatively solve problems."

Framing the invitation. Do everything you can to excite and reassure your guests about participating in a collaborative adventure. After all, you are inviting them to participate in an exhilarating undertaking, the important work of creative problem solving. Because your project will be undertaken in the company of other interesting, competent, and creative people, the journey, whatever the outcome, will be its own reward.

Excitement is key. Frame invitations in a way that inspires, intrigues, and reassures participants. Conference planners at a business school working with the Future Search people sent one puzzle piece a week for five weeks to each invited participant. To get the sixth and final piece of the puzzle, they had to attend the conference. For example, an invitation to a conference on the future of your organization might say, "The work of the conference is based on the assumption that the future doesn't just happen. The future results in part from what we do or don't do today."

It is also essential to reassure people. The Public Conversations Project dials up an activist in the Boston pro-life movement. "We would like to invite you to participate in a new kind of conversation about abortion," they say. "This is a different conversation than the one we are used to. It will not be a debate, but rather a facilitated dialogue between people with diverse views. Also invited will be several representatives from the pro-choice group." Often the invited guests are eager to participate, because they welcome the opportunity to be heard in a fresh new way by someone they desperately want to reach—people on opposing sides of an issue.[6]

III. Preparation

Take time to thoroughly prepare for the first collaborative meeting.

In South Africa during apartheid, Clem Suntner of the Shell Oil Company conducted a scenario-planning exercise about the future of the country that resulted in a slide show based on two scenarios. One was called the high road. It showed South Africa, if they eliminated apartheid, as going through a period of upheaval, then becoming a powerful and respected country that exemplified peace and prosperity to the rest of Africa. The other scenario, called the low road, showed South Africa if apartheid remained in full force, as whites keeping control for a while, then the inevitability of violent conflict and slow political and economic deterioration. The slide show was shown all over South Africa to white and black, and biracial audiences, in schools, auditoriums, hospitals, and companies. Following the show there would be an intense dialogue. The slide show is credited by many leaders as helping to break the log-jam which would have lead to violence.

Provide information about desired present and future reality that will trigger the discussion. Think carefully about what information people need to know, as in the case of South Africa, that can trigger a high-leverage, catalytic conversation. In the Mars Project, they did an "As Is" analysis and wrote down everything they knew about getting to Mars on one flip chart, and everything they did not know on another, including how they would reach their goal on a limited budget in such a short time. When the Hunger Project designates a new "hunger-free zone," they ask one well-informed person to write what they call a "What's So" report. This is a complete factual analysis of all the forces that are working in favor of reaching the goal of ending hunger in this particular region and all the forces opposing it. These kinds of analysis make people aware of what is needed and wanted to reach the goal and what's missing that, if provided, will allow it to be produced.

Many companies like Nortel, Xerox, and Lucent Technologies do the same type of exercise in their strategic planning process. A group that is being assembled to ponder the future of its company, for instance, probably should be well versed in the company's history, the strengths of key competitors, important trends affecting the company's industry now and in the future. If for example, you are preparing for a big presentation with a new customer in, consulting, send relevant materials that will help to forward the discussion in advance. You could send such materials as a brief analysis of the background of the client's problems, its competitors, or industry; your basic ideas for a proposed project that includes basic assumptions without too much detail; and other similar projects that produced successful results.

If you are hoping to generate a creative and productive discussion about a particularly hot or controversial topic, you might follow the lead of the people at the Public Conversations Project. They often talk with the participants in advance of the first meeting and ask them to ponder the following questions: What is the history of your relationship? What are the dead ends in your conversations? What do your old conversations look like? What progress or successes have you experienced? What hopes and concerns do you bring to the dialogue? When the two sides meet, the facilitators can then use their understanding of old patterns as the basis for proposing ground rules that will prevent past problems from sabotaging this fresh attempt to reach new ground together.

Establish "trim-tab" relationships between two people to set the stage for the larger group to come together. There are certain things that need to happen in preparation for the first meeting of your collaboration. One might be making contact with key individuals—or "trim-tabs"—who can bring the right people together. (When you turn the wheel of a ship, it moves a small piece of the rudder called the trim-tab, which in turn creates water pressure that moves the larger pieces of the rudder.)

For example, the people from the Hunger Project, as highlighted in the following Interlude section, always contact people who are "conveners" with the leverage to get others to come to the table and talk, as well as those who are "ripe." Terje Larsen of the Oslo peace talks was introduced by a mutual friend to Yossi Beilin. Their conversations initiated a "negotiating back channel" under Norway's auspices.

Prior to a first meeting, it is important to do some fence mending with key relationships that can act as a trim-tab for pulling a larger group together. For example, in the merger talks between British Tele and MCI the head of British Tele decided to meet personally with the head of MCI without lawyers and staff in order to speed up, not slow down, the process of the discussions between the two sides.

It could also involve a relationship between two department heads, especially where previously held stereotypes or prejudices exist. For example, we consulted Genetics Institute, a company where there was a breakdown between the head of R&D, Ed Fritsch, and the head of FDA testing, Carl Illian. The two men never talked about the bad blood that had spread to the different departments throughout the company based on their relationship. We facilitated a dialogue between the two men during a Collaborative Conversations seminar. This produced a big breakthrough in their relationship, and they started to communicate more openly, honestly, and regularly. Altering this one relationship seemed to have an impact on many others and served as a microcosm of organization learning at various levels.

IV. Facilitation

Take time to build trust, starting with greeting people at the door and saying "Hello."

One of the most exciting things about the idea of collaborating is meeting people from different professions and disciplines or sides of the political spectrum and engaging them in a genuine dialogue. Mars Project scientists and engineers loved the opportunity to teach colleagues about their occupation, as well as learn about theirs. The Israelis were very curious about what the Palestinians thought and vice versa, aside from the usual posturing and defensiveness that occur in media statements. The best marketing people are always insatiably curious about what their customers really think.

At the same time, creative collaboration isn't just like throwing peas, carrots, and potatoes into a pot. It presents a challenge in terms of basic human relationships. Imagine a CEO who has had a reputation for "command-and-control" leadership telling his team that he wants to use more of a team approach, but who acknowledges that it is hard to give up control and he worries that under pressure he may want to take it back. Imagine people suddenly being thrown together in one department as a result of a 30,000-person merger of Fleet Bank and Nat West and being told to act like a team. Imagine a group of Israelis being asked to negotiate with Palestinians who they felt may be part of a group of terrorists who bombed their cities. Imagine an African woman who has been previously excluded from talks about ending hunger being asked to come to meeting with the men who had excluded her for years.

Thus, one of the key roles in facilitating the first meetings (and others) is to take some time to build relationships. This involves making it a priority to create a intimate atmosphere where people can be authentic and vulnerable. This is necessary for overcoming stereotypes and prejudices and building trust—whether you do it through shared meals and a shared whiskey or two around a bar with good humor (like Terje Larsen in the Oslo talks) or getting everyone to an off-site where you build a shared vision and go through something like "electric fence" team-building exercises. The proof is in the pudding. As Norwegian Ambassador Holst's wife, Marianne Heiberg, said, "When Abu Ala and Uri Savir first started negotiating, they were bitter enemies. By the time they left, they were like brothers."

Small a detail as it may seem, the manner in which you greet your fellow collaborators may determine whether your group gets off on the right foot. Speak to each and every one directly, addressing each participant by name. Do your best to be warm and welcoming. Ask if they have any needs or questions that should be addressed immediately. Individual acknowledgment of each participant will help to relieve any anxiety about his or her capacity to fit in to the group. It will also help to establish an egalitarian tone by recognizing the better-known or more powerful members of your group in the same manner in which you greet the lesser known or less powerful.

Introductions. It is important to think of the first meeting as a time for building community. It might even be effective to consider the first meeting as a meeting without an agenda, except perhaps for people to simply get to know each other as human beings—not as positions in a political argument or functions in a business. Nothing stifles creativity or teamwork like prejudices, repressed feelings, or outright hostility. Nothing enhances it like finding common ground with another human being, which creates a sense of belonging and a spirit of community. Personal connections are the superconductors of creative ideas.

Find out who people are and what matters to them. If the group is new, it serves to provide the opportunity for people to kick back, let their hair down, and engage in an kind of informal conversation that they wouldn't normally have that allows them to feel relaxed and comfortable with each other.

Mediators frequently ask their disputants to come prepared with an opening statement—that contains historical background of the dispute, how the problem arose, how it feels, why it feels that way, and what they would like to have happen now.

The Future Search conferences begin with introductions in which people state briefly how they got involved in the issue at hand, their "prouds" (things they have accomplished in connection to the issue that they are proud of), and their "sorries" (things they might have done that they regret).

At AT&T, a group of employees who had never met before got together to work on a project for which they had volunteered. One by one, participants introduced themselves to the group by stating their names, positions, why they were interested in the project, and what expertise and talents they were bringing to the task at hand.

Most important word. One of our favorite community-building exercises is to go around the room and ask each person to say the one word that is most important to them and why. Once they have had a chance to identify a word, anyone who wishes can explain their selection or probe other people with questions about their word. A conversation might go like this:

MICHEL: Luc, you said your most important word was "challenge." Can you explain what you mean by that?

LUC: I mean that I want to achieve stretch goals in areas where I have talents and interests, like product development. I also want to challenge myself and my team to develop products that provide meaningful differences, not just better sameness.

FACILITATOR: Luc, is there someone in the group whose most important word made you feel curious about what they meant?

LUC: Yeah, Hal, when you said your most important word was "fun," what did you mean by that?

HAL: For me, fun is working with new people to create something new and different—something I wouldn't normally be able to participate in.

Breaking down stereotypes and historic grievances. If the group has a history of past grievances, such as the Israelis and Palestinians, Pro-Choice and Pro-Life groups, or engineering and marketing, this cannot be ignored. It is essential to create an atmosphere of real dialogue where people can see something about the other person for the first time that results in dissipating negative stereotypes or feelings. It is important to do something to assist participants in seeing each other as real human beings who have their own unique vision, uncertainties, and personal problems. Similarly, it is also important for people to treat each other as individuals who have their own particular point of view about hot or controversial issues, rather than as representatives of a particular political faction or business function who can only recite the party line.

In creating a community of commitment around a shared understood goal, begin by giving each member of the group an opportunity to introduce themselves in a personal and relaxed manner. The Public Conversations Project, which deals with such hot issues as population growth, abortion, and environment, has developed a brilliant, step-by-step approach to transforming relationships burdened by stereotypes, highly polarized issues, and old "stuck" patterns of conversation. They begin their sessions (on, for eaxmple, abortion) by asking people to share a buffet together but not to talk about where they are stand on issues. Then, following this meal and informal chat, they ask each participant (people who are frequently diametrically opposed on the issue) to take a few minutes to say something about him- or herself personally, but not yet to explain where they stand on the issue.

Later, participants are asked to say something about their personal relationship with the issue, for example, how they got involved. They are asked to speak as human beings about their particular point of view, not as representatives of a particular side. They are even asked to say where they have "grey" areas or value conflicts about their stand on the issues. Following this, questions are asked about what each other said to enrich the quality of the dialogue.

The Public Conversations Project uses similar formats for dialogues on other issues. In each case, people are asked to set aside their urges to persuade and are also asked to avoid using rhetorical questions. This format encourages the participants to speak and listen in a new way. The result is that people begin to see others as real people like themselves with concerns that often overlap, not as extremists who are antibusiness or anti-environment, or lunatics with horns on their head. This has a powerful effect on transforming the quality of their relationships with each other.

According to Maggie Herzig, associate director of the Public Conversations Project, "The person who is concerned about the environment realizes that the timber industry people are not solely motivated by profit or willing to destroy the environment to make a buck. They are also concerned about a sustainable future for their families and children, do not want to harm the environment, and, in fact, they have concerns that overlap those of the environmentalists. Suddenly, the pro-life person does not see the pro-choice person as a murderer, but as a real human being who is concerned about what will happen to a fifteen-year-old girl who gets pregnant and at the same time willing to show interest in the question about what will happen to the baby's soul, if it is aborted."

Facilitate through ground rules. Coming to an agreement over ground rules for the discussion your group is about to begin can also foster a collaborative spirit. We suggest that you start by proposing a few simple ground rules to get started that again fit the specific purpose of the meeting. For example, in the Oslo talks, Abu Ala and Yair Hirschfeld agreed on ground rules almost immediately. These had a huge impact on the talks. As you may recall, they included: (1) creating a new future, (2) no dwelling on past grievances, (3) retractability on all positions put forward, and (4) total secrecy. These ground rules kept the discussions on a positive and constructive track, prevented backsliding into polemics about the past, and made it safe to put forward ideas without the participants fearing that they would be written in law or caught in the media spotlight.

It is important for the group to own the ground rules. If you are leading the group, you might say, "This is what we have found that has worked, and what we would like to propose." Once people choose the ground rules and make them their own, they become the basis by which a facilitator, if you have one, can make appropriate interventions, as well as the basis by which people can co-facilitate the conversation themselves. **Some useful ground rules for the successful facilitation of a collaborative meeting include:**

- *Treat everyone as a colleague.*

- *Speak with good intent (nothing you say is neutral).*

- *Ask questions from genuine curiosity, not from cynicism.*

- *Openly disagree with anyone in the group.*

- *Avoid attributions about other motives, thinking, etc.*

- *Invent new options that break log-jams.*

- *Retract proposals until agreement is reached.*

- *Embrace breakdowns as part of reaching breakthroughs.*

- *Respect confidentiality.*

After listing your ground-rule proposals, ask, "Would you like to modify any of the rules or propose any additions or deletions?" Once the ground rules are decided upon, they become basis on which a facilitator or any member of the group can interrupt an unwieldy or uncivil discussion and get it back on track.

As time moves on and communication between group members becomes more complex and perhaps contentious, it may make sense to beef up your ground rules. Here are some examples of rules that other collaborative groups have found useful:

- *When you make a statement, give an example.*

- *Acknowledge and accept all differences and accept them as real.*

- *At the end of the meeting, discuss how the conversation has gone and what the group has learned about collaborating.*

Before you adopt a rule, remember: The purpose is to facilitate communication, not to make it more cumbersome. Make sure all ground rules are simple and clear.

Eat together, live together, and have fun together as a vehicle for transforming relationships. Michio Kushi, a Japanese philosopher, once said, "Sharing the same dream, eating the same food, and living in the same place results in the experience of community." It's undeniable: these three human activities belong together. Sharing the same dream gives people the feeling of a common calling, even if they had previously been enemies. Living together makes people feel like they are part of the same world. Eating together not only fills the belly but is an implicit acknowledgment that we all have the same fundamental needs—nourishment. Says Russ McKinley of Boise Cascade and a member of the Applegate Partnership—a collaboration of loggers, timber companies, and environmentalists—"It takes lots of cookies, lots of pots of coffee, lots of potlucks, and lots of helping each other out."

Many collaborations we observed have taken note of the fact that reaching lofty goals is often facilitated by sharing food and shelter. Gier Pedersen of the Oslo team spoke to us about how each day after Palestinians and Israelis went through a tough negotiating session, they would share a meal or a few drinks together. He noted that this comraderie seemed to have a powerful effect on transforming their relationship. Marianne Heiberg pointed out that sharing the same living quarters had a similar effect. Says Heiberg, "We purposely housed everyone in small hotels with an inn-like atmosphere so they could not get away from each other." Bob Manning and Matt Golombek of the Mars Project stressed co-location as a vital factor in the kind of friendly, face-to-face communication that allowed the group to solve problems without going through formal channels. Douglas Dayton of IDEO, who showed us around the offices in Lexington, Massachusetts, was careful to point out the large kitchen area with pizzas sizzling in the microwave, popcorn popping, and the coffee pot brewing.

Creating a novel, stimulating, and fun atmosphere is also a high-leverage factor. Terje Larsen lessened the drudgery of negotiations by cracking jokes all night long. Douglas Dayton was also quick to point out the toy scooters, bikes, and rollerblades that randomly laid against the walls near the kitchen area.

Joan Holmes and the Hunger Project

W hen a leader like George Bush stands before the nation in the White House Press Briefing Room the morning after Saddam Hussein's invasion of Kuwait and says, "a line in the sand has been drawn," it makes headlines. The total number of casualties on both sides numbered somewhere in the tens of thousands. When Joan Holmes, executive director of the Hunger Project, took a stand against hunger and poverty twenty years ago, the tragedy of hunger did not make headlines, even though the scourge of it was much worse than anything Hussein might have wrought. Each day 35,000 people die as a result of chronic hunger. Almost a billion people throughout the world live in conditions of poverty so severe that they do not have enough food to meet their daily minimum requirements. This is not the kind of hunger that attracts media attention, like a famine, but, as Holmes says, it is "a silent holocaust that continues day after day."

There are a several reasons I chose Holmes and the Hunger Project as an example of lateral leadership and a collaborative approach.[1] First, hunger, like many concerns facing humanity today, is a nexus issue. It is inextricably linked to solving the problems of persistent poverty, civil unrest, environmental destruction, and population growth. To face the epidemic of world hunger, a leader must grapple with all these problems and work with people and groups involved in all these areas. Unlike Holmes, many of the people leading other humanitarian groups specialize in one form of suffering and shun others. They often openly compete for resources and donations. When trouble last broke out in the Congo, for instance, relief groups engaged in a heated competition for donations, that would allow them to meet their budgets for fiscal 1997.

Second, hunger is a project that cries out for creative collaboration because the 35,000 deaths that occur each day are unnecessary. The world has more than enough food to feed the world's hungry people. As Holmes says, "Hunger is not a food, technical, or productivity problem, but a human one." Hunger exists because governments, business, and we as human beings have not organized ourselves in a way that can ensure that everyone has the opportunity to put an end to their own hunger. Traditional philanthropic agencies and relief workers, even with the best of intentions, often make matters worse, interacting with the poor and hungry by viewing them as powerless, incapable, and nonproductive (reinforcing the current situation), blindly missing that what they really need is an opportunity.

The Power of Taking a Stand

The Hunger Project is an organization dedicated to creating a new human agenda—comprised of many "strategic initiatives" designed to make the eradication of world hunger and poverty a reality. When Holmes was selected as executive director, she took a personal stand for ending hunger by the year 2000. She wasn't making a gesture. She was committing herself, and she meant business. She had to close all the escape hatches in her mind, as well as to reinvent herself many times over—from being reluctant to appear in the spotlight, to being a powerful spokesperson, from being an American in her style and approach, to finally becoming a global person.

I asked Joan Holmes what it was like to take a stand for the end of hunger and how that had affected her life. She said it was exhilarating to shift from drawing her identity from the normal concerns of job and family to a purpose larger than herself. "One of the things I noticed was that the preoccupations and petty issues that most of us are concerned with in our personal or professional lives either didn't show up on my radar screen at all, or, if they did show up, they disappeared very quickly," she says. "For example, reacting to small offenses and petty disagreements—like, why didn't this government leader come to the meeting, or why didn't so and so put the cap back on the toothpaste tube." In the face of her commitment, these kinds of trivialities could no longer have a place in her life.

From Fanfare to Despair

Not long after Holmes was appointed executive director, she took a trip to India, traveling coach on a charter airplane, standing inside her vision but with very little else in the way of pomp and circumstance or resources.

When she got to India, there were 11,000 people dying of hunger and poverty every day, and she was overwhelmed by the chronic presence and face-to-face experience of hunger. "I could see people dying in the public streets of Bombay," she recalls. "Along with that ugly spectacle of the sight of hunger, there were the sounds and smell of it as well. Within a few days, I felt overpowered by the immensity of the task."

Holmes visited the offices of the Indian bureaucrats, trained in the hierarchical tradition of the East India Company, who had tried to do something about the problem of hunger and had failed. "I'm sorry," they would say, "we're doing everything we can." Holmes also saw that there were hundreds of relief agencies that had been attempting to alleviate the problem for a long time. However, while they were helping the unfortunate, they accomplished little in the way of getting at the underlying causes of hunger. The relentlessness of the problem was brought home to her by the fact that common people she spoke to blamed *karma*—in this case, a kind of spiritual giving up.

When Holmes returned to the United States, she felt utter despair. She had made a commitment to do something extraordinary, but she had no idea how to make it a reality. She didn't even know how to get started. All she could do was stand in the space of her vision and commitment, which told her that after touching base with friends, supporters, and experts of various kinds here, she had to go back to India. "Yet her feelings of fear and despair were so profound," says former staffer Michel Renaud, "that those who took her to the airport had to physically help her get on the plane."

Paradigm Shifts

The trip, however, proved to be a watershed. Joan Holmes once again was immersed in the scenes of India—the contrasts between the international hotels like the Bombay Hilton, the tourist route with its ancient glories and modern pretenses, and the rail stations and back streets of the city, where people begged by day and laid out their mats to sleep by night. These stark scenes led Holmes to see hungernot as a statistical story, but as a human story which must be dealt with in a human way.

Holmes began to define her role as a leader and to do what she tells her staff to do: think things through. Ending hunger in places like Bombay would require leadership but not the kind offered by bureaucrats who made the forms requesting government relief so complicated that it was easier to beg. Instead, she realized, it would require a more collaborative leadership in the context of an organization that works with many different stakeholders and acknowledges the complexity of the issues that surround hunger.

It would require powerful aid and assistance from outside people and groups, but not in the way it had been attempted in the past, which had essentially involved robbing people of their dignity by treating them as helpless and dependent. Holmes also recognized that the social context which allowed for the persistence of hunger, rather than just trying to deal with the circumstances through relief, needed drastic alteration. What was needed was a shift in paradigms that involved seeing hungry people as creative and effective authors of their own destiny, not as passive beneficiaries of outside aid.

Strategic Planning

Holmes realized that to make an impact, she needed to develop a strategic-planning process that would produce concrete results. Together with her staff and colleagues in the United States. and elsewhere, she came up with a method she calls "strategic planning in action." This involves arriving at a shared vision of the solution, assessing where the world stands in relation to that vision, and providing what is missing that could make a difference.

Today, the Hunger Project has created nine "Hunger Free Zones" in India (as well as other parts of the world) that they are focusing on—leverage points for ending hunger. They have made dramatic progress in many of them. The key is to look at what's missing in the strategic sense that would produce a breakthrough, rather than shipping a few tons of wheat to a warehouse that will be captured by guerrillas the next day or will rot because there is no infrastructure of roads to get it to the hungry people.

Another of the issues the Hunger Project dealt with was female infanticide, or the killing of 3,000 girl babies a year. These girls were looked at not as a blessing, but as a financial burden to these already starving regions. Past efforts, which included talking to doctors and government agencies, proved futile. The Hunger Project gathered a wide circle of stakeholders and looked into what was missing that could make the difference. A new, updated social mentality was needed, where girls were just as important as boys. The vehicle and strategy for providing what was missing was media coverage.

A big conference was organized that brought together poets, song-writers, and movie producers and stars from the top film studios. Together they engaged in a giant campaign to transform the public attitude about the girl child. They created shorts shown in every movie theater, clips that were shown on the television everyday, and songs that were on the radio. This amazing media blitz saturated the society for a year with messages that girls are every bit as valuable as boys in modern society. Girls can take care of you in your old age, just like a son. In a country where the film stars are "gods," it created a whole other set of images for girls and women in society. The campaign was attributed to having dramatically reduced the incident of female infanticide in the areas of the state that the media was able to reach.

In the remote regions, however, the campaign was unsuccessful. So the following year, a program was launched where traditional village theater troupes would go from village to village with the same kind of message.

Lateral Leadership Is Often Invisible

Harry Truman once said that men make history, not the other way around, and in times of no leadership, society stands still. I asked Joan Holmes about lateral leadership, especially in regard to empowering people and getting them to collaborate effectively. Holmes said she was fascinated by the idea of lateral leadership and collaboration. Then she said something that I think was eye-opening, especially for those who see collaboration as group process: "It takes leadership to bring about collaboration, it doesn't just happen as many people in business, government, and the United Nations often believe."

Holmes told us, "We have developed a very collaborative approach. We often sponsor big conferences throughout the world to end hunger or look at what the next milestone is." Yet she emphasized that 85 percent of her work is not what happens at these meetings or conferences; instead, it involves getting people to collaborate on the project or bringing unlikely collaborators together. Often this is just a matter of introducing people. According to one staffer, "People often don't know who each other are, or the potential they both have to contribute to something, even though it is a common calling for both of them." Says John Coonrod, number two at the Hunger Project, "We focus on finding out who the leaders are, who the conveners are, who have the say-so in various groups to cause people to sit down and talk at a conference. We also focus on people who are 'ripe'."

At other times, this work involves breaking down barriers. For example, Holmes said it might take the form of getting government bureaucrats who have refused to speak to each other for years to rise above being prisoners of their own pettiness and discover that they have common concerns. Or the work could involve inspiring people from the government to talk to people in nongovernment organizations (NGOs). Adds Coonrod, "If we can help a government bureaucrat who has to implement a social welfare program or cut costs to see how the participation of an NGO can help him reach his goals, then it is surprising how much his attitude changes."

This is a different kind of leadership than many of us are accustomed to. Charismatic leaders make headlines, but they just as often take positions that create opposition and splinter groups. "The key to lateral leadership is to bring people together across whatever deserts and mountains there are that divide them," says Coonrod. Interestingly enough, the kind of lateral leadership that makes a difference by orchestrating people and events behind the scenes often doesn't show up. Although it has a powerful impact, people are not aware of those who are doing it.

Coonrod points out, however, that just because lateral leadership may not fit our pictures of powerful leaders doesn't mean that it doesn't exist, or that it is not important. As complex problems involve creating new patterns of relationships and interaction, Coonrod believes that this kind of leadership is key to creating a new future for humanity as we cross into the twenty-first century. It is important that we look at this leadership with rigor, and decode its principles.

Coonrod considers Holmes and himself as examples of lateral leaders, but he also speaks of people in other occupations, like staffers in Congress who, while their bosses are pontificating and taking positions, take the intiative to find out where people stand on issues, build common ground, and draft the legislation that will actually get passed.

Toward a Collaborative Organization

Joan Holmes is a highly skilled executive, especially in dealing with people. Once during a trip to Canada she asked Veronica Pemberton, then the national director of the Hunger Project in Canada, "How's it going?"

Veronica sputtered off the latest results and then burst into tears saying, "It is not going well at all. I inspire the volunteers but tend to ride roughshod over the staff, and they have lots of resistance to me." Joan responded, "You have trouble being your stand." Veronica answered, "That couldn't be. I say and do things all day long to make it happen." Joan replied, "I think you may have misunderstood me, I said, I think you have trouble 'being' your stand." "Then I got it," Pemberton told me, "It is *who you are in your stand*, not only *what you say or do* that makes a difference."

"It's Joan's natural ability to take total responsibility, to be authentically grateful, to give others the gift of her presence that makes her stand one that inspires and empowers others to support her. When she speaks to you, you feel that you are the one person who can make a difference for the end of hunger. A few years ago at the Africa Prize presentation, Joan stopped and talked to me for a minute, being completely present to me before she was ushered off to meet Bill Clinton and Nelson Mandela on stage," offered Pemberton.

Holmes is constantly talking about the vision and her commitment to the end of hunger, even at staff meetings. Pemberton went on to say, "I didn't understand this at first, but later I saw that what she was doing was reframing our perspective from our personality quirks and small concerns, by returning us to why we came to our vision. She also was always very grateful, delighted, and supportive whenever anyone would show any commitment to the end of hunger. If someone acted like a jerk, she wouldn't make them wrong, she would think in terms of 'what's missing' that, if she could provide it, would serve to transform the person's behavior." Pemberton went on to tell me, "While I have never heard her force her views on anyone or give an order in a meeting, she can be very cut and dry when something needs to be done."

In many ways, Holmes has designed a very different kind of organization that is ahead of its time. In the early eighties, long before it became an advertising slogan for Continental Airlines and Burger King, Holmes talked about how the individual could make a difference. "She gave each person in the organization the feeling that they were 'the whole project,' that they were responsible for the whole of it, not just their part."

At the same time, she strongly believes in the interconnectedness of the issues. In the early days of the organization, long before it became fashionable to speak in terms of multidisciplinary teams and processes, Holmes spoke in terms of the alignment of wholes (all the people involved in the project). She made this real through global conference calls at a time when nobody had ever heard of a conference call, through the e-mail before many people had heard of the Internet, and through long meetings designed to give people the big picture. She created a global office in New York that was separate from the U.S. office, which tended to be territorial. She created tons of strategic relationships with people in business, government, and academia.

On the Ground in the Hunger Free Zone in Mpal, Senegal

Creating an extraordinary combination of people to end hunger in Africa, for example, involved seeking out African women, who have traditionally been left out of leadership roles in their society. This presented some dilemmas to Joan Holmes and other Hunger Project people. Michel Renaud tells of a conference being held in Senegal to introduce the Hunger Project to the highest level of government and business and to initiate a strategic plan to end hunger in that country. Ten villages of the Mpal region were chosen for on-the-ground projects as an initial application of the strategic planning-in-action methodology. The villages were commonly known as "the forgotten villages of Senegal." Michel told us, "We invited twenty high-level financial contributors from the U.S., Europe, and Canada so that they could see firsthand what they were funding and so that the people in Senegal could see that people from around the world were standing behind them.

"We also invited government ministers who controlled the social programs, academics who wrote nutritional and agricultural policy guidelines, other NGOs, business people, and leaders of peasant movements. We also invited the leaders of thirty women's groups who had never participated in any discussion—even though it is women who often suffer the most from hunger, and women who bear primary responsibility for health care, education, and nutrition. For example, in Africa, agricultural production was going down in the late 1980s. Part of the reason was that farmers were being marginalized. It turned out that the many aid workers only talked to men and didn't know that 90 percent of the farmers were women.

"I got a call from Dr. Charlie McNeil the night before the big meeting, alarmed that none of the women had responded to the invitation. These women had very good reason to refuse attendance, as they had never been invited before, and they felt resentful and were particularly concerned that they would not be listened to. Charlie and I got on the phone and called each one of them up and convinced them to come. On the first day of the meeting, they sat in the back of the room. On the second and third day of the meeting they sat in the front of the room, and everyone remarked on what an intelligent and powerful impact they had."

Michel tells the story of a meeting that took place in Mpal subsequent to this original meeting. "When I arrived in Mpal, a desert area, everything was yellow, covered with dust from the desert. There were no trees, no crops, and people were walking in a slow listless way. All of the young people had left the local area to go to Dakar. They saw no future in Mpal."

Michel tells how they had to do something differently. "The old approach was very top-down and specialized. People from relief agencies would come in and say, 'We are committed to feeding you, the hungry people, and we have the knowledge and skills that you need to follow.' Implicit in this was the notion that 'you are the hungry people, you haven't done a good job feeding yourself, so now you must listen to us.'

"We took an approach that was totally collaborative. We gathered all of the people together—village leaders, state agencies, NGOs—and had a planning session. We starting by asking the village leaders, 'What do you need? What will make a difference in eradicating hunger and poverty based on your commitment, your knowledge, your experience?' We asked others the same question, looking at everyone as an important participant. We produced a plan that represented the collective wisdom of all involved. Amazingly enough, we then partnered with them in making those things happen."

Michel told me that this partnering included planting fruit trees in strategic places to protect soil erosion. It also included providing irrigation in conjunction with a Swiss organization that came as a third-party NGO to bring irrigation facilities at low costs. Women organized themselves to start some cottage industries that allowed them to buy food, seed, and farm tools. There was a complete turnaround in the region.

Four years later, Mpal is a different place. The yellow tinge has been replaced by the green of crops and the purples and reds and yellows of fruit trees on the horizon. Cattle abound. "The energy of the people is totally different," contends Renaud. "There is a new attitude of entrepreneurship. The young people don't want to flee to Dakar anymore, because they see a future for themselves in the village."

Chapter Five

It Happens in Conversations:

An Introduction

In the work we have done as learning leaders and in personal transformation programs over a fifteen-year period, we have engaged many people in extraordinary conversations that touched their lives with new possibilities, transformed their relationships, and helped them to break the grip of paradigms that limited their creativity and effectiveness. There is a moment in each of these conversations where people's faces seem to be illuminated with a quality of radiance, where their hearts open, and they experience moments of true insight that enable them to see things differently, and to alter their actions.

Years ago, we asked ourselves if it was possible to have these same kinds of extraordinary conversations with a group of people—an assembly of stakeholders who were trying to achieve something impossible, like exploring the surface of Mars, or solve a problem that was intractable, like hunger, or resolve a bitter conflict like the one between the Palestinians and Israelis. This is a challenge, given that most groups are prone to inauthentic communication, gridlocked thinking, and defensive routines.

We have discovered through years of research with groups in science, business, government, and other fields, that the answer to this question is a decided yes! In the following two chapters, you will be introduced to a powerful five-phase method to help trigger such powerful conversations. These are conversations that have the power to transform who people are, as well as the way they think and interact, especially in conversations that previously would have been considered difficult or impossible.

In these very enlightening conversations, we have often seen the faces of everyone in the group illuminated as they break through stereotypes and prejudices, build shared understanding that leads to breakthrough insights, and take concerted, innovative action. We call these extraordinary conversations "collaborative conversations." Many examples follow in the pages ahead.

Collaboration Happens in Conversations

Whether we are speaking about a new era—such as democracy and the Declaration of Independence, scientific revolutions like the development of the atom bomb, or geo-political breakthroughs like the Israelis and Palestinians at Oslo, the landmark events of human accomplishment are rarely the result of individual actions, but rather of people thinking and interacting together in a collaboration of some kind.

The medium for that collaboration is a conversation. It is important to see a collaboration not just as one conversation, but a network of conversations. This series of conversations must help us find our path through the inevitable maze of personality issues and conflicting views and perspectives, until we build a basis for shared understanding that results in a creative solution.

Normally, most conversations we have in group meetings focus on such topics as strategic planning, problem solving, conflict resolution, and so on. Collaborative conversations focus on topics as well, but they also focus on process. We have discovered five phases (or principles) of a collaborative conversation that provide guiding ideas for how to navigate your way more easily through almost any conversational topic. This powerful, concise, step-by-step structure allows you to have more creative and collaborative conversations. Figure 5.1 shows the five phases. Later, we will look at other conversational recipes or templates that offer you some guiding ideas on how to make a strategic plan, creatively solve a problem, or negotiate a conflict as part of your collaborative project.

Ordinary Conversations Focus on Topics	Extraordinary Conversations Balance Topics and Process
• Designate possibility	**1.** Clarify purpose of conversation
• Talk about strategy	**2.** Gather divergent views/ perspectives
• Solve a problem or issue	**3.** Build shared understanding of divergent views and perspectives
• Settle a conflict	**4.** Create "new" options by connecting different views
	5. Generate conversation for action

FIGURE 5.1
**Differences between Ordinary Conversations
and Extraordinary Conversations**

How the Thinking Behind the Idea of Collaborative Conversations Developed

Physicist David Bohm, in *On Dialogue,* emphasized the importance of dialogue in creating not just shared vision but in "shared meaning that perhaps leads to something new." He believes that this could be applied to solving many of the world's problems—especially those that arise from fragmentation, separation, and misunderstanding.[1]

Bohm, however, was more interested in using dialogue to repair the damage caused by excessive fragmentation in our society rather than using it to create or accomplish something. This attitude was summed up by one of Bohm's disciples, Bill Isaacs, who at a conference we attended said that dialogue is not about building community, but about inquiring into the nature of community. Collaborations, in contrast, are based on inspiring visions and are deeply purposeful but are focused on practical, down-to-earth, day-in/day-out accomplishments that are carried out in conversations.

Years back, we began asking ourselves how we could incorporate the spirit of dialogue into these conversations, but with a view toward creating new value and actually accomplishing something extraordinary. Thus, we distinguished the term "collaborative conversations."

We were inspired by profound yet practical examples of collaborative conversation (the Camp David Accords example below) that we found in Roger Fisher's and Bill Ury's book *Getting to Yes*. (They both were also helpful role models in terms of structuring a difficult conversation in a way that produces results. More will come later in Chapter Seven.)

The Camp David Accords Is a Consummate Example of a Collaborative Conversation

The example of the Camp David Accords that I mentioned in Chapter One bears recapping here, because it is essential to understanding the nature of a collaborative conversation. Former President Jimmy Carter was a facilitator of the conversation. Both heads of state, Menachem Begin from Israel and Anwar Sadat from Egypt, wanted peace, yet they had stereotype perceptions of each other and were sharply divided in their views on such thorny issues as what to do with the Sinai Peninsula that was captured by Israel in the Six-Day War.

Yet something was different; just the two men making, what Yossi Beilin calls, basic people-to-people contact in the intimate setting of Camp David constituted an historic moment. As Beilin pointed out, "Every time people talk and have a dialogue, they come back and tell me that they are amazed to find out that the enemy doesn't have horns on his head." This discovery creates a clearing for treating each other as colleagues working on a joint problem.

Carter played a key role in making this possible, as well as creating the conditions for what Bush and Folger call "empowerment" and "recognition." He started by asking Sadat what the occupied Sinai territory meant to Egypt. Sadat answered with great authenticity and vulnerability that giving up the Sinai was a loss of face, that the land was always part of Egypt and was sacred ground of the Pharaohs. You could see from the expression on Begin's face that, what Joe Folger calls, a "moment of recognition" had occurred. This so-called moment is an example of effective collaborative conversation out of which shared meaning develops. All of a sudden, you begin to view the person you have been negotiating with as human. This often changes the dialogue to one of compassion and understanding rather than prejudice and thinly disguised contempt.

Carter then asked Begin what the Sinai meant to Israel. He said, with simplicity, that the Israelis didn't want tanks and missiles ten miles from their border. Here again, Carter could see from the expression on Sadat's face that shared meaning had developed through another moment of recognition.

At this point Carter pointed out that the two men were *empowered* to make choices for their countries, the whole Middle East, and the world. They could live with the seething hostility they had for each other, they could go to war again one day, or they could find a way to make peace by giving up their winner-take-all positions, looking instead toward their national, community, and family interests. Carter asked them to invent some new options, a kind of "brainstorming."

Both Begin and Sadat began with the shared goal of peace. Both now had a new shared understanding which lead to a idea that had never occurred to them before. The land would be returned to Egypt, but a demilitarized zone would be created that gave Israel the security it required. This solution paved the way for a separate peace treaty between Egypt and Israel and dramatically changed the political landscape of the Middle East.

Note: The principles of a collaborative conversation that come from this example can be used not only in foreign affairs but also in any government agency, corporation, university, school, or law office. They can be used to reach goals, solve complex problems, or resolve disputes.

Previewing the Five Phases of a Collaborative Conversation

Breakthroughs in any field come when people declare possibilities that were previously never imagined and collaborate to achieve them. The purpose of a collaborative conversation is to increase the velocity by which we transform a possibility into a reality. This not only involves reaching goals and solving practical problems but also transforming the process or way people think and interact. In reality, while we would often like to have collaborative conversations, they seldom occur. This leaves many of us facing a number of dilemmas.

How do we make sure that the speaking and listening at the big meeting coming up on the calendar are purposeful rather than just hot air? How do we build a climate of trust and shared understanding among people who see things completely differently from each other? How do we handle difficult conversations where there are heated or controversial topics in a way that results in a breakthrough solution rather than a blowup? How do we move the conversation from a place where we are basically trying to figure out how to do the same thing better, to a place where we do something creative, innovative, and different?

The five phases of a collaborative conversation will give you a powerful assist in dealing with these and other dilemmas. They represent, on the one hand, a powerful, structured, concise, step-by-step process for making sure that creative thinking and teamwork happen by design, not by chance, and in a way the results in the creation of new value. On the other hand, the five phases represent a set of guiding ideas or principles for people to keep in the back of their minds in any conversation.

Like a good golf swing or tennis serve, a collaborative conversation can be divided into several components, each of which can be separately analyzed and honed. In a master stroke, however, each flows seamlessly into the next. So it is in a collaboration. In Chapter Six, we will explore in more detail each of the phases of a collaborative conversation. Each phase will be shown through the triple- and double-loop learning approach described in Chapter Two and as shown in Figure 2.1, Triple-Loop Learning (see page 63). First, we will look at *who you need to be* in the phase. Second, we will examine the mental models, metaphors, and analogies that are useful in guiding your *thinking*. *Third*, we will provide *things to do* and *pitfalls* to watch out for.

The Five Phases of a Collaborative Conversation

I n this chapter, we will be looking at each phase of the collaborative conversation in more depth. For each phase, we will provide an example of an extraordinary conversation that illustrates the phase, look at who you need to be, how you need to think (mental models, metaphors, and analogies), and what you can do, as well as potential pitfalls to watch out for.

---

1. Clarify the purpose of the conversation.

2. Gather divergent views and perspectives.

3. Build shared understanding of divergent views and perspectives.

4. Create "new" options by connecting different views.

5. Generate a conversation for action.

FIGURE 6.1
The Five Phases of a Collaborative Conversation

PHASE 1.

Clarify the Purpose of the Conversation

Extraordinary Conversations

In South Africa, until the recent resolution, the situation appeared to be a classic win-lose situation. The whites were going to win and the blacks were going to lose, or vice versa. Then, as time went on, both F. W. DeKlerk and Nelson Mandela realized that the situation, based on the kinds of antagonistic relations people were having, was going to become a lose-lose situation very fast, with both sides suffering the consequences.

DeKlerk thought that the whites could hold on to power for a little while by sheer coercion of physical force, talking down to blacks, and not listening to their concerns. Then he asked himself, what kind of South Africa are we going to live in if we take this approach? Wouldn't it be a nation where blacks and whites were chained together with violence and hatred?

Mandela realized that the black majority which made up 80 percent of the country's population was going to eventually win, but then what kind of South Africa were they going to inherit? From either side, it looked like it would be a South Africa in ruins. So, in 1990, the two leaders began to explore the possibility of a different future through a series of conversations—something that required tremendous courage given their respective constituents.

Up until this point, the purpose that motivated the conversations between Mandela and DeKlerk was winning control of South Africa's future. In fact, it drove all of the speaking, listening, and actions between blacks and whites in South Africa. But now, these two men began to see the need to clarify (or alter) the purpose or the nature of their conversations.

They began to speak and listen in terms of "what can we create together for the benefit of South Africa," rather than winning for their respective sides. Mandela mentioned in his autobiography that over time he noticed a shift in the way DeKlerk listened to him. During one of DeKlerk's visits to Mandela at Robben Island Prison, Mandela told DeKlerk that he wanted to bring about peace and was equally concerned with recognition of the African

National Congress (ANC) and the white minority's reaction to it. DeKlerk responded by saying he wanted to recognize the ANC but asked Mandela to consider minority rights. Heartened by this candid interchange, several days later DeKlerk freed almost all the political prisoners in South Africa.

These early conversations led to further discussions in which these two men created a vision of South Africa where blacks and whites would build a new society together. This took tremendous courage on both of their parts, at a time when the notion of such a collaboration was something that had been both unthinkable and undiscussable. It wasn't just these two leaders who altered their conversation and relationship, they brought their whole parties with them with a view to creating a South Africa that could compete in the world marketplace and provide for the needs of all its people—black and white.[1]

Clarifying the Purpose of the Conversation Is a Matter of Distinction

A collaborative conversation is a conversation that is purposeful by nature. It suggests people with different views and backgrounds thinking and interacting together but also creating and generating not only something that never existed before. We engage in collaborative conversations to accomplish something that we passionately care about, such as a shared vision for a company, solving the problem of pollution, or eliminating family conflicts. A collaborative conversation, then, is distinct from conversations where we indulge ourselves in giving our opinion on things we are not responsible for, finger pointing, or gossiping about others.

It is important to clarify the specific purpose of the conversation that is powerful and distinctive from all the other conversations we might have. For example: Are we here to talk about our vision based on an image of aspiration, or merely to talk about the whole discouraging complexity of the situation? Are we going to talk about a quick-fix for this problem, or dig down into fundamental causes and solutions? The purpose acts as a guiding light that allows us to navigate our way through the often confusing process of eliciting diverse views, building shared meanings, and coming up with creative ideas. It is important to understand that how you "frame" the purpose will have a significant impact on whether you have deeply spirited, high-leverage, catalytic conversations, or whether you run into breakdowns later on.

Examples of Purposes for Collaborative Conversations

- *To declare new possibilities or opportunities*

- *To create a community of commitment that will stand for the possibility*

- *To create a strategic plan*

- *To reach goals, solve problems, or resolve a dispute*

- *To improve the way a group thinks and interacts*

Who You Need to Be in This Phase

We've discovered that it is *who you are* in a situation that often matters the most, not just *what you do*. To be effective in each phase of a collaborative conversation, it is often important to think of what you want to create with others and then ask yourself how you need to be different. This will automatically shape your behavior.

For example, if I am someone who draws my identity from my commitment to being the center of attention and a chatterbox, I will do whatever is needed to get a word in edgewise, whether or not it throws the conversation off track. If, on the other hand, I draw my identity from my commitment to having conversations that make a difference, and being a deeply purposeful, clear, and focused person, I will behave quite differently. Think about this phase. Then ask yourself: Who do I need to be? Once you distinguish that, come from that stance into the conversation, or, to make it even more simple, think of trying on a new role for the duration of the conversation.

Mental Models, Metaphors, and Analogies

Think of purpose as a navigating beacon. We have already spoken of one metaphor that will help us to understand the nature of purpose, and that is to think of it as a guiding light that assists us in seeing where we have been, where we are now, and where we are going in the conversation. Here are a few other ways of thinking about purpose that allow you or your group to construct a shared mental model that highlights the importance of taking time on this phase. In fact, this phase often takes more time than people expect.

Think of clarifying the purpose as focusing the conversation like a laser beam. David Bohm pointed out in *On Dialogue*, that most group conversations are incoherent.[2] People come into a room and starting giving their opinions without listening much to each other's opinion or questioning their assumptions. The conversation has no direction; it just kind of fills the space like incoherent light in a room. People are not thinking out loud, they are thinking apart. Clarifying the purpose of the conversation captures all of that energy and light into one focus like the red light of a laser beam.

Think of the purpose as a container that can hold whatever happens in the conversation. A purpose is like a container for the conversation in that it helps people think in terms of the conversation at hand, rather than getting it mixed up with other conversations. It reminds people to speak in a focused way, as well as to give the other people the gift of their presence—a high quality of attention and listening. The container is a powerful image for recognizing that a collaborative conversation may cool down or heat up. The container has to be both cold- and heat-resistant, enough to contain reasonable discussion as well as shouting matches where people disagree and where there is emotional upheaval. This range of emotion may be all part of fulfilling the purpose.

Examples of Clarifying the Purpose of the Conversation

What is the purpose the collaboration is supposed to accomplish? A good example of the importance of clarifying the purpose of the conversation (or network of conversations) comes from Bill Gates of Microsoft who, when he started his company, had a conversation with his partner about the future of the business. The partner started talking about selling both computers and software. Gates said in essence that he did not want to have that conversation because, while computers were going to be saturated, the software market could expand forever. He wanted to talk about software. The partner saw the wisdom in this approach—and the rest is history. Similarly, in the early days of Intel, Andy Grove and the people running the company had a conversation where they decided that there wasn't much market for personal computing and instead decided to focus on making microchips. Since that conversation, Intel has never built a personal computer, yet "Intel Inside" is seen everywhere.

Note: It's important here not to confuse clarifying the purpose of a conversation (phase one) with clarifying the purpose or setting the goal of the collaborative project. The conversation to clarify the purpose of the project will involve going through all five phases of a collaborative conversation. What we are emphasizing here is that each conversation you have should have a clear and explicit purpose.

Clarify how you will "frame" the purpose. When the Hunger Project was formulated, there were 35,000 people who died each day and an abundance of organizations already in existence whose purpose was to deal with the problem. These other organizations that were attempting to deal with chronic hunger and starvation essentially saw their purpose as "providing relief." The Hunger Project saw the limitation of this approach, as illustrated by the old saying of "give a man a fish and he will be hungry the next day; teach a man to fish and he will be able to feed himself forever." They created a charter to be a "strategic organization" that was distinctly different, one that was dedicated to ending hunger permanently, not giving temporary relief. They also created a declaration of principles that supported the charter. These principles included seeing people as self-reliant rather than beneficiaries and solving problems collaboratively with different experts rather than working in isolation. These few principles provided an underlying structure to literally thousands of conversations and influenced the way people took action on a day-in, day-out basis.

Things to Do

Public inquiry questions to assist in clarifying the purpose of the conversation. If you have questions concerning the purpose or frame of the conversation, pull together your group of collaborators and ask the following questions. Answering these kinds of questions requires taking a reflective stance rather than simply following a recipe.

- *Is there a clear purpose for the conversation consistent with what matters to all of us?*

- *Have we clarified a purpose for the conversation that is attainable? Are the issues and problems we have defined solvable?*

- *Will the way we have framed the goal or problem give us the results we want?*

- *Will the conversation move the collaboration and learning along?*

Potential Pitfalls of This Phase

- *Watch out for imbalance between community-building and task-oriented conversations.*

- *Watch out for having too many purposes in a conversation.*

- *Watch out for pursuing a purpose that is not well framed.*

- *Watch out for engaging in conversations that are not purposeful or that undermine collaborative efforts—such as gossip or backbiting.*

---

1. Clarify the purpose of the conversation.
2. **Gather divergent views and perspectives.**
3. Build shared understanding of divergent views and perspectives.
4. Create "new" options by connecting different views.
5. Generate a conversation for action.

FIGURE 6.2
The Five Phases of a Collaborative Conversation

PHASE 2.

Gather Divergent Views and Perspectives

Extraordinary Conversations

Donna Sytek, Speaker of the House in New Hampshire, convened a small group of key stakeholders to discuss juvenile justice. Known as the "Tea Party," they met at each other's homes to get away from the legislative arena. The group included the Deputy Commissioner of Corrections, the Director of the Division of Children and Youth Services (DCYS), the Chairman and Vice Chairman of the Corrections and Criminal Justice Committee, and the legal counsel to DCYS.

"There was a perception among constituents that young offenders were getting away with a slap on the hand when they had committed a serious crime," says Sytek. "The amazing thing was that the attitudes I expected my colleagues to bring to the table weren't the attitudes they had. The person from DCYS said, 'These delinquents really need to have more of a punishment than they are currently getting under my system.'

"The person from adult corrections, who everyone expected to say, 'Let's hammer these seventeen-year-olds,' said instead, 'I think that they really need to have treatment.' It was a total reversal of what I expected. But these were practical people who were not just interested in the position they represented but in solving a shared problem.

"It's very easy for people to come to unanimity when a group all comes from the same perspective," says Sytek. "But not so easy when people come from different sides of the fence."³

See Divergent Views as a Source of Strength

In the first phase of a collaborative conversation, your group may have settled on a challenge or goal for a passionate pursuit, or decided to work on a problem. Your challenge during phase two: gathering divergent views and perspectives, is to make sure you have all the different stakeholders at the table and then enlist them to share their knowledge and experience in a creative and productive way.

Think about the following scenarios. Israelis and Palestinians are in one room who, due to years of a ban on official contacts, are actually curious about each other's views. In another room you have right-wing Republicans, like Phil Gramm, with liberal Democrats, like Ted Kennedy, who look at each other with unspoken disdain. You've got a multidisciplinary team in a company—but some who are thinking, "what can salespeople tell engineers?" Then you have parents who support the current principal in the same room with the parents who want to throw her out. How can these people possibly work together?

Who You Need to Be in This Phase

Take a look around the room and see the extraordinary combination of people assembled. You may also want to notice *who you are* in conversations like this that may lead to unintended results. For example, do you present yourself as someone who dominates the conversation and doesn't listen, or someone who treats other people's truth as the enemy, or maybe as someone who tends to be cool, aloof, distant, or shut down? Ask yourself in what ways you need to transform who you are in order to produce the results you would like. Then, start thinking of yourself differently, such as someone who is warm, social, gregarious, spacious, and gracious, and who sees other people's truths as something to learn from, who doesn't have to win and who can just listen. Of course you have to be yourself, but make a commitment to try on new roles for this part of the conversation.

Mental Models, Metaphors, and Analogies

Empowerment. Adopt a stance that one of your guiding principles in the group is to empower people not only to come to the table but also to speak up with authenticity and vulnerability. Often there will be hierarchical differences at the table, so it is important to treat everyone as colleagues, acknowledging potential roadblocks. You could say, "As CEO, I really need to hear where you stand on this new acquisition and I'm afraid you will just tell me what you think I want to hear. This makes me wonder what kind of climate of communication I have been creating around here." By simply acknowledging these feelings and differences, you can begin to get past them. It is also important to acknowledge unresolved issues. For instance, "Two years ago I came to a meeting and you asked me for my suggestions. I started giving my suggestions and you cut me off and dismissed every one. Since that time, I haven't said anything. I'm not sure I can trust you." Creating a confidentiality agreement can also be vital to empowerment.

Recognition. When people jump in and participate in a collaborative conversation, they also need to feel recognized. This is important because people don't just have ideas, they identify with their ideas. They *are* their ideas. So if an individual puts an idea forward and nobody listens or responds to it, they will feel unacknowledged and they pull back from the group or cause trouble. Another dimension to recognition is that, if we want to gather different views and perspectives, it is important to recognize and validate different opinions and assumptions. Remember, it is more important at this point to get the differences on the table than it is to agree.

Shared pool of information. Instead of thinking in terms of putting the different views and perspectives out on the table with a view that this might lead to an argument, think in terms of creating a shared pool of information where opinions, frames of reference, and data are needed to reach a conclusion. It helps to step back from your opinions and facts in order to be able to consider other's. For example, "Here's what I think. How do you see it differently?" Or "Here's my examples and data. Do you have different ones that we need to consider?" It also helps to be able to adopt a beginner's mind and a basic attitude of learning. If an argument ensues, don't be too concerned. Keeping this image of the shared pool of information in mind, you may discover that as you listen to others, your unilateral opinions and assumptions may begin to collapse. As you begin to embrace other views, you see the truth emerge from a clash of dissenting opinions.

Examples of Gathering Divergent Views and Perspectives

John O'Rourke, marketing director of Adidas USA, was assigned to develop a new tennis-shoe range and new basketball-shoe range. O'Rourke had very little budget for design and development. Instead of hiring a big design outfit, he hired two small design companies and asked them to put their youngest, most talented designers on each of the ranges. He met with each designer and said he would select the shoes that seemed best, being fully up front about what he was doing. The two designers sweated out the process, then met on the same day with a focus group, where they saw each other's work for the first time. The focus group gave feedback about each range and about each designer's work. O'Rourke then asked both of them to work together on the final shoe designs. The result was a smashing success.

Things to Do

Create space for "chaotic communication." There is often a degree of chaos created in this phase of a collaborative conversation that stems from the massive amounts of "new information" generated by people speaking to each other for the first time. Says Margaret Wheatley, Future Search consultant, "I found that it was only after I'd been through a few searches that I could trust going into the chaos and messiness and know that it served a purpose." Wheatley observed, "It was during this period that I learned from natural scientists how chaos and messiness are part of the path to higher forms of order. There is a self-organizing property to people sharing information. As different people in a system learn of new information, they often expand their views, as well who they are. Order does not come from the facilitator who imposes control from tightly woven group processes. I facilitate the creation of order by having people share information in the same room. It is like an energy that swirls around, creating new forms and shapes that suit the present. It's surprisingly simple . . . its product is the compelling and synchronous visions that the group creates. It happens without anyone trying to control it."[4]

      Give up the need to be in agreement. The key to creating a real quality of dialogue is to teach people how to give up the need to be in agreement. Assist people in seeing that disagreement is often needed to light the spark of creative collaboration and that it will not lead to a blow-up if we learn not to take it personally. Keep in mind that a collaborative conversation is an effort to break the age-old patterns that keep divergent mental models apart. The goal is to hear a new mix of voices that you haven't heard before. Yes, there will be dissonance, but on its heels will be new harmonies—new ideas and new solutions.

Slow down the conversation. We've all seen it: the fast-talking, expressive types jumping into a group conversation without prompting, their thoughts ricocheting off the walls and each other, often whizzing by the people who can't keep up. All the while, the quiet types sit silently, taking it all in. In a group discussion with AT&T managers, my partner Susan consciously slowed down the conversation to give everyone in the room a chance to speak. One woman who had been quiet for most of the morning piped up, "I never felt comfortable speaking up because I process information slowly. I never had the time in a meeting to figure out what I think, but today I did." The other people in the room were gratified to hear from her. One man spoke for the group when he said, "You've always been a question mark to me, because I never knew where you stood." It may be helpful in these situations to say, "Let's take a break for a few minutes to mentally digest this."

Time spent in the "confusion room" is often the fastest route to clarity. Anyone who has written a paper or presentation on any topic, or worked out a treatment plan, or engaged in any other creative act knows that there is a period of confusion before the final product is uncovered and put together. But we usually try to bury that part of the process and pretend it never happened rather than celebrate it. The period of chaos and confusion plays a vital role in solving complex problems. As physicist Richard Feynman noted in his Nobel-prize lecture, "Real science is confusion and doubt, ambition and desire, a march through the fog . . . The inefficiency, the guessing of equations, the juggling of alternative physical viewpoints are the key to discovering new laws."[5]

Potential Pitfalls of This Phase

- *Watch out for relating hierarchically rather than as colleagues.*

- *Watch out for thinking diversity is an issue of minorities, not thinking styles.*

- *Watch out for not including the views of bright people who process things more slowly.*

- *Watch out for one or two people monopolizing the air time.*

> 1. Clarify the purpose of the conversation.
>
> 2. Gather divergent views and perspectives.
>
> 3. **Build shared understanding of divergent views and perspectives.**
>
> 4. Create "new" options by connecting different views.
>
> 5. Generate a conversation for action.

FIGURE 6.3
The Five Phases of a Collaborative Conversation

PHASE 3.

Build a Shared Understanding of Divergent Views and Perspectives

Extraordinary Conversations

Rene Jaeggi, CEO of Adidas, who has the good looks and broad shoulders of a Steven Segal, and Andre Kolizinski, his blond, Polish deputy of Eastern Europe with a sharp, triangular goatee, were both speaking, and all eyes and ears of the other executives were on them. I had been invited to sit in on a meeting between this top group of managers. The setting was a parlor in a spectacular lakeside hotel on Lake Teegensee, near the Black Forest at the German and Austrian border.

"We are at war," said Jaeggi, as he started off the meeting that morning. The company was in a tough battle with Reebok and Nike. Jaeggi set up the meeting several months earlier with the idea of addressing a shared strategy and operation issues such as branding and sourcing, as well as to give people a chance to really talk.

JAEGGI: *(after a day of polite executive discussion):* This conversation is too superficial. *(He pointed to a mirror in the front of the room.)* We had better be prepared to be open and honest, as well as to look in that mirror and see something ugly!

KOLIZINSKI: Okay, I'll start. When you sent me out to Eastern Europe to bring costs down, you told me you respected me because I was smart and tough, as well as human. To do what you asked, I soon found out, I would have to close some factories. But as soon as I did that, you started to throw tons of obstacles in my way. And this has not only been holding me back but costing me some dignity and pride. Please help me to understand the reasons.

JAEGGI: *(clearly moved):* You're right to bring that up. You're absolutely right. The reason I threw those obstacles in your path is not because you're not a good leader or manager. Maybe it's because I'm too soft. I just don't have the stomach for closing factories and throwing lots of people out of work as if we have no responsibility in the problems that led to this.

KOLIZINSKI: *(wiping his eyes, raised his index finger to the sky):* You have just given me my left ball back. And I now understand how you feel. You need to cut production costs but you care about the people in those factories. Maybe I can consolidate them, as well as shift some of our sourcing operations in the Far East to our own factories.

JAEGGI: Yes, I can back you in doing that, yet we have to talk to our Hong Kong sourcing office to do it right.

KOLIZINSKI: *(dryly):* You have just given me my other ball back. *(He stands up, walks over to Jaeggi, and gives him a manly sort of hug and extends his hand. After a handshake between the two men, Kolizinski sits down again. He then bangs his fist on the nearest table.)* Now THAT was a real conversation!

Shared Understanding Makes it Possible to Agree on Goals and to Iron Out Conflicts

Clearly, as people begin to express their different views and perspectives, new shared understandings are reached—even amongst close associates. This is because people begin to explain their views on the issues at hand. It becomes clear that past misunderstandings were the result of people making false assumptions about each other's position. Often you hear people say, like Kolizinski at dinner that night after the day's meeting, "Rene always talks so tough. I never knew he had such real compassion for people."

However, gathering diverse views is just as likely to result in heated arguments over negotiable assumptions, emotional reactions, and a whole slew of defensive routines as it can lead to creative team-work. Phase three involves creating shared understanding by inquiring into each other's thinking, expressing emotions constructively, and recognizing and dispersing defensive routines.

It is very important in this stage to have a spirit of curiosity about how other people see their world, themselves, the situation they are in, what they want to achieve, and how. As people learn to set aside their positions for the moment and begin to ask questions and listen in a deep way to build shared understanding, they start to see things about themselves and each other they hadn't recognized before. This new awareness can create new openings for possibility and action.

Who You Need to Be in This Phase

Instead of considering yourself as a heavyweight in a bout or contest, think of yourself and the others as colleagues trying to solve a joint problem. Instead of considering yourself as someone who has to dominate the conversation by shouting others down or trying to get others to accept your views, think of yourself as someone who is curious and asks questions with a real sense of curiosity, as well as one who actually enjoys listening. As you begin to view yourself in this way, adjust your behavior accordingly, again trying on these different roles and suspending old ones, at least until the conversation is over.

Mental Models, Metaphors, and Analogies

Authenticity and vulnerability. Often people don't speak authentically because they're afraid this will make themselves or others uncomfortable and lead to an upset or misunderstanding. Or they strut around, posturing with shows of strength, not admitting to any doubts about their own views or showing any feelings. This elicits the same from the other side. Speaking authentically gives people valid information, without which there can be no shared understanding. Showing vulnerability, such as holding yourself or your views in question or showing your feelings, allows people to look beyond the posturing and see you as a human being. People are often afraid their emotions will make them look weak. Yet showing too little emotion is often a bigger mistake in failing to eliminate misunderstandings than showing too much. Emotions can act like superconductors of communication that penetrate a closed mind or heart.

Open-minded and open-hearted listening. Many people come to a conversation saying they have an open mind, but really don't. They view things through a structure of interpretation filled with stereotypes and prejudices—twisting it by adding their own meaning. To get beyond the hostile attitudes and emotional reactions this creates, put aside stereotypes and prejudices and sit down with your "enemies" and listen with an open heart. This means taking a stance to see who they are. View their past actions with compassion and understanding, as a result of the pressures, circumstances, or events they found have themselves in, not as something personal. Also, adopt a stance to listen to what people are saying right now with the intent to deeply understand versus judge and evaluate. It is amazing the effect this can have on eliciting a similar response and creating new openings for shared understanding.

Balance persuading with certainty and questioning with curiosity. Most creative people tend to be passionate advocates of their own views, but they often fail to question their own reasoning or to ask questions of other's views. Balancing advocacy and inquiry is a powerful antidote. It starts with making statements, then explaining your reasoning, as well as inviting questions. Urs Althaus, an executive I consulted for in Europe, would passionately advocate his views on an issue and then suddenly stop and say, "Tell me how you see it differently." Balancing advocacy and inquiry also involves asking people questions about how they developed their views with the intent of building shared understanding. "Can you help me understand how you arrived at that conclusion?" "Were there any significant events or examples that may have contributed to the development of your thinking?" The ladder of inference, as shown in Figure 6.4, is a tool that helps with this distinction. (The ladder of inference will be discussed in more detail in Chapter Seven.)

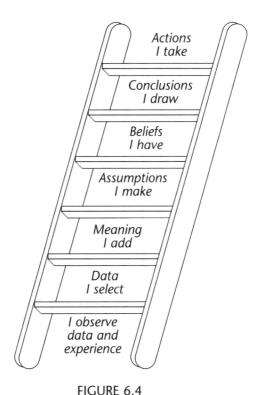

FIGURE 6.4
Ladder of Inference

Establishing a trading zone. When you collaborate with people who have different views and backgrounds, you create a shared work context—such as reaching a goal or solving a customer problem—that pulls you beyond the boundaries of your profession. It is helpful in these situations to think of the metaphor of the trading zone, where you can exchange something of value without having to agree on everything or even understand each other's basic assumptions. For example, the marketing person and the engineer don't have to see eye to eye in order to coordinate their activities in customizing a product for a client. Neither do two elected officials. Ted Kennedy, liberal Democrat from Massachusetts, and Orrin Hatch, Republican from Utah, are bitter rivals who disagree on many things and are philosophically far apart. Yet they often create a trading zone and exchange various kinds of assistance to help each other shape and pass certain bills, dropping some of what they worry about and focusing on the overlap.

Examples of Building Shared Understanding: Seeing What It Feels Like to Be "Them"

This example comes from Bill Ury, co-author of the negotiating classic, *Getting to Yes*. In 1996, Ury was involved in a conversation between the Turks and the Kurds who were busily killing each other in Turkey at an alarming rate. Though the media wasn't paying much attention, it was a major war in which over 25,000 people had been killed and thousands of villages destroyed. According to Ury, "I was facilitating an off-the-record conversation between a group of leading Turks and a group of leading Kurds, with extreme nationalists on both sides. One of the Turks was described to me as someone in the room who said they would 'just as soon shoot a Kurd, as talk to a them.'" Somehow, Ury was able to keep all of the people in the room talking with and, above all, listening to each other until a powerful moment of recognition.

According to Ury, "The fellow who was described as a right-wing Turkish nationalist, given to violence, said he wanted to say something. 'I have never really thought in my life what it felt like to be a Kurd,' he said, 'it just never occurred to me.' The Kurds had not been able to speak their language, their culture was suppressed, and, as a result, they wanted to secede and have their own state. The Turk went on to say that spending this time together talking for two or three days and sharing meals had kept him awake at night, and created a conflict in him because suddenly he saw the other side of the story."

He concluded, "If you had told me two months ago that I would be in this room talking with Kurds about these kind of things, I would have felt I was living in my worst nightmare. Now I feel like I am living in a dream." A dream in which he could see a new future. He then publicly stood up and thanked his adversary, for helping him see that there was another side to the issue. Ury told us, "To me, where all that came from was the power of having a collaborative conversation."[6]

Things to Do

Learn the stories of others. It is impossible to resolve differences without understanding them. Misunderstandings and problems have come to mean the same thing. Instead of assuming you understand others enough, assume you need to understand them more. It may help to think that the current misunderstanding or problem is a result of two stories—yours and theirs—where there are different interpretations. You are well versed in yours, but not theirs, so ask questions that reveal how others see things, their priorities and concerns. Remember the example of Andre Kolizinski—"I never knew [CEO] Jaeggi really cared about the people in those factories we were going to close." You also have to tell people your story. It's a mistake to assume people know how you see things or your priorities and concerns.

Listen *to* what they say: *listen for* what they mean and how they think. The distinction is very powerful in helping people to build shared understanding. On a basic level, it is not only important to "listen to" people's words but also to "listen for" what they mean by what they are saying so as to build shared meaning. For example, "As we gathered the different views and perspectives about the company's vision and values, you just said you were committed to service, quality, and innovation. Can you help me to understand just what you mean by those words?" Or instead of simply listening to people's conclusions and disagreeing, again ask questions and listen for the underlying reasoning process, emotions, or witnessable events by which they reached those conclusions. "What led you to that view?" "Can you give me an example so we will both be operating in the same world?" (Refer again to the ladder-of-inference exercise on page 181.)

Discuss the undiscussable. Often in listening to people tell their story or share their views, you might notice that they start to sugar-coat things or avoid certain issues that are on everyone's minds. In ordinary conversations, people often make hot or controversial things undiscussible by not talking about them or by sending mixed messages. This is defensive routine designed to avoid embarrassment or threat to ourselves or others. In extraordinary conversations, however, people focus on discussing the undiscussable. Tom LeBrecque, chairman of Chase Bank, once invited his executive group to an offsite meeting without saying why. When they arrived, he said that the purpose of the meeting was to "address the issues we have not addressed with each other." The first day, according to one executive, was a "bloodbath." The second and third days were a "miraculous healing." The left-hand-column exercise, as shown in Figure 6.5, is a tool that helps to discuss undiscussable issues in a way that is positive and constructive without damaging relationships. (A more detailed explanation of the left-hand-column exercise is in Chapter Seven, page 230.)

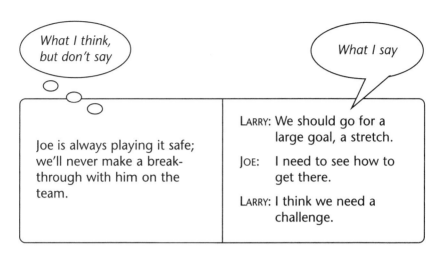

FIGURE 6.5
Left-Hand-Column Exercise

Use verbal aikido. "You don't care anything about quality," said one executive in a biotech firm. "No, *you* don't care anything about quality, or the possibility that if we release these drugs without good testing, we could all go to jail," said the other. In heated arguments with misunderstandings, someone may start making nasty attributions about you or your motives. Instead of feeling like you have to step up to this hostile energy coming at you by responding in kind (which will attract more of it), use "verbal aikido." This means stepping to the side and letting this hostile energy pass you by without responding. Or it might mean somehow using the force of the other person's attack to shift the conversation. For example, you might say, "We have shared goals but disagree on how to reach them, which is now starting to lead to personal animosity. Look, instead of making nasty attributions about each other, let's slow down the conversation and try to understand each other better here. I have a question . . . " The likely response might be something like, "Yes you're right, I didn't really mean what I said. Let's find a way to go forward together. Your question was . . . ?"

Potential Pitfalls of This Phase

- *Watch out for passionately advocating your views without inquiring.*

- *Watch out for people talking too fast without understanding; to get to an agreement faster, slow down the conversation.*

- *Watch out for thinking you have shared understanding when undiscussables lurk.*

- *Watch out for sending mixed messages or pretending you have not received one.*

---

1. Clarify the purpose of the conversation.

2. Gather divergent views and perspectives.

3. Build shared understanding of divergent views and perspectives.

4. Create "new" options by connecting different views.

5. Generate a conversation for action.

FIGURE 6.6
The Five Phases of a Collaborative Conversation

PHASE 4.

Create New Options by Connecting Different Views and Perspectives

Extraordinary Conversations

When people with different views or backgrounds collaborate on a shared goal, they often have incompatible beliefs and thus find it difficult to "talk the same language." Harvard Professor Peter Galison's study of boundary cultures offers some insight into this issue. "What happens at the boundary between different languages?" I asked Galison during one of our conversations. "Often, it is not just a matter of finding a translator, but an establish-

ment of a new local 'pidgin' or Creole language" in their trading zone that allows them to think and interact together. These new languages make it possible to connect different frames of reference and create or innovate something that never existed before.

One historical example of a highly successful trading zone where this happened is the large group of people who came together in the MIT Rad Lab to invent radar during World War II. The group included wave physicists and radio engineers, neither of whom knew anything about constructing radio sets. The physicists had certain abstract techniques for quantifying microwave patterns. The radio engineers had certain ways of doing their calculations based on home appliances that used copper wire circuits which would have leaked the radar waves. Talking together proved to be very complicated, even with translators who understood both fields. The war would have been over before they produced any results.

According to Galison, "The first thing they did was restructure the layout of Rad Lab 4-133 so that the physicists, radio engineers, and administration people, who previously worked in separate floors and office cubicles doing abstract research, all worked in one or two rooms—such as the Antennae Lab and Receiver Lab. The idea was to put all the people in the project in the same place so they could think and interact and so that the discussion would be grounded in producing specific components for the radar device. This worked much better, they reasoned, than the previous approach of delivering presentations to each other that did not go into enough detail or writing papers that went into too much."

Then they did something creative and worked out a kind of common language based on the physicists' interpretation of Maxwell's equations of wave theory and some of the calculational techniques of the radio engineers used for practical devices. Galison explains, "Their shared discoveries of radar, which grew upon ideas from both sides, were extremely important for the war effort."[7]

This and the Manhattan Project began to transform what was then called "pure science"—where people had worked in isolation—to much more of a collaborative process. "Interestingly enough," says Galison, "both groups learned so much as a result of the collaboration that neither the practice of wave physics or radio engineering was ever the same."

Exploring Creativity Through Collaboration

In the last section, we discussed "Building Shared Understand-ing" so that people can expand their views and perspectives to include those of others and get on the same wavelength during their conversation or network of conversations. Phase Four of a collaborative conversation involves playing with or looking for ways to creatively connect differ-ent views or perspectives with an eye toward creating dramatically new, surprising, even delightful solutions.

As mentioned in Chapter One, Arthur Koestler, the controver-sial science writer and philosopher, in his weighty tome, *The Art of Creation,* says that most people's thinking is the result of a single frame of reference. While a person may be familiar with many different views and perspectives, most people operate from one frame of reference at a time. Creativity occurs when a person (or group of people) can relate what are normally different views and perspectives in a flash of insight Koestler calls "bisociation." "The creative act, by connecting previous-ly unrelated dimensions of experience," asserts Koestler, "is an act of liberation—the defeat of habit by originality."[8]

The most famous example of all time is that of Archimedes, who was asked by the king to measure the volume of a gold crown. Archimedes told the king the only way he could do this was to boil down the gold in the crown into a brick. His thinking was bound by the frame of reference which said that volume is determined by the size of the container something fills up (a pint, quart, gallon). When he took his bath later that day, he noticed the water being displaced and exclaimed "Eureka!" He had connected two different frames of refer-ence—the crown's volume and the water in a bathtub that was dis-placed when he sat in it.

One of the basic premises of this book is that the act of creation (or the bisociation act) is more likely to occur when you have people from different frames of reference thinking and working together on a shared goal or grounded in the same problem. The dilemma is that these people with different frames of reference may not in the end pro-duce *creative tension,* but *emotional tension* which results in disillusion-ment with the whole process—especially when the positions or views seem irreconcilable. Therefore, this phase of the collaborative conversa-tion is intended to assist people in handling these conflicting emotions.

Who You Need to Be in This Phase

You are an author of your own destiny. You are a creator, or an inventor, not someone who is a product of circumstances, a direct report, or a passive consumer. Think of yourself as someone who has the ability to invent new options (choices), at all times, under all circumstances and conditions, instead of someone who is trapped by the whole discouraging complexity of the situation. Consider yourself as someone who is a creative synthesizer, juxtaposing crazy combinations of people and ideas instead of someone who only likes to deal with familiar people or ideas. Finally, think of yourself as someone that creates something new, invents a tradition, and leaves a legacy of something beneficial and a life full of satisfaction.

Mental Models, Metaphors, and Analogies

Creation versus artistic creativity. Some readers at this point may question, How can I be part of a creative collaboration if I am not a creative person? I can't draw. I don't write. If I am completely honest, I fell asleep by the second act of *Phantom of the Opera*. Our answer is that there is a distinct difference between creation and artistic ability. The "ability to create" means being able to bring something into existence that did not exist before. "Creation" is something that is possible in all fields—science, business, government—not just the arts. It has more to do with a passion to bring something to pass, to work in crazy combinations, or perhaps a desperate need for new answers, than anything else. Together these constitute what Henri Poincare called a "a condition of ripeness." Also, while it is usually thought that creativity comes from creative individuals, our research in places as disparate as the software companies of Silicon Valley, the Newport Jazz Festival, or the halls of Congress say that creativity just as often happens with people who collaborate in groups.

    Explore white space to create "what's missing" versus improving what already exists. Imagine that 200 years ago human rights did not exist. Imagine a country without TV, a billboard for ABC televisions says. Imagine that half the world, two billion people, have not received their first telephone call. The point is that courageous and creative people do not merely focus on what already exists—their relationship with the despot king or government, the dials on the radio, or land-line phone terminals. They're too busy exploring white spaces between what already exists and inventing "what's missing" that never existed before—e.g., the Bill of Rights, computer TVs, global mobile phone systems (GMS) that allow you to call your wife from a department store in Singapore or down the street from your neighbor's garage. Keep in mind that it is hard to create something new if, instead of focusing on "what's missing that will make things better," we are always focusing on "what's wrong." As Jimmy Ballard, the renowned golf coach once told me, "It is easy to find the fault. It's hard to find the cure."

Invent new options by expanding your view to include others. People who are attempting to collaborate are often confronted with wicked problems, dilemmas, and conundrums where there are no simple or obvious answers. This can lead to arguments, anger, depression, or discouragement. There are always more possibilities and options than people are aware of, no matter how convinced they are otherwise. The key to creating or inventing new options is to expand your view to enclose opposing views that may look incompatible at face value. This involves focusing on what really matters and dropping what really doesn't, or focusing on areas of overlap and forgetting areas that cannot be resolved at the present time. A good example is the balanced budget amendment. Both Democrats and Republicans wanted to balance the budget but disagreed on spending cuts for social programs. They then focused on creating a balanced budget that would do minimum damage to social programs and would actually increase education spending.

An Example of Creating New Options by Connecting Different Views

In the pre-Oslo security talks that dealt with issues such as how a peace accord with Israelis and Palestinians would be implemented, there were seemingly incompatible positions. According to Professor Everett Mendelssohn who was instrumental in facilitating these talks, "The Palestinians said they needed access to the holy sites in Jerusalem. The Israelis said they needed security. Then we began to look at how these two concepts interacted.

"I said to the Palestinians, 'If you have totally open access and there are people in your ranks that want to do harm, then you create a problem for Israeli security, that, you in their shoes, would not find acceptable.' Then I said to the Israelis, 'If you deny access to people's holy sites and to the graves of their ancestors, how can you expect to have security? It was partially for access that you fought to create a country here.'

"Then," he continued, "you turn the situation around. 'Is there a way that you can frame the question so that you can create access and provide security in some equal measure? What do you think this is? What would it look like?'" He told us that they uncovered some ways by which both security and access could be achieved, without either side giving up what really matters. This discussion led to some plans, as well as a collaborative thinking process that helped model the talks that would lead to the breakthrough of the Oslo Accords.[9]

Things to Do

Put the challenge or problem in one sentence. This is an important part of the creative process that involves *formulation, preparation, illumination,* and *verification,* as shown in Figure 6.7. George Lois, a giant in advertising who came up with the campaigns of Lean Cuisine and Avis's "We try harder," emphasizes that the first stage of creativity, *formulation,* involves coming up with a one-sentence definition of the problem. Lois was once asked by Volkswagen to design an ad campaign. Lois said he needed time to think. After a week, the client called him and said, "Do you have it yet?" Lois replied, "No, call me in a week." The following week Lois called the client very excited. "I've got it!" "The solution?" the client asked. "No, the problem," Lois responded, "How to sell a Nazi car in a Jewish town." This led to a successful solution—the idea of the Volkswagen Beetle, a design which was intended to humanize a car that at the time, people might have been prejudiced against.[10]

Brainstorm multiple options. Brainstorming is sometimes thought of as a mindless process where people slap ideas up on a flip chart. At IDEO, David Kelly has created a structured brainstorming process that has resulted in some award-winning designs, like the Apple mouse, the stand-up Crest toothpaste tube, and the Motorola flip phone. He gets the whole project team in one room—it is an honor to be invited—and gets everyone interacting with each other and putting ideas on the board. The brainstorming session starts with a one-sentence defini-

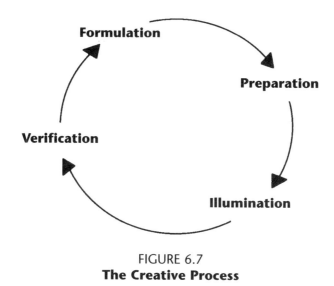

FIGURE 6.7
The Creative Process

tion of the problem. Then people start generating lots of options according to these rules: (1) one conversation at a time, (2) encourage wild ideas, (3) care and nurture versus judgment. People then take a break and resume for a "back to brainstormer" session. The intention is to see if connecting the main categories of ideas leads to different associations of a new idea or even a new way of seeing the whole. "Most combinations of ideas so formed would be entirely sterile," says Henri Poincare. "But certain among them, very rare, are the most fruitful of all."

Use metaphors to incubate, care, and feed ideas. Reaching goals and solving problems involves creative thinking. Metaphors are an intuitive method of perception that allow people to express what they know on a vague, intuitive level, but can't say. Metaphors bring about a connection between two things that seem only remotely related. Philosopher Max Black describes this as "two ideas in one phrase." For example, *a warm voice, a sweet smile, a sharp light.*

People in a creative collaboration with different views and backgrounds often use metaphors that employ colorful symbols to help others intuitively understand what they would like to create but find hard to put in words. Metaphors achieve this by combining two distant and different areas of perception into one embrasive image or symbolic representation—*a lean organization, a docking station for your personal computer, doctors without borders.*

For our purposes, metaphors can be created consciously and used by an individual or group when challenges or problems arise to jump-start the process of creative thinking. As people begin to be able to express the insight the metaphor represents, they work to reconcile its contradictory meanings. By connecting their different experience and frames of reference in new ways, the result is often a Eureka insight!

According to Ikujiro Nonaka, business professor at Hitosubashi University near Tokyo, a Honda team in Japan was given the charge to design a car based on the principle of "Let's Gamble." The leader of the project, Hiro Watanabe, came up with a metaphor for a new kind of car that would challenge the thinking of Detroit. He called it the "Theory of Automobile Evolution." This metaphor combines two different ideas one wouldn't usually consider—the automobile, a machine, and evolution, which refers to living things.

He and his team postulated that if the car were to evolve, it would do so according to "machine minimum/man maximum," taller and cheaper, but also more comfortable and solid than traditional cars. The evolutionary trend articulated by the team came to be embodied in an image of a sphere—short in length and tall in height—giving more room to the passenger and taking up a smaller parking place in crowded Tokyo. This gave birth to the Honda City Car, or "Tall Boy," a very popular car in Japan.[11]

Use analogies to distinguish what is missing and solve practical problems. While a metaphor can start the creative thinking process, analogies are useful in working out practical problems. They provide a more structured process of distinguishing "what's missing that could make a difference" by combining in one sentence how two ideas are alike or not alike.

Nonaka offers a powerful example of an analogy that comes from the Canon team that developed the revolutionary minicopier. They knew that for the copier to be successful, it had to have minimal breakdowns. To ensure this, they decided to make the product's photosensitive copier drum, which is the cause of 90 percent of all maintenance problems, disposable. To be disposable, the drum would need to be cheap and easy to make. How could they build a "toss-away" drum?

The Eureka event came one day when the team leader, Hiroshi Tanaka, sent out for some beer. As the group talked over the design issues over a few beers, Tanaka picked up one of the beer cans and wondered out loud, "What's the cost of making this can?" The question led the team to look at whether the same process for making a can of beer could be used to make the photocopier drum. "By brainstorming how the copier drum was like or not like a beer can, the minicopier team was able to come up with a process technology that could manufacture an aluminum copier drum at a low cost."[12]

Potential Pitfalls of This Phase

- *Watch out for prematurely thinking that you have exhausted all possible options.*

- *Watch out for merely trying to improve what exists versus creating something new.*

- *Watch out for focusing on what's wrong versus what's missing that could help.*

- *Watch out for jumping ahead in the creative process before allowing time to formulate the idea; prepare by stuffing your mind full of facts and giving enough time to incubate.*

---

1. Clarify the purpose of the conversation.

2. Gather divergent views and perspectives.

3. Build shared understanding of divergent views and perspectives.

4. Create "new" options by connecting different views.

5. Generate a conversation for action.

FIGURE 6.8
The Five Phases of a Collaborative Conversation

PHASE 5.
Generate a Conversation for Action

Coming up with shared goals, shared meaning, and creative solutions is essential to collaboration. Yet there is one missing piece, without which nothing will bear fruit. That missing piece has to do with action. The medium for taking action, once again, is a conversation. In the same way that you move an impossibility to a possibility by making a declaration—a shared commitment to a collaborative objective—you move a possibility into reality by taking experimental action and making powerful promises and requests.

It may be helpful to think of the creative process as a spiral originating with new ideas that you cannot quite express, that are then developed through metaphors and analogies and finally culminate in a sketch, prototype, or scale model. This becomes a shared work space that allows you to see if you have a shared understanding of what to create and how, as well as to test your mental conception through a prototype to see if it really works.

The Wright Brothers were able to have a good sense whether their plane could fly because they were excellent model builders. The Beatles would talk about an idea for a song and then go to the studio late at night to play around and record it. Software designers, such as those working on the Microsoft Project, often would bring in project managers (the users) to see if what the engineers defined as "great code" was something they could really use.

We have found through experience that, in addition to experimental action, there is a certain language that promotes action versus reflection. In this section, we will look at how making bold statements and requests tends to lead to action, and which types of language do not.

Who You Need to Be in This Phase

Think of yourself as someone who not only declares new possibilities but also makes powerful promises and requests based on your commitment, instead of someone who will only promise when there is guarantee or evidence that makes the promise predictable. Think of yourself as someone who, when you say you will do something, honors your word, instead of someone who honors their moods, reasons, or excuses. Think of yourself as a pragmatist hero, the person not necessarily involved in the newsworthy or dramatic part of the project but someone whose obsessive-compulsive behavior in the nuts and bolts may be responsible for the difference between implementation and another good idea gone up in smoke. Think of yourself as a tinkerer with a desire to act by building something one chunk at a time, not as a blue-sky type that gets easily bored with the details.

Mental Models, Metaphors, and Analogies

Speak in a generative way. Normally, most people and groups use language to make *predictions,* saying things like, "I'll do my best," "I'll try," or "That's a definite maybe." They do not distinguish this way of speaking and listening from making a clear promise or request. In addition to making predictions, these people or groups tend to use language to represent or *describe* what already exists, or to *explain* their way out of things, seldom realizing that it doesn't create or produce anything. There is another way of speaking and listening that is based on using language in a generative way that goes beyond the predictions, beyond the descriptions and explanations. This way of speaking and listening can carve out a new possibility between white spaces, elicit the passion in people's minds and hearts, and cause people to jump into action.

Conversations for possibility. John F. Kennedy declared that the United States would put a "man on the moon by the end of the decade." Colin Marshall, chairman of British Airways, declared that his company would become the world's number-one airline. Declaring a vision that represents the triumph of the human spirit over resignation leaves us feeling empowered. Yet to realize a possibility, you need to use a different kind of power. As Tracy Goss says in her book, *The Last Word on Power,* "Power is the speed at which we convert a possibility into a reality."[13] Notice that nothing can proceed until people move into the world of action.

Conversations for action. The power to transform a possibility into a reality is one in which we have to make bold promises and requests that launch us into the world of action. You can talk about all kinds of possibilities and get people excited about them or even build community regarding a project. Yet, until you ask people to join you in a project or begin to exchange a series of promises and requests, nothing happens.

Network of commitments, communication, and support. In a collaboration, the hierarchical structure often becomes an irrelevant issue. Authority is based on knowledge rather than position, and things are prioritized according to what's next on the project. It is normal that a project manager will find himself working for someone who is his or her subordinate on another project. As people make promises and requests to anyone in the group—like "Can you help me sort through this?"—the chain of command is replaced by a network of commitments, communication, and support. It is like passing a ball of energy back and forth until the collaborative project is brought to completion. There is an implicit self-organizing structure to this commitment network that surpasses any organization chart.

Rapid prototypes versus elaborate planning; creative frenzy versus leisurely pace. There's a story about how aircraft engines are built. All new aircraft engines have to pass the chicken test to prove that new engines won't ingest birds in flight and crash. This means that the testers go down to the supermarket, buy a couple of gross of chickens, and fire them into the big engine on the runway. A few years back, Rolls Royce built an engine and invested a quarter of a billion dollars into it. The problem was that it didn't pass the chicken test. The idea is to do the chicken test at the earliest stage possible, perhaps, in this case, where you have only invested twenty-five million, not a quarter billion.

Members of the Mars Project didn't have time to elaborately plan and prepare everything. Instead, they used a system, according to chief engineer Rob Manning, based on rapid prototypes and trial and error. According to Manning, it took this iteration: "We would get together as a group, say 'here is what we need to do,' try it out, and then come back as a group and try to figure out what went wrong and how to start over and pick our feet up and go another iteration. We did this over and over again going through another five or six cycles of this process in a hurry, with a fixed budget." A creative, frenzied pace was normal during this project.[14]

Example of a Collaborative Prototype and Learning Process

Around 1990, home appliance developers at Matsushita Electric in Osaka, Japan, were working on a new breadmaking machine that could knead dough in a proper way. They were frustrated that no matter how many times they tried, the bread crust would turn out dark brown and hard, and the inside would be too soft and doughy. Team members drove themselves crazy trying to figure out the cause of the problem, even x-raying the dough kneaded by the bread maker and the dough kneaded by professionals in bakeries.

Finally, a software programmer, Ikuku Tanaka, proposed a creative solution that involved studying the bakers at the Osaka International Hotel, which had a reputation for making the best bread in town. Perhaps it could be used as a learning model. Tanaka then began training as an apprentice with the head baker to study kneading technique, noticing that the baker had a distinctive technique for stretching the dough.

After a period of trial and error, working closely with engineers on the project, Tanaka came up with the product specifications for the bread maker—which had special dough-stretching ribs that reproduced the chef's bread-stretching techniques and the tasty bread made at the Osaka hotel.[15]

Things to Do

Alter your strategies and plans as you take action. You always have to adjust your strategy and plan based on what you said you would do, what you accomplished, breakdowns, or opportunities you didn't anticipate. When there is a breakthrough to be reached and you are doing something you have never done before, you have to take an action to see what it produces and then go back and see if you have to alter your strategy a bit. In reaching a goal in a business, you might discover that your thinking is flawed, that instead of going for it on your own, you need to reach out and create a strategic partner. You might come to a negotiation with a strong position and discover that, in light of your conversation with others and their respective positions, that what you are asking for is unrealistic. Instead of focusing on your position, you need to focus on your interests.

Make bold promises. Making bold promises has a powerful impact on transforming your possibility into reality. If you are keeping all your promises, either your promises are not big enough or you are playing too small a game in life. The Mars Pathfinder mission involved promises that the members of the group could not guarantee. "We were actually a pretty crazy collective," says Bob Anderson, chief geologist.

"We said: We'll do a mission where we'll develop a new landing technique and we'll cut costs by 90 percent." That one bold promise, which became the basis of an "immutable timetable and budget," resulted in other promises in every aspect of the mission that moved the whole mission forward, causing people to think outside the box and take creative and bold action.

Four conditions necessary to make a promise viable:

• *A committed speaker: someone who makes a bold promise and then follows through*

• *A committed listener: someone who holds you accountable and encourages you to make bold promises that stretch your mind and skills*

• *Conditions of satisfaction: what will be delivered? produced?*

• *A time frame*

Make bold requests. Many people have difficulty asking for what they want or need assistance with. They make requests that are overly polite. They may hint or expect others to be mindreaders. They may be afraid that others will reject them. If you make a request and people say "yes," the possibility you stand for moves forward. Yet even if they decide to decline, the possibility is brought further into reality. For example, their decline might bring other issues to the surface that need to be discussed or will make you realize that there has to be another way to achieve the desired result. A request asks others to take action. Just as with a promise, a request need not be fulfilled to move your collaboration forward. To be viable, it requires the same conditions:

• *A committed speaker and listener*

• *Conditions of satisfaction or fulfillment*

• *A time frame*

Give people the power to say "no." No promise is honestly made, no request is legitimately accepted, if the person who takes on the task did not have the right to turn it down. Any coerced action or involuntary participation is likely to further undermine your collaboration down the road—if not immediately. What makes it possible for people to pursue a promise as something they believe in and have the internal commitment to do? The knowledge that they made a free and honest choice. What makes it possible for people to honestly agree to a request? The sense that they have the free and honest chance to decline. That freedom really empowers both the person making the request to ask for that they want and the person who is on the receiving end. "No" should not necessarily be interpreted as a signal that people are not committed to the project but, perhaps a basis for inquiry. "Here's why I asked you to do this. I respect that you have declined, but could you help me to understand your reasoning? Perhaps there is another approach?"

Potential Pitfalls of This Phase

- *Watch out for setting ambitious goals and then reducing them when anxiety comes up.*

- *Watch out for making vague or inexplicit promises to other collaborators.*

- *Watch out for making complaints instead of requests or speaking in a nongenerative way.*

- *Watch out for planning too much before attempting a pilot test.*

Chapter Seven

Coaching, Practical Applications, and Tools for Creative Collaboration

I would like you to be able to read this chapter and say to yourself, "Wow, I can do this!" It doesn't take a genius or highly skilled professional to facilitate a collaborative conversation, or project. Part I of this final chapter helps makes this point by opening with a conversation I had with Bill Ury, who had just returned from the Amazon and the Kalahari where he studied how indigenous people facilitate difficult conversations. It also provides simple but powerful guidelines for facilitation that anyone can use. Part II provides some structured, step-by-step, easy-to-apply conversational templates for doing specific things, like strategic planning, creative problem-solving, or conflict resolution. Part III provides some ideas on collaborative tools that serve to focus the conversation, create a shared mental model, and make it possible to take creative and effective action.

PART I.

Coaching and Facilitation

How Bushmen Facilitate Difficult Conversations

I asked my colleague, Bill Ury, who refers to himself as a "renegade anthropologist," about his recent work. "Recently, I was on an expedition into a place one would not normally get into. My interest was in how these indigenous people converse about reaching their goals and resolving their problems. I did some interviews and just observed." This is something Ury had previously done in other parts of the world, including the Papua Indians in New Guinea and the Bushmen in Africa's Kalahari desert.

Ury noticed that, while each of the fifteen tribes of about 200 to 300 people he studied has its own language and culture, when they have an issue to resolve, they all basically work off the basis of building a shared understanding until it results in a real consensus. "It could be a conflict—a personality conflict, something over jealousy, something over someone's land. These people talked things through and thoroughly—something that we impatient Americans (or Europeans) don't do. "The impatience," says Ury, "can be a real barrier to having collaborative conversations."[1]

The elders act as facilitative leaders. Everything that happens gets talked through. If there is a question of where to plant a field or where to go on a hunt, it gets talked about by men and women sitting around and having a kind of dialogue. Ury said that the elders had a special role to play as facilitative leader. "Usually it is one of the elders who listens for a long time, and listens for what the sense of the group is, and waits until the end of the conversation to distill what the group has decided." In other words, the elder's decision is not unilateral. After the elder has finished speaking, people can still disagree. He or she is basically summing up the collective wisdom of the group. For example, he may ask for an apology, if that is called for.

When the Bushmen have an issue to solve, all of the adult men and women sit around the campfire, everyone is given a chance to have their say, and everyone is listened to. "It can be quite emotional in the beginning, with lots of accusations, laundry being aired, and so on, explains Ury. "Every once in a while, people talk simultaneously. And then things start to settle down. It might take two or three days to get to the bottom of the issue. The point is they do not let the issue rest until a real shared understanding or a consensus emerges about how to handle the problem, and until the relationship is restored."

I wondered what happened when the Bushmen or others got stuck. "For one thing," Ury said, "they do not believe in just letting something go or dropping it until it is resolved." If the discussion reaches an impasse, then one of the elders may intervene at a certain point. There is a kind of hierarchy, but it is a type of facilitative leadership very much in the sense of the anthropological joke that "one word from the chief and everyone does what he pleases."

People look to the elders and value their opinions because of the work the leaders have done over the years into forming relationships and reasoning with people. An elder may ask others who have been shy or lurking behind the group to speak up (empowerment), or he may reframe a certain point so that others understand it better.

No exit strategies. One of the elders' main functions is to hold the container for the group, making sure that no member of the group leaves until some resolution has occurred. "These people have a belief that, if you prematurely close a conversation and don't resolve an issue, it will come back to haunt you later," Ury says. I have seen this happen countless times in business with a devastating impact on both results and relationships.

"Unlike Americans," Ury says, "the Bushmen are not quick to use the exit strategy and prematurely bring the conversation to closure, or do things like hang up the phone and leave." I recalled in the Oslo story, when everyone wanted to leave, how Terje Larsen held them together in a million different ways. I also recalled a story about an event which took place just before the Oslo agreement signing at the White House. Arafat didn't like some aspect of the agreement and said if it wasn't changed, he was going to pack his bags and leave. Peres, nonplussed, said, "I haven't even unpacked my bags yet and I will be at the airport before you." Arafat backed down and the agreement was signed.

Trance dances. If the Bushmen did not believe in fighting to the point where it could damage relationships or running away, how did they resolve logjams? Ury said they just keep talking all day until some kind of resolution occurs. Then something amazing happens: "They do a trance dance as a way to find the wisdom they need to get to the bottom of things or to heal the relationships from any rifts that have been created." These dances usually happened around the campfire at night. Professor Ury witnessed one in the middle of the Kalahari. "The men stamp their feet, the women sit there clapping. Some of the men sit there clapping as well. And after an hour or so of stamping and chanting, a few of them fall to the ground in a trance. And, as they put it, they are asking the gods for answers to the problems that are troubling the group. When they wake up from their trance, they communicate the wisdom they have elicited from the world of the spirit."

The Importance of Coaching and Facilitation

When people want to reach breakthroughs, bringing together extraordinary combinations of people is an excellent way to generate creative tension, which in turn is released by engaging in collaborative conversations. Like an orchestra leader, a facilitator can play a powerful role in drawing out people, building shared understanding, and helping people construct powerful insights so that the whole becomes greater than the sum of the parts.

At the same time, bringing together extraordinary combinations of people with divergent backgrounds, views, and perspectives can also result in counterproductive emotional tension. As a result, collaborative conversations can often be *difficult* conversations, and a facilitator can play a powerful role in making them easier. In fact, the dictionary definition of facilitator is "to make easier."

One of the key roles a facilitator has today, in what Xerox's John Seely Brown calls "knowledge ecologies of different specialists," is to act as a translator and language creator who can provide people a lexicon to help them communicate. Being a specialist and a generalist helps here. Recall what Rob Manning said: "My only prerogative as chief engineer was to be able to go around and ask any question I wanted." This not only allowed him to see whether people were on track and to coach them by asking further questions, but to learn enough about each department's work so that he could help people to see the big picture.

Manning also set aside time at the beginning of the project to have each team member from different departments explain his or her profession and how they were going to approach this particular job assignment. People said, "Oh that's how a electronic or (mechanical) engineer really thinks, I never understood that before."

Creating "Pidgin" or Creole languages and metaphors can also help. Douglas Dayton, of IDEO, told me a story about the early days of

Apple Computer. Steven Jobs was looking for a way to tell people in the MAC team just what kind of computer he wanted to build. He wanted to do so in a way that would tell engineers, computer scientists, industrial designers, and software folks what really needed to be done, as well as to allow them to coordinate their actions in the trading zone of the first MAC.

Jobs eventually came up with the metaphor of "a bicycle lying against the garage." He wanted them to design a computer that would be simple to get access to, easy to find, and upgradable. Dayton remembers how excited he was by the metaphor and how it allowed him as an industrial designer to coordinate his actions while working on the first mouse with other people on the project.

In more personal terms, a coach or facilitator can do a lot in a collaborative conversation simply by showing up and giving people the gift of his or her presence (quality of attention). For example, people who have strong views about an issue and wind up with disagreements always have strong feelings. Beneath the business suits and the air of rightness and invulnerability is a human being who wants to know that there is at least one person in the room who understands his feelings.

Also, people want to know that there is at least one person who has really listened to what they said and deeply understands their point of view. It doesn't matter if the facilitator is neutral, as long as this primary emotional need is met. And yes, just having the facilitator in the room—even if he or she has no skills in mediation—will tend to have the effect of preventing extravagant displays of emotions and unreasonable thinking and attitudes.

What Is Coaching and Facilitation?

The role of a coach is to create a relationship with people and groups where they continuously expand people's capacity to produce the results they truly desire.

Images of aspiration. Ron Lippet, one of the founders of Organization Development, discovered by running community building conferences in years past that people in communities want to come together, but don't know how. He said that one of the best ways to bring the group together is for the coach or facilitator to focus the discussions on "images of aspiration" that are future oriented, rather than focus on "past problems or grievances."

Focusing on images of aspiration—such as striving for peace, ending hunger, doubling your business—tends to center people on their passion to have an impact on their work. Focusing the conversation on the problem tends to center the conversation on what people don't want or on the whole discouraging complexity of their present situation. The facilitator plays a key role in making sure that people declare and assert that a solution is possible, no matter how much it may appear otherwise. This tends to elicit feelings in people that are shared by all the different stakeholders, no matter what their differences.

This provides a good opportunity to share one of the most interesting collaborations we uncovered in our work.[2] According to one article we read, this example "involved an unlikely collaboration of Jack Shipley, an avid environmentalist; Jim Neal, a longtime logger from northern Oregon; and others (representatives from the U.S. Bureau of Land Management [BLM], and timber companies like Boise Cascade) regarding the management of the Applegate Watershed, a half million-acre area in southwestern Oregon.

Together Shipley and Neal, who were frustrated with the various groups' polarization, decided that there must be a better way to deal with the issues of resource management (especially timber) than the gridlock, antagonism, and legal battles they were experiencing. They spent six months talking to groups and in one-on-one conversations, nurturing the idea that they could do timber sales that kept an economic view, yet were ecologically viable. They found that there was considerable overlap between the desires and interests of the environmental groups and the industry groups. They decided that it was worth a try to get all the protagonists together and hash out the issues face-to-face. The meeting ultimately involved sixty people.

According to Jack Shipley, they started the meeting, by asking people to introduce themselves by their name, not their company or affiliation, and tell a little bit about themselves and their families. It became clear to people that they had shared goals for the community. The idea was conceived to create a collaborative partnership that would look for creative solutions for managing the natural resources in the area. However, before long, haggling broke out about who was going to be on the board of directors

Someone stood up and said, "If we are going to do this right, it doesn't make any difference where the individuals come from, or what their background is, as long as they are willing to find solutions. If we focus only on the problems, we'll be back in the same old place." According to Shipley, "That had a lot of logic in it. We could move beyond individual representation of each group. He articulated what we were all wanting to have happen, but didn't know how to say."

That was a turning point, and they were able to quickly set up some guidelines and appoint a nine-person board of directors representing corporations, foresters, the BLM, environmentalists, and various community interest groups. With weekly meetings for three months consecutive, it wasn't long before they had established a real dialogue that allowed them to create a thirty-page document that defined the territory in which they were operating and their mission statement. The document included a profile of each member, including their goals and priorities.

The group then went on to test out their intentions in a series of successful projects where they really broke from the ranks—a non-appealed timber sale that included some rather unusual approaches to logging, such as lifting the trees out by helicopter and many watershed restoration projects on private land. These have only added to the positive feeling surrounding the partnership in the community.

The Applegate Partnership has continued to meet weekly for the last four- and a-half years. At each meeting, someone steps forward to facilitate. The facilitator's job is to keep the discussion on track and to ensure that people are civil to each other. According to Shipley, "We were very good early on at forgetting our shared goals and sliding back—getting off track or occasionally throwing poison darts across the room at each other. Part of the reason this happened is that everyone wanted it to work so much that they were afraid to say anything bad or express their feelings. Then it would come out sideways. Each member had a job as co-facilitator to point this out when it happened, and say, 'Okay, let's not beat around the bush.' That was helpful.

"We learned that if we disagreed, it was fine. We could talk about it, and usually we would reach some kind of resolution. In fact, we have become quite comfortable at having adverse conversations. We really encourage people to express their different views—diversity is our strength. For example, at one meeting someone from the BLM was the facilitator. Then an issue came up that he had strong opinions about and that impacted the BLM. He asked to step down and have someone take over so he could fully participate."

Building a Relationship as a Facilitator with Group Members

It is impossible to emphasize the importance of building a real relationship with all parties in a collaboration. The fact is that people will not authorize someone to coach them who they do not trust or admire and respect. Though some people may gain this respect just by being a skilled professional, in many cases that will not be enough.

Dr. Everett Mendelssohn of Harvard University told me the reason he was selected as a facilitator in the Israeli-Palestinian security talks was that, "I have been around for a long time. I had talked with various Israeli leaders and with Arafat. I speak some of both languages. I have studied the entire region for a long time."[3]

Terje Larsen spent over two years pounding the street surveying 300 to 400 families as a way to meet people and build up his understanding of the region. He would listen and say, "I understand. Norway understands." If he or she is a good facilitator, both sides will think that they are on their side, while at the same time they'll respect that the facilitator has to act in an impartial way. In the typical group within a government, business, school, or hospital, the facilitator should be someone who not only commands but is also liked and respected—someone who is friendly and frank, clear-minded as well as compassionate.

It is important to learn about the people you are facilitating and, to understand their goals and aspirations. It is also important to talk to them about the approach you will use in the collaborative conversations. Finally, make sure that both the individual and the group feel they have the power to say "no" to your offer to facilitate them. Giving people the power to say "no" often gives people the power to say "yes."

Expand the Group's Capacity to Produce Desired Results: Basic Versus Developmental Facilitation

The facilitator's role in a collaborative conversation involves many things—but it must result in expanding the ability of the group to reach its goals. There is an important distinction to be made between "basic facilitation" and "advanced or developmental facilitation."[4] Basic facilitation may be the best approach when people in the group are under pressure to produce a particular outcome—like a strategic plan or decision—and want someone to maximize synergy and stumbling blocks but do not have the time or the inclination for deeper interventions that might be more personal. Advanced or developmental facilitation also involves enabling the group to reach a particular outcome for that meeting, yet includes making deeper interventions that will help people to break the grip of counterproductive thinking and attitudes.

Let's use dealing with emotions as an example for how basic and developmental facilitation might work. Let's say Hans, a production engineer, says no to a request by Roddy, a marketing vice president, to assist him on a customer issue. Roddy, who feels that his request is reasonable, becomes very angry and pounds on the table. "You don't care about customers. You don't want to cooperate. All you care about is yourself . . . " The "basic" facilitator's response to this emotional outburst might be, "Let's just let Roddy express how he feels." All feelings are valid, and perhaps it is not a good idea to try to argue him out of them. In effect, the facilitator chooses to *bypass* the reactive behavior. This transactional or single-loop learning approach is aimed at changing Roddy's reactive behavior, not the thinking or attitudes that caused it.

In the *advanced* approach, the facilitator may choose to *name or engage* the reactive behavior, with a view toward getting at the underlying thinking and attitudes that caused it. "Roddy, you're obviously angry, upset, and made several accusations about Hans. Are you sure you didn't jump to conclusions when he said no? Are you sure they are based on something solid or are they just your reactions? Why not check it out and ask Hans why he said no?" These questions take Hans and the group in the direction of transformational or double- and triple-loop learning.

Governing Values of Collaborative Leaders and Facilitators

If you want to create a group based on the principle of lateral leadership, collaborative conversations, and so on, there are three governing values that you as a facilitator may want to adopt and invite the group to do the same. This becomes the basis for how you go about your role as a facilitative leader and provides a platform for your interventions.[5]

1. Commitment to the truth (or valid information). One of the high-leverage roles a facilitator plays is encouraging people in the group to speak authentically so that they know what each other really thinks and feels. Another is to encourage the group not only to express their thoughts and feelings but also to test implicit assumptions and inferences that may be invalid. On the most basic level, a facilitator can help to ensure that people have the necessary facts by doing a factual analysis of the situation. Finally, it can be used to clarify his or her approach.

2. Free and informed choice. People feel empowered when they they have choices and disempowered when they don't, which can lead to counterproductive attitudes or behavior. It is part of the facilitator's job to empower people by reminding them that they do have choices. For example, they can choose to speak up or choose to remain silent (and perhaps be misunderstood). They can choose whether to have the facilitator opt for a basic "let's-just-get-the-results-for-today" approach or to go deeper, which may bring up feelings and attitudes. They can choose to share their authentic thoughts and feelings or keep them private. The facilitator can remind them that they have choices at any time.

3. Internal commitment. If people have valid information and a commitment to the truth, they will generally have an internal commitment to the process.

Roles of the Facilitator:
Who You Are in the Conversation

Who we are, our way of being, naturally shapes what we do more pow-erfully than any technique or list of things to do. So it is important to think about "who you are" or "who you need to be" in order to fulfill the purpose of the conversation or collaboration. For example, if the collaboration requires bringing people together who have lots of stereo-typed perspectives about each other or are even enemies, you may need to be a community builder and be very social, in order to help people build bridges, get to know each other, and start to build trust. It is not essential that you be an expert at every role to make a difference, but a combination of two or three roles appropriate to the situation can be very powerful. Review the four roles below and ask yourself which one best reflects who you are and seems most natural. Then ask yourself which one of these roles is missing in your approach that, if developed, would make a difference: (1) community builder, (2) creator of space, (3) intervener, (4) go-between.

1. Building a community of commitment. In the Oslo story, Terje Larsen had a kind of "Aha!" experience where he realized he could make a difference in the Middle East. He was an effective community builder in the Oslo talks because he was not only a committed vision-ary but also a very social person for whom it was natural to bring peo-ple together. The passion he showed should lay to rest the notion that a facilitator is someone who is neutral.

Larsen passionately believed in what he was undertaking and his role in it. At the same time, he knew that his success as a facilitator depended on being able to build a community of commitment between the different people involved: Norwegians, Arabs, Israelis. His role was always to *hold the intention* for the entire process, to provide the con-tainer for the conversation. He did this by holding the possibility that a breakthrough solution was possible, no matter what was happening, by organizing lodging in intimate and remote settings with good food, and by encouraging people not to give up.

Interestingly enough, though his role (as well as his wife's) in the talks cannot be overestimated, they were out of the conference rooms during most of the negotiations. He did not feel that he was a skilled facilitator and observed that when he was in the room, he became part of the gallery that the two different sides played to. He was frequently running around fetching faxes or making sure people had breakfast, snacks, and ate together—a powerful way to build a community.

As Yossi Beilin said, a simple meal, has the latent purpose of bringing people together: to build trust and to see that they do not have horns on their head. In the Applegate Watershed Project, Jack Shipley told us that the first meeting of sixty or more people took place at his house on the back porch for a barbecue.

Russ McKinley, from Boise Cascade lumber company, told us about the history of the problems and the changes that had occurred in the Applegate area: "I think the biggest problem the BLM had [before the Applegate Partnership] was that they would not go into the local communities and sit and listen to people. They always demanded that people come to them, provide input without any chance for dialogue. I happen to believe that if you want to get the local people's support, you have to eat their cookies, drink their coffee, and talk to them, in their homes, at their grange halls, or sit on a bank with a fishing rod and be able to cut firewood along side them. That's what it takes."[6]

2. Creating space. Creating space is a key design element of a collaborative conversation in many different ways. In the Israeli-Palestinian security talks (which, as previously discussed, were a prototype for the Oslo talks) Professor Everett Mendelssohn said that success was made by providing physical space. This meant giving the group a place to talk, far away from the spotlight of the media, and where group members could feel safe.

Mendelssohn's colleague, Jeff Boutwell of the Academy of Arts and Sciences in Cambridge, Massachusetts,, told me an amusing story about the security talks. "One night in London after we had made significant progress on security and Palestinian access to holy sights, an alarm sounded in the hotel. Soon we were escorted out into the street in our pajamas. It turns out that there had been an IRA bomb threat in the hotel."[7]

In government offices, businesses, and schools in day-in, day-out terms, physical space can mean many things, such as having a room available where you can go and talk in an undisturbed fashion. One idea I've had is that each organization ought to have a room called the "Dialogue Lab" that facilitates people in having a real quality of dialogue. It could include white boards and flip charts as well as guidelines posted for various tasks and on-call facilitators who can be brought in on twenty-four-hour notice.

There are two other dimensions to providing physical space. First, as Mendelssohn said, give people "intellectual space." This means reaching an agreement that anyone can explore possibilities, put out any wild ideas, float trial balloons, "sorta-kinda" agree to something without feeling that just because they said it, they must commit to it. This means complete retractability until you reach a final agreement.

Second, creating space means facilitating the dialogue itself in a way that encourages people with diverse ideas and perspectives to open up and talk about the things that matter to them. I have seen many facilitators who actually shut down the conversation because they imposed an overly structured protocol on the group—with too many interventions and not enough trust in the wisdom of the group to see its way through chaos.

Harrison Owen, the founder of Open Space Technology, has created a simple method that almost any group can use to create space for people to open up and talk.[8] The ground rules are as follows: (1) The people who come to the meeting are the people who are supposed to come, (2) People talk about what they are passionate about, and (3) The Law of Two Feet: If you feel you are not getting value from the meeting or contributing, you can always exercise the law of two feet and leave. The people in the Open Space usually gather in a circle at the beginning of the meeting and declare their passion. Then the group breaks up into subgroups interested in that topic. After the groups are done with their tasks, there is reporting back to the larger group.

Harrison, who I interviewed a few years back, told me an interesting story about how the process works. He was asked to facilitate a meeting of a cluster of big organizations in Mexico that were embarking on a joint venture. He told people the ground rules and how to write on flip charts what they were passionate about after which they would break into small groups. Then he left for a while. He went outside, put a sombrero hat on, and took a nap under a tree. It turned out to be a long nap. He was found and awakened at the end of the day by the representatives of the various companies. They were excited to tell him that they had reached a breakthrough solution to some of the issues they were facing.

3. Intervening. We have discovered that creating space often has to be balanced with skillful interventions. When serving as a facilitator and you spot a group getting off track, keep in mind the old Chinese saying, "If you don't change the direction in which you are going, you are likely to wind up where you are headed." Intervening involves interrupting the dialogue and making statements or asking questions that are intended to further the purpose of the conversation.

Such interventions could take many different forms, such as asking the group to clarify the purpose of the conversation or the way they have framed it. It could involve asking people who are not participating to give their honest opinion about a hot or controversial topic, and seeking to make sure their views are understood. Or the intervention could involve spotting a particular defensive behavior and calling the person or group's attention to it.

There's an interesting story about Chris Argyris of Harvard, who was at a board meeting with the chairman of a big company. The chairman got up first and said, "I don't want to preempt every else's remarks, but . . ." Argyris, two minutes into the meeting, interrupted: "Excuse me," he said, "when you spoke was it or was it not your intention to preempt?" It appeared to Argyris that the chairman who had asked for a collaborative meeting was going to basically tell everyone what to do.

The governing values mentioned earlier—commitment to the truth (or valid information), free and informed choice, internal commitment—are supported by the following ground rules for effective groups which you can use to facilitate any meeting where it seems appropriate. The group co-facilitates by being mindful of these ground rules.[9]

Ground Rules for Effective Groups

1. Test assumptions and inferences.
2. Share all relevant information.
3. Focus on interests, not positions.
4. Be specific—use examples.
5. Agree on what important words mean.
6. Explain the reason behind one's statements, questions, and actions.

7. Disagree openly with any member of the group.

8. Make statements, then invite questions and comments.

9. Jointly design ways to test disagreements and solutions.

10. Discuss undiscussable issues.

11. Keep the discussion focused.

12. Do not take cheap shots or otherwise distract the group.

13. All members are expected to participate in all phases of the process.

14. Exchange relevant information with nongroup members.

15. Make decisions by consensus.

16. Do self-critiques.

Examples of How to Intervene

• **What's the problem?** Group members are talking to others in an imperious way or treating others as subordinates.

How to intervene: Interrupt. Point out the behavior. Suggest that in the spirit of free and informed choice, it is important that we treat each other as colleagues.

• **What's the problem?** The conversation is becoming hot, passionate advocacy without inquiry. Emotions are flaring and misunderstandings are occurring.

How to intervene: Interrupt. Point out the behavior. Slow down the conversation by asking questions to help to build shared understanding. Ask members to explain their reasoning or to give examples, so that everyone is operating in the same world.

• **What's the problem?** Group members are indicating through their statements that they do not feel free to speak with openness and candor or mixed messages to others.

How to intervene: Interrupt. Point out the behavior. Suggest that dialogue cannot be achieved without authentic conversation. Remind people there's a ground rule about being free to authentically disagree and discuss undiscussable issues. Suggest the left-hand-column exercise (as discussed later in chapter).

Figure 7.1 shows a useful diagnosis-intervention cycle.[10]

4. Go-between. In general, it is not a good idea to have serious conversations with one group (or group member) while the other group is not present, as this can lead to distrust of the facilitator. It is especially important not to accept the kind of role where someone comes to you at the beginning of a meeting and suggests mentioning something to someone in the group that they feel uncomfortable saying themselves. If you do, you may unwittingly collude with the defensive routines of the group, which might be to send mixed messages or to make hot issues undiscussable.

However, a skilled facilitator may need to break the rules,

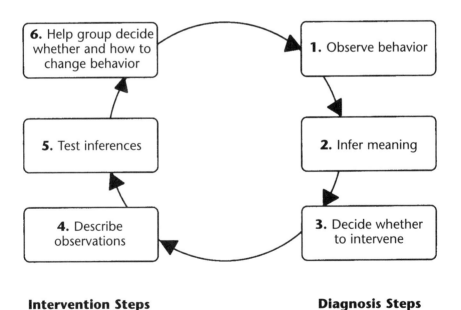

Intervention Steps   **Diagnosis Steps**

FIGURE 7.1
Diagnosis–Intervention Cycle

change the rules, or invent new rules in order to further the purpose of the group. As such, there may be times when you want to step out of your role as a facilitator and act as an intermediary or go-between.

For example, Roger Schwarz, a professional facilitator, was in a meeting where he was trying to help management and labor settle a dispute. The meeting started off amicably, but then people seemed to retreat into hardened positions with cheap shots and name calling. The meeting threatened to blow apart. Schwarz noticed that he could either continue in a neutral facilitator capacity and watch all the work he and the two groups had done so far go to waste, or he could step out of his role as a facilitator and act as a mediator. He went and talked to the union group privately, helping the groups to see something they hadn't seen before and the dispute was settled.

Terje Larsen attempted to play a very neutral role in the Oslo talks but was often drawn into the role of passing messages from one group to the next. This was partly because in between each phase of the talks, the Israelis and Palestinians had no way of communicating: the phone lines from Israel to Tunis (the PLO headquarters) had been blocked due to the fact that the two countries didn't recognize each other's existence. (In fact, in the Arab countries Israel was not on the map.) Larsen said, "I often had to put a spin on what was said to maintain a positive atmosphere of negotiation." For example, "Are they serious about wanting peace?" "Yes, I think so." "Is Rabin informed?" "He must be."

One thing worth mentioning is that a go-between often has to tolerate a certain amount of emotional tension, as both sides usually expect this type of facilitator to express their respective views, and may attack him or her when they feel this has not been done accurately. "Have you called them? What did they say? Did you get the message across? Idiot!" As Larsen said, "we had to take our beatings." He recalls one evening sitting on the phone at about 3 A.M. after speaking with Abu Ala, who had spoken to him in this way, waiting for a phone call from the Israelis. He noticed that as he reached for the phone, his hands were shaking because he was afraid he was going to explode at the next person who talked to him. It is worthwhile noting that on the days of the signing of the peace accord, the phone lines were reopened and the maps were redrawn.

PART II.

Applications

Conversational Recipes for Collaborative Projects

We found that the five phases of a collaborative conversation were excellent general guidelines but that other conversational recipes needed to be provided for specific applications, such as strategic planning, creative problem solving, or conflict resolution. The ideas, methods, and tools of guest facilitators are used here with appreciation.

APPLICATION #1.

Transforming Team Talk

As mentioned in the Introduction, people in groups often get trapped in old and unproductive patterns of conversation. As Dr. Louis Koster of Venice, California, who coaches diverse groups in organizations (like Doctors without Borders in Bosnia), says, "Fifty percent of the communication in groups is gossip and complaining."

This way of speaking and listening keeps people from seeing each other's desire to make a difference or from seeing the possibility of creative collaboration. Dr. Koster, believes that the key to transforming the way groups interact is to make sure that each person can distinguish the generative conversations that they have—where their speaking and listening has made a difference—from the times that they indulged themselves in just giving their opinions, gossip, and complaining.

As people begin to have new and more creative and productive new conversations, the group is freed up to do strategic planning, solve complex problems, and resolve bothersome conflicts. Koster suggested the following conversational recipe. It can be used by any assembly of stakeholders or by a team within any organization.

1. Ask group members to say what the culture of the group is—what works and what doesn't.

2. Ask groups members to explain how their speaking, listening, or actions contribute to what doesn't work in the culture—for example, complaining and gossip.

3. Ask other group members to describe what a particular individual does that contributes to the effectiveness of the group.

4. Engage in dialogue about what you want the group to accomplish in the future, both in terms of results and the group's culture.

5. Make personal and group commitments.

Facilitator guidelines. It is essential in this kind of process to make the distinction between the way people usually talk—such as indulging in opinions, gossiping, or complaining—to a more generative conversation in a way in which people view it as an opening to a new possibility for speaking in a way that is creative and effective, as opposed to people taking this as an evaluation or judgment.

Also, so this doesn't just become an interesting conversation that is forgotten about later, ask people to write down in a journal the people in the group that they gossip or complain about. If appropriate, give people a chance to acknowledge this publicly or off-line as appropriate.

The facilitator should also point out that while most team members are quick to talk about the need for strategic and structural changes, they are hesitant to observe how their behavior contributes to the group's problems and how it may need to change. Acknowledging what they do in step two is a way to recognize and disperse organization defensive routines (those things people do to avoid embarrassment or threat, like making issues undiscussable).

When it comes to acknowledgment of people's contributions, discuss the importance of giving up being shy about being generous in acknowledging others. After all, some have said that history is a struggle for recognition.

APPLICATION #2.

Strategic Planning in Action

Joan Holmes of the Hunger Project talked to me about the importance of having strategic goals, but says she prefers "strategic intent." This implies looking at the areas where you would like to have an impact, analyzing the current situation, and declaring stretch goals that are "impossibilities" and where there is a deliberate mismatch between aspirations and resources.

The power of a group of stakeholders holding this intention in their minds as they inquire into what's missing to realize it, and taking creative, bold, and effective action, can be awesome. This becomes the basis of what Holmes calls "strategic planning in action," a process that applies to many collaborations.

Start by asking yourself or the group members about what you want to collaborate on in general terms—fast company growth, a new legislation for schools, ending hunger—then use the following template:

1. Describe the current reality: "What's so" fact analysis.

2. Declare a stretch goal or impossibility.

3. Inquire: What's missing that, if provided, will make a difference?

4. Delineate the major milestones, priorities, timetable, budget.

5. Take action. See what's accomplished and not accomplished. Look for what you see now that you didn't see before. Adjust.

Facilitator guidelines. With respect to what you want to achieve, encourage people in the "what's so" analysis to honestly acknowledge what's working—all the facts and circumstances pulling for the success of the project. It is empowering for people to know all the forces, facts, and circumstances that are aligned with them in succeeding. Let's take, for example, an airline. "People are looking for an airline that can give great service and cheap fares. We have great fares next to competitors."

Also, encourage people to acknowledge what's *not* working—people, forces, facts, and circumstances pulling against the project's success. It is important to do this in a way that helps people understand what's not working in way that is empowering and encourages them to take action. For example, "Our airline has the worst record of on-time arrivals and customer satisfaction in the business. That's just what is so. If we can look at this as an opportunity, rather than an invalidation, we can begin to take steps to impact it."

In facilitating people to choose a stretch goal or strategic intent, encourage them to pick something that is really challenging and that will require them to stretch who they are, their talents and skills. At the same time, assist them in making sure they are choosing a goal that is attainable and not pie in the sky—for example, "to be the world's favorite airline."

In looking at what's missing that will make a difference, identify the most high-leverage elements or small actions that can have a large impact, just don't make a laundry list of things to do. Use these high-leverage factors to spearhead the project, allocating resources and budget accordingly.

APPLICATION #3.

Complex Problem Solving

I spoke to Roger Fisher, co-author of *Getting to Yes,* to ask him what his ideas were on the subject of creative conversation. Fisher was intrigued by two ideas I mentioned—first, clarifying the purpose of the conversation, and second, enabling people in groups to think and work together. "It's having them work together that is the key aspect," he said, "to reaching a goal or solving a problem."

Fisher had an interesting approach to this process. He said that there are two main challenges in helping adverse groups think together in solving problems. For example, an elected official will see the problem from a political perspective. A executive will see the problem from a business perspective. A psychiatrist will see the problem from a psychological perspective, and so on. The issue is that, while one person is talking about the problem, the other is talking about the solution, while someone else is looking at action ideas.

The second challenge is that the dialogue can be chaotic, jumping from topic to topic, from a statement of the problem to a suggested solution and then back again. The chart in Figure 7.2 can be used to create some bridges in shared understanding as well as to create some order in the discussion so people can think together.

1. What's the fundamental problem?

2. What's the fundamental cause?

3. What's a fundamental solution?

4. Ideas for action

Facilitator guidelines. Post in the conference room four large blank pieces of flip chart paper on the wall, or a black board divided into a pie with four pieces (such as the one in Figure 7.2). Each piece of paper (or pie section) will be used to record statements that fall into the following categories: (1) Problem definitions, (2) Problem causes, (3) Problem solutions, and (4) Action ideas.

Ask the people to sit facing the flip chart or blackboard, not each other. This creates an atmosphere of seeing each other as colleagues thinking and working together on the same problem rather than as adversaries.

Start the discussion, following the ground rules that one person talks at a time. As each person speaks, the facilitator simply records what they say on the appropriate piece of paper, without trying to control the discussion by saying, "First we'll look at the problem, then the solution," in a linear fashion which can prevent emerging ideas from surfacing.

Problem Definitions	Problem Causes
Problem Solutions	Action Ideas

FIGURE 7.2
Complex Problem Solving

Fisher says that once all the ideas have been put out and the conversation simmers down, the facilitator goes through each key idea. According to Fisher, "I walk them right down the ladder of inference." In so doing, people see not just what the other person's idea is, but the perspective and reasoning process from which they said it and what it means to them. For example, people may ask each other, "What's your particular perspective on this? What lead you to that view? What examples are you basing it on?" Figure 6.4 (on page 181) shows the ladder of inference, a useful tool to help people become more aware of and to share the reasoning process behind their conclusions, beliefs, and actions.

After people have had a chance to go through this process and build shared understanding, four new pieces of paper can be put up, in which people answer the questions again. "The result," says Fisher, "is quite often a breakthrough solution."

APPLICATION #4.

Creative Negotiation and Conflict Resolution

Whenever there are two positions in a negotiation,
the solution will never be one of those two positions.
A successful solution depends on finding
a third positionthat must be created or discovered.
—SHIMON PERES, 1997

I asked Bill Ury to summarize his approach to negotiation in conflict resolution over the past fifteen years. He said, "First of all get people talking about how they see the situation, how they see themselves, how they see each other. It is important to get people talking about perceptions essentially, and emotions. I like to make sure that there are some structured opportunities for people to ask questions and to listen to not just the other person, but what they themselves are saying. This makes it possible for people to identify the key interests behind the positions they and others are taking, which are the real concerns. It also creates the platform for people to move into a brainstorming conversation where they look at ways of reframing the problem so that they can meet the interests of both sides. I ask them to focus on identifying which options are most promising, while working with them to try to flesh them out and make them as operational as possible as options for decision making."

Joint Brainstorming Exercise

1. Sit with a partner from the other side of the conflict. Say hello, talk about personal interests, family, etc. Be prepared to introduce your partner to a third party.

2. Talk again with your partner about an area where you feel misunderstood.

3. Write down a statement about what the other side's interests are, in a way that you feel he or she will accept.

4. (If you are in a group) consolidate these statements in a way that no one will find objectionable.

5. Engage in a joint brainstorm session for solutions.

Facilitator guidelines The following exercise can be done with two people, a group where there are conflicts, or conflicts between groups. It was contributed by Roger Fisher who was facilitating a dialogue between representatives from Ecuador and Peru during a cease fire in the war over their joint border. Similar to Oslo, participants in this situation were not authorized to make a commitment on behalf of any person or organization, but they are charged with trying to understand each others' perceptions, ideas, and points of view.

Chairs are placed in a semi-circle and participants from one country (interest group) were asked to sit in every other seat, while participants from the other country took the seats in between them. Fisher then issued the following charge to the group:

1. *Talk to the person next to you for half an hour and be prepared to introduce that person to the group.*

At the end of the half hour, each pair has established the beginning of a relationship with the person next to them who is from the opposing side and has said something positive about him or her to the rest of the group, what they do, their family, their education, something personal.

Fisher continues: Then you acknowledge that there is an issue or problem between the two sides and that the communication or collaboration is weak on this issue. "You probably think the other side misunderstands you." Then each person is paired with another person from the other side. The next instruction is:

> **2.** *You have an hour in which to talk without interruption and tell that person something that you think they misunderstand.*

All they can do is ask questions. They should be thoughtful questions, like "What caused you to feel that way?" or "What caused you to think like that?" Then the role is reversed, and the person who was talking has to listen and ask questions.

Next, the group is divided into two small groups (or more) composed only of one side—in Fisher's case, the Peruvians and Ecuadorians—and the next instruction is given:

> **3.** *Write out what you think the other side's interests are, in a way that the other side would accept as a group.*

The Peruvians wrote things like "They have a fear of invasion. They think our army is twice as big as theirs. They think we want to fight on their territory for the purpose of espionage."

> **4.** *Once each group comes up with a statement, the groups get together in front of a flip chart and try to draw up a consolidated statement that the other side will not object to.*

Says Fisher, "Having spent so much time on the other side's interests, they are now in the position to do some 'joint brainstorming.'"

> **5.** *Brainstorm new options for solution.*

Automatically, the first things they generate are options to meet the other side's fears. For instance, "This is crazy. They don't trust our military. Let's get them to meet." Says Fisher, "They are inventing options to meet the other side's concerns."

PART III.

Collaborative Tools

*Instead of asking, What is the information that matters
and how do we most efficiently manage it?,
companies must start asking, What are the relationships
that matter, and how can the technology most
effectively support them?*
—MICHAEL SCHRAGE,
Wall Street Journal, *March 1990*

The shift from hierarchies to networks not only also means a shift from looking at people as things but to the connections between them. It is our observation that collaborative tools can provide an excellence vehicle for enabling people to make connections, and for focusing conversations where people build shared understanding and come up with creative, innovative ideas. Here are a few examples of tools we have found to be very useful that are available to almost everyone at reasonable costs. Some readers may be aware of most of these, but putting them all in one place may spark some ideas.

Tools for Focusing the Conversation: Deep Dives and Discussions for Decisions

The simplest tools for focusing a conversation is an agenda and a room. However, the agenda can be too cramped to provide the intellectual space to allow emergent ideas to be expressed. It is good to balance meetings with agendas (where your group needs to make decisions) with meetings without agenda (where the group can explore issues in more depth). The agenda for a one- or two-day conference can easily be set up to divide those issues that need in-depth discussion into two categories: Deep Dives and Discussions for Decision. See Figure 7.3.

Meeting Agenda	
1. What is our strategy?	Deep Dive
2. Company values	Deep Dive
3. Joint-venture partner	Discussion for Decision
4. Revisit marketing plan	Discussion for Decision

FIGURE 7.3
**Meeting Agenda for Deep Dives
and Discussions for Decision**

Tools for Moving from Creative Chaos to Order: *Post-It Pads*

When people are exploring creative or collaborative terrain, new ideas emerge that are difficult to articulate. Also, there are often a lot of random bits of information that float around one's mind. A good device for eliciting and arranging ideas and information is a pack or two of post-it pads. For example, Art Kleiner, who collaborated with Peter Senge on the book *The Fifth Discipline,* met with Peter in the basement of his house one day, and asked him about his ideas for the book. As Senge spoke, Kleiner wrote each main idea on a post-it pad. When all the main ideas were expressed, Kleiner organized them into five columns. To Kleiner, the columns looked like skills or disciplines. This is how the book was given the title *The Fifth Discipline.*

Tools for Building Shared Understanding: *Napkins, Flip Charts, White Boards*

The best tools for building shared understanding and focusing the conversation are those that allow the conversation to be represented in physical space. These include napkins, a blackboards, flip charts, etc. Each person's scribblings or drawings become a basis for others to talk about their understanding of the situation and for creating new shared understandings, as well as what John Seely Brown calls "co-constructing insights" into the situation that just didn't exist before. If you have any doubts about the importance of having such collaborative tools, try to do a collaborative project without one. I was involved in designed a coaching seminar and the first step was to create an outline on the computer. It was a group of three, and the person who was at the computer tended to become lost in outer space as they wordsmithed on the keyboard, while the other two spouted on, rolled their eyes, or fell asleep.

Tools for the Electronic Workplace: *Conference Calls, Groupware*

One of the most often overlooked tools for collaborative conversation between people in different parts of the world is a simple "conference call." These allow people in entrepreneurial (and large organizations as well) to connect, collect ideas, and create some innovative solutions at very low costs. Today, many phones are equipped with this feature. If not, the telephone company can hook up anywhere from three to hundred people in just minutes.

The World Wide Web makes it possible to have meetings that are electronically distributed over time and space, with colleagues, in other groups, organizations, or regions, where people can send out messages and respond when it works for them, rather than have to show up at a particular time. It is important to keep in mind that, while groupware increases the quantity of interactions similar to the telephone or the fax, it doesn't necessarily increase the quality. Some people report that they feel scattered, disconnected, and discombobulated.

According to Peter and Trudy Johnson-Lenz, who coined the term, *groupware* means "intentionally chosen group processes plus software to support it." There are several software packages that have been designed to facilitate groups in creating shared goals, choosing team roles, as well as establishing facilitator guidelines. One I saw was an experimental package by the name of "Lotus Teamroom." If you use a groupware approach, build in human connections, like saying hello when you go into the teamroom, and don't just keep it limited to rigid protocols such as policy and procedure.

Tools for Handling Difficult Collaborative Conversations

The tools we have just described provide for a physical space that will make a collaborative conversation possible. The following tools help to provide intellectual and emotional space during difficult collaborative conversations.

Use the "ladder of inference" to penetrate illusions and to build shared understanding. The ladder of inference is a tool that can be used for more creative, productive reasoning, constructing a shared mental model, or dispatching prejudices of people in the group toward each other. The ladder is a simple but powerful model for understanding the steps in our reasoning process as we make sense of what is happening in preparation for taking action. (See Figure 6.2 in Chapter Six.)

The ladder of inference is placed on the top of a field or pool of data that consists of everything people say and do. Our reasoning processes begin with selecting what events or data we will pay attention to and treat as something that matters. That data go on the first rung of our ladder. For example, I might focus on Jill coming late to a meeting. Then we move to the second rung of the ladder by interpreting or adding meaning to what we have on the first rung. I might think Jill doesn't really care about this meeting and doesn't respect me enough to be on time.

We might go through several steps making interpretations this way and then draw the conclusion that Jill is not a collaborative person or team player. We may then take action based on that conclusion by complaining to the boss.

The first lesson to learn about the ladder of inference is that people automatically jump high on the ladder and do not notice the gaps in their reasoning process where they jumped to conclusions. Using the ladder of inference involves helping people see where they have jumped to a conclusion in their thinking regarding something substantive—like a strategic-planning process, for example—and have forgotten to test their inferences and assumptions. This can be to some extent natural, but it can lead to problems in groups and intergroup communication if people with relatively the same data have reached a different set of conclusions.

Walking people down the ladder of inference is vital not only to penetrate the stereotypes and prejudices people have of each other, but also to help people see the steps in their reasoning process.

Ladder protocol questions to surface and test assumptions or penetrate illusions:

- What led you to that view? Did you jump to conclusions?

- Can you help me to see the steps in your reasoning process?

- Can you give me an example?

- Here's what I think about this; do you see any gaps or inconsistencies?

Ladder protocol questions for creative and productive reasoning. Walk the group up the ladder to develop a shared view or to think together. The ladder of inference can also be used to help groups think productively. This involves basically walking up the ladder.

- What data do we all agree on here?

- What meaning does that have for our group?

- What assumptions or beliefs can we all make about that?

- What conclusions and actions can we take?

Use the "left-hand-column exercise" to encourage people to discuss the undiscussable. People in groups are often subject to any number of defensive routines. A defensive routine, according to Chris Argyris, is anything people do to avoid embarrassment or threat to themselves or others. One of the most prevalent is to send mixed messages or to make certain hot or controversial issues or feelings undiscussable. This leads to distortion of communication and coverup of the distortion, as most people do not actually admit to themselves or others that they are doing this and, to a large degree, are unaware of it.

The left-hand-column case involves asking each person in the group to take a piece of paper and draw a line down the middle. Each person remembers a recent conversation which may have been difficult. In the right-hand column, people write down everything they said in the conversation, as well as just enough of what the other person said to sum up the story. *He said this, I said that,* etc. In the left-hand column, people write what they thought, but didn't say. This includes any issues they have suppressed to not make waves, any evaluations and judgments, any emotions.

After people have written this out, they exchange cases with another person in the group and go through the following protocol questions.

Protocol questions for debriefing left-hand-column:

1. What did you notice about what was in your left-hand column?

2. What did you keep undiscussable?

3. What emotions did you conceal in your left hand column?

4. How did what you say or not say contribute to the results?

Protocol questions for breaking through prejudices and judgments. After you have done the left-hand column, circle any evaluations or judgments you made about other people in the group and then refer to the ladder of inference.

1. What assessments or judgments did you make about other people?

2. Were these assessments based on valid information?

3. Where did you jump to conclusions or add meaning?

4. What could you have said to that person from your left-hand column that would have served them and improved your relationship?

Do a role-play. A role-play is an excellent way to prepare for handing a difficult conversation. Start by writing down a left-hand-column case of a conversation you are going to have with a person in your group that you expect will be difficult. Write down in the right-hand column what you think you will say and what they will likely say in response. Write down in the left-hand column what you think you will defer saying, as well as the emotions you might be concealing.

After you have done this, role-play your conversation with your partner, taking on the role of the other person. This can lead to many insights about how to approach the person, as well as allow you to release some pent-up feelings. Then, switch roles. Put yourself in the other person's chair and have your partner play you. This can be even more eye-opening and have a powerful impact on transforming defensiveness into learning.

The Sounding of the Tone

This book has been a daring adventure for me, an exciting, thrilling adventure in many ways. The adventure was one in which I engaged in conversations with some of the most creative, generative, and collaborative people alive on the surface of the planet today. I never stopped marveling, as I spoke to people in various professions about the subjects of lateral leadership and creative collaboration, who generously gave me their time. How many brilliant, wise, creative, compassionate, bold, and effective people there are in the world just waiting to have an opportunity for someone to ask them to make a meaningful contribution! I am speaking of Rob Manning, Terje Larsen, Shimon Peres, Joan Holmes, John Seely Brown, Robert Bush, and many others.

This book has been a conversation, or rather a network of collaborative conversations, a process of inquiry and reflection that has led to many questions, many hours of listening, and many moments of insight. There are a few powerful insights that I would like to share with the reader by way of closing that are personally meaningful and that I offer with the aim of making a contribution to you. First, while I was writing this book, I came across an article about Sir Isaac Newton who discovered the Laws of Motion. There was a quotation from Alexander Pope that said, "Nature and nature's laws lay hid in night. God said, Let Newton be!, and there was light." Newton was always in the act of discovery.

A day or so later, I watched a film about Picasso. I could see from the film that, while his personal life was in shambles, he was always in the act of creation. He never stopped creating, whether it was a new art form like Cubism, a new painting like *Guernica* or the *Child Holding a Dove*, a new sculpture, a new work of pottery. The stories of Newton and Picasso reminded me of what I was experiencing in writing this book: to live one's life as a creator and author in a continuous nonstop process of creation and discovery is closely akin to what it really is to be a human being—something soul-satisfying and enlivening.

I am not only talking about creating something like a famous painting or a groundbreaking book, or discovering a new approach that has real value to others in cultural or economic terms, but everyday creations and discoveries as well— planting a tree, building a rock garden, cooking a meal, meeting your neighbor and discovering you have shared interests.

The other profound moment of insight I had in writing this book had to do with the sheer joy of creating with other people something that previously appeared dizzyingly impossible, that you could never dare to imagine realizing on your own. Yet at the heart, the real insight was how one's possibility for creation and generation, whether in science, government, business, education, or other fields, exponentially increases ten times or more by bringing together a crazy, creative combination of people. I saw the power of consciously and intentionally creating new patterns of relationship and interaction that defy barriers of history, separations of language and culture, division of knowledge, and division of labor to achieve what could never be. I saw this most powerfully in the story about the Mars Pathfinder Mission, the story about the Israeli-Palestinian peace accords and especially embodied in the spirit of Oslo, the story about hunger, the story about the Applegate Partnership, and so many more.

As we stand on the evening of the millennium, in a period of relative peace and prosperity, with people who are perhaps more creative and educated and skilled than ever before in human history, with technological breakthroughs in every field, there are unquestionably many possibilities in our midst. And yet, to realize those possibilities requires people to take the lead. As Joan Holmes said, "It just doesn't happen." This means each of us acknowledging our passion to have an impact, daring to take a stand that a difference can be made, declaring possibilities in every field that represent our highest human aspirations, and then sounding the tone so that others who hear it may come to the tone, as creators and collaborators, to do what has never been done, to create what has never existed before.

The Twenty-first Century

When Geniuses Collide

Alfred North Whitehood said that the eighteenth century was the century of genius. During the writing of this book, I have wanted to say many times that the twenty-first century will be the century where geniuses collide.

I restrained myself from doing so because I wanted lateral leadership and creative collaboration to be viewed as something ordinary people, gathered together in extraordinary combinations, could readily undertake. I submit that this point has been proven many times in this book, through the numerous examples that have been cited.

So now you and I are free to consider what will happen in the years ahead when people who already are extraordinary come together with others from different fields to make an even more extraordinary combination.

I think this possibility gives all of us something to look forward to. No doubt, great creations, inventions, and miraculous events will occur in the hour of the unexpected.

Notes

Chapter One
Collaboration—An Idea Whose Time Has Come

1. Arthur Koestler, *The Art of Creation.* London: Hutchinson & Co., 1964.
2. I am grateful for my conversation with Michael Schrage where he shared many insights on creative collaboration. See Michael Schrage, *No More Teams.* New York: Currency Doubleday, 1989.
3. William Irwin Thompson, *Darkness and Scattered Light.* New York: Anchor Press/Doubleday, 1978.
4. Ethan Bronner, "Amid Gloom, Jews, Arabs Seek Peace Personally." *Boston Globe,* July 16, 1997.
5. I am thankful for the informative conversations with historian Pauline Maier of MIT on the writing of the Declaration of Independence. See Pauline Maier. *American Scriptures.* New York: Alfred A. Knopf, 1997.
6. The stories of David Kelly Designs (now known as IDEO) comes from Tom Peters in *Liberation Management.* (New York: Ballantine Books, 1992) as well as interviews with Douglas Dayton and Haven Tyler at IDEO Boston.
7. I appreciate my conversation with Bob Anderson, staff geologist for the Mars Project.
8. I am thankful for the time spent talking with Donna Shirley, manager of the Mars Exploration Program.
9. I appreciate conversations with Robert Claur, project director at the Space Physic Research Laboratory and professor at University of Michigan, Ann Arbor.
10. Based on an article by Michael Lewis, "The Subversive." *New York Times,* May 25, 1997.
11. I am grateful for the conversation with Donna Sytek, Speaker of the House in New Hampshire, where she shared her insights into the importance of collaborating in drafting successful legislation.
12. Again, from Tom Peters, *Liberation Management,* New York: Ballantine Books, 1992, and conversations with Douglas Dayton, IDEO Boston.
13. I am grateful to the interesting and informative conversations with Robert Bush and Joe Folger about the importance of empowerment and recognition in collaboration. See Robert A. Baruch Bush, and Joseph P. Folger, *The Promise of Mediation,* San Francisco: Jossey-Bass, 1994.
14. Thanks to Sharon Press, of the Dispute Resolution Center, for information on mediation work being done in Florida.
15. I am appreciative of the time staff sergeant Rick Murphy of the Ottawa, Canada, police department spent talking about the collaborative work they are doing between the police and members of the community.

16. Louie Koster, M.D., and president of Strategic Humanitarian Development, was gracious enough to share about his experiences in collaboration, especially with the "Doctors Without Borders."

17. Nicholas Delbanco, *Group Portrait*. New York: William Morrow & Co, Inc., 1982.

Interlude
The Mars Pathfinder Mission

1. I am grateful for the opportunity to speak with Rob Manning, Bob Anderson, Matt Golombek, Donna Shirley, and Tom Rivellini of NASA's Jet Propulsion Laboratory as well as Eleanor Foraker from ILC about their insights into the role of collaboration in putting the lander and Rover on Mars.

Chapter Two
How to Be a Collaborative Person

1. David Makovsky, *Making Peace with the PLO, The Rabin Government's Road to the Oslo Accord*. Boulder, CO: Westview Press, Inc., 1996.

2. Again, a special thanks to Matt Golombek and Rob Manning for their time spent telling us of their experiences on the Mars Project.

3. Scoring Artist Grant Hill: "The NBA's Rimbrandt." *Houston Chronicle*, Feb. 8, 1996.

4. "Fools Gold," *Reputation Management*. March/April 1997, New York.

5. Tracy Goss, *The Last Word on Power*. New York: Currency Doubleday, 1996.

6. Donna Markova, Ph.D., coined the terms "river story" and "rut story." See Donna Markova, *No Enemies Within*. Emeryville, CA: Publisher Group West, 1994.

7. Goss, Tracy, *The Last Word on Power*.

8. Chris Argyris of Harvard University has contributed much to the work of organizational learning; he has numerous books, among them, *Overcoming Organizational Defenses*. Needham Heights, MA: Allyn and Bacon, 1990; *Strategy, Change, and Defensive Routines*. Boston: Pitman, 1985; and *Knowledge for Action*. San Francisco: Jossey-Bass, 1993.

Interlude
Passionate Diplomacy in the Middle East

1. Excerpts from a speech by Yitzhak Rabin at the signing of the Oslo Peace Accord on September 13, 1993. See David Makovsky, *Making Peace with the PLO, The Rabin Government's Road to the Oslo Accord*. Boulder, CO: Westview Press, Inc., 1996.

2. Taken from a letter sent from Yasser Arafat to Yitzhak Rabin, recognizing Israel's right to exist in peace, September 9, 1993. See David Makovsky, *Making Peace With the PLO, The Rabin Government's Road to the Oslo Accord*. Boulder CO: Westview Press, Inc., 1996.

3. I was totally taken and inspired by the story behind the Oslo Peace Talks and am very grateful for the conversations with the Israelis: Former Prime Minister Shimon Peres and Yossi Beilin; Palestinian: Hasan Asfour; and the Norwegians: Terje Larsen, Marianne Heiberg, and Gier Pedersen. Two books that were also helpful were Jane Corbin, *The Norway Channel*. New York: The Atlantic Monthly Press, 1994; and

David Makovsky's, *Making Peace With the PLO, The Rabin Government's Road to the Oslo Accord*. Boulder, CO: Westview Press, Inc., 1996.

4. Jane Corbin, *The Norway Channel*. New York: The Atlantic Monthly Press, 1994.

5. Ibid.

Chapter Three
The Building Blocks of Creative Collaboration

1. I am appreciative of the time Roger Ackerman, CEO of Corning Incorporated, spent with me talking about his success and management beliefs.

2. Robert Reich, *The Work of Nations: Preparing Ourselves for 21st Century Capitalism*. New York: Knopf, 1991.

3. Charles M. Sennott, "Economic Order Chaining." *Boston Globe,* July 22, 1992.

4. I am grateful for the stimulating conversations with John Seely Brown, chief scientist of Xerox's Palo Alto Research Center in California.

5. Charles M. Sennott, "Economic Order Chaining." *Boston Globe,* July 22, 1992.

6. The first time I heard the term "lateral leadership" was in conversations with Roger Fisher, co-author of *Getting to Yes,* and have applied it to the kind of leadership necessary for effective collaborations.

7. Again, a special appreciation to Rob Manning of the Mars Project for his impassioned conversations.

8. I am especially grateful for conversation with Joan Holmes, director of the Hunger Project.

9. Joseph L. Dionne, "It Takes a Global Village." *Chief Executive,* April 1997.

10. Again, I am appreciative of conversations with Donna Shirley of the Mars Project.

11. Margaret Wheatley, *Leadership and the New Science*. San Francisco: Berrett-Koehler Publishers, 1992.

12. Again, a special thanks for conversations with Tom Rivellini about his work on the Mars Project.

13. Again, I would like to acknowledge the work of Chris Argyris of Harvard University in the area of learning organizations.

14. I am thankful for conversations and assistance from John Coonrod, Joan Holmes' assistant at the Hunger Project.

15. I am grateful for conversations with Michael Schrage and his insights into the fact that collaboration is accomplishment-oriented as well as the significance of shared space. See Michael Schrage, *No More Teams!* New York: Currency Doubleday, 1989.

16. A special thanks to Robert Schaffer for the time spent in conversation on his breakthrough strategy. See Robert Schaffer, *The Breakthrough Strategy*. New York: Ballinger Publishing Division, 1988.

17. I am thankful for the conversation with John Reingold, project manager of Microsoft Project.

Interlude
Future of the Firm

1. The idea of the hundred-year lag between the inventions of the 1700s and development of the management and organization structures to take advantage of it was

proposed in a paper written by John Seely Brown and Paul Duguid, of the University of California at Berkeley called" Organizing Knowledge."

2. Again, I am grateful for the time that Roger Ackerman took away from his vacation to speak with me about his leadership beliefs and style and the successes at Corning.

3. I am especially appreciative of the conversations with John Seely Brown on the work they are doing at PARC, as well as his view of the future of the organizations which I found stimulating and enlightening.

4. I first heard of the idea of the "knowledge creating" company from Ikujiro Nonaka, business professor at Hitousbashi University, in a Harvard Business Review article published in *The Learning Imperative: Managing People for Continuous Innovation*, a *Harvard Business Review* book by Robert Howard, ed. Boston: Harvard Business School Press, 1993.

5. Thanks to Tom Moran of Xerox's PARC for sharing about his work on the "Live Board" and other collaborative tools.

6. I am appreciative of my conversation with Peter Galison, Professor at Harvard University and winner of the MacArthur award for his insights into the "trading zone" concept as it applies to collaborations between divers people. See Peter Galison, *Image & Logic,*.Chicago: The University of Chicago Press, 1997.

7. I am grateful for the stimulating conversation with Paul Blasch, Jim Hubbard, and Bennett Goldberg at Boston University's Photonics Center.

8. Thanks to David Bell for the time he spent talking to me about the Eureka Project at Xerox's PARC.

Chapter Four
Close Encounters of the Creative Kind: Launching Your Collaboration

1. Ryuzaburo Kaku, "The Path of Kyosei," *Harvard Business Review*. July/August 1997.

2. This story is from papers from the Eracism group and letters to the editor from *The Times-Picayune,* June 30, 1993.

3. Taylor, Jim and Wacker, Watts, with Howard Means, *500 Year Delta*. New York: HarperBusiness, 1997.

4. I am appreciative of conversations with Marv Weisbord and Sandra Janoff of Future Search, a planning organization. See Marvin R. Weisbord, *Discovering Common Ground*. San Francisco: Berrett-Koehler Publishers, 1992; and Marvin R. Weisbord and Sandra Janoff, *An Action Guide to Finding Common Ground in Organizations and Communities*. San Francisco: Berrett-Koehler Publishers, 1995.

5. We are grateful for touring the offices of IDEO in Lexington, MA and the time spent in conversation with director Douglas Dayton and Haven Tyler.

6. I am grateful for the various conversations with Maggie Herzig and Bob Stains of the Public Conversations Project. The work that they are doing in promoting effective and productive dialogue is inspirational.

Interlude
Joan Holmes and the Hunger Project

1. I am grateful for the time that Joan Holmes took from here intensive schedule to

share about the Hunger Project. Also I am appreciative of conversations with John Coonrod, the director of programs at the Hunger Project, as well as two friends and former Hunger Project staffers, Michel Renaud and Veronica Pemberton of Renaud Pemberton International in Montreal, Canada.

Chapter Five
It Happens in Conversations—An Introduction
1. David Bohm has researched and written extensively on dialogue. He has made a significant contribution to the work of dialogue. See Bohm, David, *On Dialogue*. Ojai, CA: David Bohm Seminars, 1990)

Chapter Six
The Five Stages of a Creative Collaboration
1. Mandela, Nelson, *Long Walk to Freedom*. New York: Little, Brown and Company, 1994.
2. Bohm, David, *On Dialogue*. Ojai, CA: David Bohm Seminars, 1990.
3. Again a special thanks to Donna Sytek, Speaker of the House of Representatives in New Hampshire for her insights on collaboration.
4. Margaret Wheatley is an sssociate professor of Management in Brigham Young University's Marriott School of Management. This quote is paraphrased from a chapter called Future Search Conferences and the New Science in: Marvin R. Weisbord, *Discovering Common Ground*. San Francisco: Berrett-Koehler Publishers, 1992. Also see Wheatley, Margaret, *Leadership and the New Science*. San Francisco, Berrett-Koehler Publishers, 1992.
5. Gleick, James, *Genius: The Life and Science of Richard Feynman*. New York: Vintage Books, Random House, 1992.
6. I am appreciative of the interesting and useful conversations with William Ury about his work in collaborative mediation. See Fisher, Roger and Ury, William, *Getting To Yes, Negotiating Agreement Without Giving In*. Boston: Houghton Mifflin, 1981.
7. The story about the Rad Lab at MIT came from Professor Peter Galison, Harvard.
8. Koestler, Arthur, *The Art of Creation*. London: Hutchinson & Co., 1964.
9. I am appreciative of conversations with Professor Everett Mendelssohn, chairman of the History of Science Department at Harvard and conversations with Jeffrey Boutwell of the American Academy of Arts & Science in Cambridge, Massachusetts, who together sponsored a series of meetings between Israeli and Palestinian people to discuss points of security and sharing of intelligence. What started out as an academic exercise in early 1993, lead to specific agreements and was in a way a prototype for the meetings that lead to the Oslo Accords.
10. Lois, George with Pitts, Bill, *What's the Big Idea*. New York: Doubleday, 1991.
11. Ikujiro Nonaka in a Harvard Business Review article published in *The Learning Imperative: Managing People for Continuous Innovation*, a *Harvard Business Review* book by Robert Howard, ed. Boston: Harvard Business School Press, 1993.
12. Ibid.
13. Goss, Tracy, *The Last Word on Power*. New York: Currency Doubleday, 1996.

14. Again, thanks to Rob Manning of the Mars Project.

15. Ikujiro Nonaka in a *Harvard Business Review* article published in *The Learning Imperative: Managing People for Continuous Innovation,* a *Harvard Business Review* book by Robert Howard, ed. Boston: Harvard Business School Press, 1993.

Chapter Seven
Coaching, Practical Applications, and Tools for Creative Collaboration

1. Again, a special thanks to Bill Ury, coauthor of *Getting to Yes.*

2. I am appreciative of the conversations were Jim Shipley shared his experience of collaborating with the Applegate Partnership.

3. Again, I am thankful for the informative conversation with Dr. Everett Mendelssohn of Harvard University.

4. The ideas of basic and developmental facilitation come from Schwarz, Roger, *The Skilled Facilitator.* San Francisco: Jossey-Bass, 1994.

5. The governing values are from the work of C. Argyris and D. Shön, *Theory in Practice: Increasing Professional Effectiveness.* San Francisco: Jossey-Bass, 1974.

6. I am appreciative of conversations with Russ McKinley, from Boise Cascade, about his involvement with the Applegate collaboration.

7. Again, thanks to Jeffrey Boutwell of the American Academy of Arts & Science in Cambridge.

8. I am grateful for conversations with Owen Harrison on his Open Space Technologies.

9. The ground rules are from Roger Schwarz, *The Skilled Facilitator.* San Francisco: Jossey-Bass, 1994.

10. Reprinted with permission from from Roger Schwarz. *The Skilled Facilitator: Practical Wisdom for Developing Effective Groups.* San Francisco: Jossey-Bass, Inc. 1994.

Index

"f" refers to the figure

About the Author

Robert Hargrove is the founder of Robert Hargrove and Partners, in Brookline, Massachusetts. He has worked with over 30,000 people in coaching programs that are designed to shift fundamental thinking and attitudes that in turn produce a shift in behavior. His work is grounded on expanding the capacity of people in groups to achieve the results they truly desire. He is also the author of *Masterful Coaching: Extraordinary Results by Impacting People and the Way They Think and Work Together.*

Robert is a sought-after inspirational and thought provoking speaker, represented by the Washington Speakers' Bureau. He is an executive coach, group facilitator, and consultant to organizations in government, business, and education in the United States, Canada, and Europe.

Specific program topics include Lateral Leadership, Strategic Planning in Action, Creating a Collaborative Organization and Effective Enterprise Web, and Masterful Coaching with a Results Orientation.

Robert and his group have extensive experience in consulting large organizations such as: Adidas, Fidelity Investments, Ciba Geigy, Royal Bank of Scotland, AT&T, Genetics Institute. According to René Jaeggi, former chairman of Adidas, "Robert is a business guru par excellence." Humanitarian efforts include work with the United Nations Commission on Refugees and dispute resolution in South Africa.

Robert Hargrove is the founder of the Institute for Creative Collaboration, which does research in collaboration and applies this to fieldwork in projects that involve radical innovation, complex problem solving, negotiation, and conflict-resolution services.

For more information on Robert Hargrove and the Institute for Creative Collaboration, call (800) 800-4508.